EA   ON
FOR   ED
      N:
    NS

LIST OF CONTRIBUTORS

Helen H. Beebe, Helen Beebe Speech & Hearing Center, 505 Cattell Street, Easton, PA 18042

Gillian Clezy, The School of Communication Disorders, Lincoln Institute for Health Sciences, Melbourne, AUSTRALIA

Elizabeth B. Cole, School of Human Communication Disorders, McGill University, 1266 Pine Avenue West, Montreal, P.Q., H3G 1A8 CANADA

Mary Eager Koch, Helen Beebe Speech & Hearing Center, 505 Cattell Street, Easton, PA 18042

Daniel Ling, Ph.D., School of Human Communication Disorders, McGill University, 1266 Pine Avenue West, Montreal, P.Q. H3G 1A8 CANADA

Marietta M. Paterson, Department of Special Education, 339 Teachers College, University of Cincinnati, Cincinnati, OH 45221

Helen R. Pearson, Helen Beebe Speech & Hearing Center, 505 Cattell Street, Easton, PA 18042

Doreen Pollack, 14285 Marina Drive, Aurora, CO 80014

EARLY INTERVENTION FOR HEARING-IMPAIRED CHILDREN: ORAL OPTIONS

Edited By

Daniel Ling, Ph.D.

Professor, Otolaryngology and Education
School of Human Communication Disorders,
McGill University, Montreal

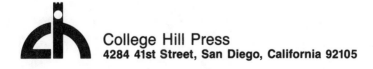

College Hill Press
4284 41st Street, San Diego, California 92105

College-Hill Press
4284 41st Street
San Diego, California 92105

Library of Congress Cataloging in Publication Data

Main entry under title:
    Early intervention for hearing-impaired children: Oral options.

    Bibliography: p.
    Includes index.
    1. Hearing impaired children. 2. Deaf—Means of communication. 3. Hearing impaired children—Education. 4. Children, Deaf—Language. I. Ling, Daniel. [DNLM: 1. Education, Special. 2. Hearing disorders—in infancy & childhood. 3. Speech—in infancy & childhood. 4. Verbal learning—in infancy & childhood. 5. Hearing disorders—rehabilitation. WV 271 E12]
HV2391.E27   1984   362.4'28'088054   84-7642
ISBN 0-933014-33-3

Printed in the United States of America

Contents

List of Contributors, ii

Preface and Acknowledgments, vii

This book has been written both for newcomers to the problems of hearing impairment (parents, students, and professionals practicing in related fields) and for those already working with hearing-impaired children who want to know more about programs currently being offered by others. Like its companion volume (*Early Intervention for Hearing Impaired Children: Total Communication Options*) it introduces and discusses four programs that are regarded by many as being of exemplary quality. The oral options described in this book vary in the emphasis placed on different aspects of work with young hearing-impaired children, but all contributors emphasize the utmost use of residual hearing. All four work in different settings: a hospital clinic, a private center, a university project, and a program for training speech–language pathologists. They represent practice in the United States, Canada, and Australia. Their work encompasses a range of relatively new strategies in intervention with hearing-impaired children and their parents, much of it reflecting the influences of recent developments in technology, advances in linguistics, and expanding knowledge in speech perception and speech production. Much of the work described differs from that of the more traditional oral programs. The type of programs the contributors describe are becoming increasingly widespread as the results of their work are recognized, although there are still many areas throughout North America and the English-speaking world where early oral options of any sort do not yet exist.

Relatively little has been written about oral options in early intervention by people who are, themselves, actively engaged in the work. This book therefore makes an important contribution, particularly because its focus is on what actually happens in such programs and largely, if not entirely, avoids contentious comparisons between one form of intervention and another. The authors state their philosophies and describe their work and results. Their bias is *toward* communication through spoken language rather than *against* alternative methods. As with the companion volume, the purpose of this book is to prevent rather than foster prejudice or controversy. Options are esentially choices, and the goal of these books is to provide the facts that will help parents and professionals make wise choices for individual children, not choices between methods, for (and it bears repetition) no one method or collection of methods can meet the needs of all children and their parents. Various options should exist for children, so that their individual needs can be met and their human potential developed.

The authors of the chapters in this volume were selected from among many on the basis of recommendations received from numerous people—parents and professionals—who are familiar with early intervention for young hearing-impaired children and their parents. All were asked to follow an outline which specified the information to be included. They were asked to begin with a brief history of their programs, a description of their philosophies and the types of children they teach, their enrollment procedures, and their goals. The bulk of each chapter consists of a detailed account of the treatment procedures they employ with notes on how assessment and evaluation are carried out. They were also asked to provide case histories that would illustrate the characteristics of children and their parents which lead to success (as each author defined it) and the factors that appear to be associated with failure. Particular emphasis was to be given on how individual differences among staff, parents, and children were handled. Finally, all were asked to say what has happened to graduates of their programs, to summarize what they consider to be their "golden rules" for success, and to express their views on the viability of their own and other options for early intervention. They were all urged to avoid polemics. The ground rules for writing were, therefore, the same as those provided for authors in the companion volume. Similarities and differences between and among options should therefore become apparent to readers of the two volumes. Comparisons of the options described are also made and discussed in the concluding chapter written by the Editor.

Readers will appreciate that points of view expressed by the authors are not necessarily shared by the editor.

Daniel Ling

ACKNOWLEDGMENTS

The editor thanks the four authors who so ably contributed the chapters describing each of their programs. He also thanks his colleagues at McGill University for their assistance in reading draft chapters. His deep appreciation goes to Carole Shevloff-Ammendolea who typed and proofread so much of the material. Final acknowledgment goes to his wife, Jane, for her understanding and generous support.

1
EARLY ORAL INTERVENTION: AN INTRODUCTION

Daniel Ling

ORAL EDUCATION

Oral education is so called because its primary emphasis is on communication through speech. It has undergone many important changes during the several hundreds of years of its recorded life span. Initially, the emphasis was on the "wonder" of teaching speech to deaf children and adults who had become mute. Today emphasis is on prevention of mutism rather than its cure through the early detection of hearing impairment and the development of spoken language from early infancy (see Markides, 1983, for a brief history of oral education from ancient times to the present day). The greatest changes have been very recent. They have been brought about through technological advances, particularly the development of hearing aids (Bess, Freeman, & Sinclair, 1981). Although hearing aids have been available for over 30 years, they continue to improve. Where hearing aids have been used, they have led to better standards of achievement, and greater success in meeting the overall goal of oral education; namely, to fit children to take their place in a world in which most people communicate by talking.

Oral education cannot be considered as a single, unitary process. Many different forms of treatment are required to meet the varied needs of children among whom hearing problems may range from slight impairment to total deafness. Fortunately, very few children are totally deaf. Hence, the majority of them can benefit from hearing aids. However, even total deafness is not an insurmountable barrier to intelligible speech (Ling, 1976). Many children with mild or moderate hearing impairment who use hearing aids well can learn spoken language with very little, if any special help. Those who have severe or profound hearing impairment usually need a great deal of special help. Some such children can use hearing as their main avenue for learning but generally use speech reading (lip reading) to bottom curve shows her unaided responses, and the top curve, her aided responses. With aided responses such as these, this child can hear all but the very high sounds of speech at a distance of at least 2 yd. She can not only detect most speech sounds, but she can also discriminate between them. Without a hearing aid, she cannot hear speech at all. Many children with unaided hearing levels comparable to this child are not fitted with appropriate hearing aids and cannot, therefore, overcome their hearing impairment to the same extent through audition. One should use residual hearing to the greatest extent possible, even though it is not essential to hear all the sounds of speech in order to learn to communicate through speech (Bess et al., 1981).

Hearing impairment does not imply simply a loss of auditory acuity. There is more to hearing than being able to *detect* and *discriminate* between sounds. These are the basic skills, but children also need to be able to *identify* sounds and strings of sounds (as in sentences) and to *comprehend* their meaning. For this, most hearing-impaired children (and their parents) need both training and extensive experience. The principles underlying the provision of auditory training and experience are discussed in a later section entitled "Oral Education: Theory and Practice." Several of the auditory strategies employed in practice are presented in the following chapters by the four contributing authors.

Children's Needs

Young children make no far-reaching decisions on their own: their needs are met on a day-to-day basis by their parents. Children who are hearing impaired have the same basic needs as those with normal hearing, such as warm, responsive, loving care, acceptance, stimulation, and an enriching environment. Given these, most children will flourish. Beyond these basics, children who are severely or profoundly hearing impaired need to be helped to learn how to communicate. Reaching a decision on how best to encourage communication is a task for the parent. Communication is essential to growth and language and is best learned in early infancy (Bloom & Lahey, 1978), but the child's needs for language and communication should not pressure parents into making hasty choices between program options. In order to avoid choices that are based on an inadequate understanding of the issues, it is best for parents first to be aware of the facts and implications of their children's hearing problems and study the intervention options available. The type of intervention program selected will largely determine the range of skills their children will eventually have as adults. It is therefore important for parents to take

FIGURE 1-1. Thresholds of unaided (bottom curve) and aided (top curve) hearing in the better ear of a profoundly hearing-impaired child.

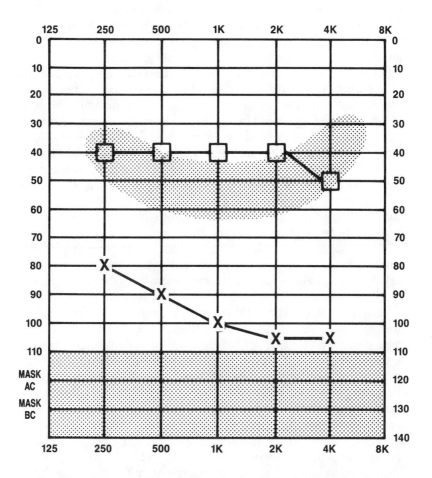

sufficient time to think through their goals and aspirations for their children and to reach rational decisions on how best to meet their short-term and long-term needs. Undue delay in beginning to meet a child's communication needs can be damaging both to the children and to the relationship between them and their parents. To optimize opportunities for children while information on which to base choices is being collected, audiological follow-up and hearing aid selection can be undertaken and use made of their residual hearing prior to enrollment in any kind of parent–infant program.

Parents and Families

Parents, particularly those who have normal hearing themselves, are usually shocked, bewildered, angry, depressed, and generally find it hard to cope with the discovery of hearing impairment in their children. According to Luterman (1979) and Shontz (1967), most go through a typical mourning reaction which includes shock, recognition of the problem, and denial, before they can accept the situation sufficiently to take constructive action and become involved in early intervention work with their children. The most potent early intervention, however, is that which parents and families are involved (Bronfenbrenner, 1975) and in which they learn to interact effectively with their children who have special needs (Bromwich, 1981). Compared with professionals, parents are with their children longer on both a day-to-day and a year-by-year basis, have closer bonds with them, and have more opportunity to interact with them under real life conditions. Once the early reactions to the discovery of deafness have given way to acceptance and the ability to work constructively, they can therefore do more for their children than any professional.

Some parents are unable for various reasons to provide for their children's needs themselves to the extent that they might like to. They include single parents who must work during most of the child's waking hours, and parents who are hearing impaired and want their children to learn to speak but cannot themselves provide an adequate spoken language environment. If family members or friends are not available to be with their children at home and follow the guidance provided by the early intervention center, then half- or full-day admission to an early intervention program may be advised. If so, parents should choose to place their children according to the aims and philosophy of the program, the method of communication used, the qualifications of staff, the availability of support services (audiology, psychology, etc.), the opportunities for parents and staff to interact, whether the children can interact with normally hearing peers, and the achievements of former pupils with similar hearing impairments and background. More detailed information on parents and families are provided by the authors in these two volumes.

Parents need the professionals for three things: counseling, information, and guidance. Parents who abrogate their roles as the persons primarily concerned with their child's development of communication skills substantially reduce the child's potential for success, whatever form of early intervention is chosen. This is not to say that parents should devote their whole lives to their hearing-impaired children. Time for themselves and other members of their families is an essential for healthy living.

Professionals and Programs

The professionals represented by the authors in this book are all highly qualified and experienced teacher/clinicians. They carry out their work with knowledge and skills relating to many areas, including child development, audiology, early education, counseling, speech acquisition, and language development. The majority of professionals do not have adequate training for this type of work and can only acquire the necessary background for it through experience. Those who have had the opportunity to work with master teacher/clinicians in the course of obtaining experience are fortunate. Thus, standards of work in general are not so high as those reported by the contributors to this book. (See also comments relating to this problem in the companion volume.)

The basic requirement of oral education is that the children served are taught to speak and to understand speech. Teacher/clinicians offering oral options therefore have to be able to monitor both their own and the children's utterances. This requirement prevents most hearing-impaired people from working as professionals in oral programs. This is unfortunate because many hearing-impaired adults could otherwise serve as excellent role models.

The programs described in this book all provide auditory–verbal options. They focus upon the development and use of residual hearing and place less emphasis on visual cues than some other programs which adopt strategies that are best described as auditory–visual. This difference requires clarification. In auditory–visual programs, hearing and speech reading are regarded as complementary, both as a means of learning to interpret speech and as the preferred mode for everyday communication (Erber, 1982). Auditory–verbal programs, on the other hand, offer acoupedic or unisensory-based training involving the use of residual hearing alone, that is, without speech reading, for a part of each training session. To those with little background in speech science, using defective hearing alone for part of each training session may seem to reduce rather than increase the child's prospects for development. This is not necessarily so. Stone (1983), for example, has reviewed and has shown experimental support for this practice, which appears to result in better performance both for hearing alone and for hearing-plus-vision when speech reading is added. In Stone's program the technique is used with groups, whereas in early intervention programs it is used in one-to-one communication. Both stress the difference between *hearing* (a physiological phenomenon) and *listening* (a learned skill). The view of those who apply unisensory techniques is that the consistent presentation of simultaneous auditory and visual stimuli tends to detract from the development of listening skills (Vaughan, 1981); and that the crucial thing is not how much information can be presented to a child, but how much of it can be perceived and in what way the child can learn to process it. This position is clearly contrary to that held by those who advocate simultaneous multisensory stimulation either in oral options that offer auditory–visual training or in total communication settings. Certainly, if unisensory training were to be used by unskilled professionals who were unable to match verbal material with the auditory capacities of the children, the procedure could be disastrously ineffective. Those who practice it effectively have to know speech science and the child's auditory potential very well.

The assessment of a program requires more than looking at its label. Some programs labeled as oral are in fact total communication programs, since the children also use sign language and finger spelling. Several research studies comparing oral and sign language education have justly received strong criticism because the researchers grouped the children they studied according to program label rather than actual practice (see Nix, 1975). The recent increase in the number of programs that are now described as total communication is in part due to change in program title rather than practice. Thus, most options now described as oral are more likely to be so than formerly. However, the only way to be sure that a program successfully follows a stated philosophy is to see the program in action, talk with the staff, and meet graduates of the program. The content of the following chapters should provide guidelines to readers on the factors that need to be studied.

Cued speech is an oral option that has recently become available and can be very effective with totally deaf children. Devised and reported by Cornett (1967), it has been studied mainly with children of school age. Results of an independent study by Nicholls (1979) demonstrate that it permits excellent reception and development of spoken language even by totally deaf children. Although it has also been employed successfully with infants who are hearing impaired, the lowest chronological or mental age at which it can be effectively used remains to be established. It is not yet clear whether Cued Speech can add significantly to the acquisition of oral skills by children who have moderate or severe hearing impairment, but nothing has so far been found that detracts from its use with children who are totally or near-totally deaf. The alternatives to Cued Speech for such children are few. They include tactile aids (Proctor & Goldstein, 1983) and cochlear implants (Ling & Nienhuys, 1983), both of which can supply information that supplements speech reading. Speech reading without additional cues of some sort has many limitations (see Nicholls, 1979, for a review). However, if it is supported by the use of residual hearing, as it is in programs offering auditory–visual options, its use can lead to superior levels of spoken language and educational achievement (Erber, 1982; Geers, 1983).

ORAL EDUCATION: THEORY AND PRACTICE

In this section, the theory and practices relating to oral options are considered. The purpose here is to examine oral education from a somewhat broader perspective than could be provided in the four programs described in subsequent chapters. Assumptions underlying oral options are challenged, while controversy over methods is avoided. Treatment of the topics is therefore similar to that provided on total communication in the companion volume.

The philosophy of oral education is that hearing-impaired children should be given the opportunity to learn to speak and to understand speech, learn through spoken language in school, and later function as independent adults in a world in which people's primary mode of communication is speech. The theory is that spoken language has emerged as the universal means of basic communication not by chance, but because the central nervous system and physiological nature of mankind render it the most efficient means of human communication; and that only oral education can give hearing-impaired children access to the auditory and/or articulatory codes on which spoken language is based. The theory also extends to written language, which is regarded as parasitic on the spoken form, and includes the notion that spoken language skills provide children with knowledge that helps them master various aspects of reading and writing. The most extensive discussion of oral education is to be found in Mulholland (1981).

Evidence in support of the theory of oral education is patchy and inconclusive. Many children, regardless of their degree of hearing impairment, achieve high levels of speech intelligibly and learn effectively through the use of spoken language (Karchmer, Milone, & Wolk, 1979; Lane, 1976); but some acquire so few oral skills that alternative methods of instruction become essential. Thus, while it seems reasonable to accept that, in general, speech is the most efficient form of basic communication among those who hear normally, there is doubt about the extent to which some hearing-impaired children can be given access to the acoustic and/or articulatory codes that underlie the acquisition and use of spoken language. The theory as stated does not, however, suggest that all children can acquire high levels of speech communication; just that oral education is the only way to access the codes of spoken language. Evidence to date does not contradict this point of view, but if it is true, then the quantity and type of oral education that is required by individual children and the range of options under which it can be effectively delivered have to be defined.

The notion that spoken language skills are a help in learning to read and write receives considerable support (Truax, 1978). However, since there are children with little or no spoken language who can read and write, it is clear that reading and writing skills do not depend entirely on spoken language. Since many educational skills are developed through the written form, the relationship of speech to reading requires much more study. The importance of this question is indicated by the results of a large survey of school-aged hearing-impaired children by Jensema and Trybus, which showed that educational achievements were positively correlated with speech but not with sign (Jensema & Trybus, 1978, Table 19, p. 17). These results strongly suggest that emphasis on speech communication in the early years, as advocated by the authors of the following chapters, may have considerable positive influence on subsequent academic performance.

Widely divergent levels of spoken language skill are to be found among children in oral programs. A substantial proportion can become highly competent and go on to receive most of their education in regular schools with minimal support services (Lane, 1976). Some acquire few spoken language skills and have to be placed in different types of programs. Others function at less than satisfactory levels of competence that lie between these two extremes and receive most of their education in oral schools or classes (Conrad, 1979). The degree of oral competence achieved does not necessarily depend on the degree of hearing impairment (Karchmer et al., 1979). Other factors are involved. These include the presence of additional handicaps, the teaching procedures used, the teacher/clinician's competence, and parental involvement. Such variables influence the results obtained through either of the two main intervention options; oral or total communication.

Children need a sufficiently intact central nervous system and reasonably good cognitive skills in order to learn the acoustic and/or articulatory codes underlying spoken language (or the comparable codes underlying sign language). Children with additional damage that results in language learning problems are more commonly found among hearing-impaired children whose deafness is due to prenatal or postnatal infections or birth injury than among normally hearing children. This is because whatever causes the deafness may also impair the child's ability to process verbal material presented either through speech or sign. However, whenever certain procedures fail to accomplish their purpose, professionals tend to blame the client rather than look for reasons related to themselves or their programs (Stubbins, 1982). Problems can stem from inadequate procedures.

Oral teaching procedures have changed over the years with advances in, for example, technology, the development of early intervention programs, and knowledge about speech and language acquisition. However, while specific studies suggest that these advances now permit more children to have better access to the codes underlying spoken language (see Bess et al., 1981), there have so far been no extensive comparisons between the achievement of children taught orally in recent years and similar children taught in previous decades. In any case, even if advancing technology has helped some children with useful residual hearing to gain better oral communication skills, it has, so far, done little for totally deaf children, because alternatives to hearing aids, such as wearable tactile devices and cochlear implants, are only just coming into use. Their effects on oral education remain to be evaluated. To a great extent, how well procedures are developed and applied depends on the knowledge and skills of the teacher/clinicians working in any program. Professional competencies have never been studied in relation to hearing-impaired children's achievements in early intervention programs, although many of these competencies have been clearly defined (Zeitlin, du Verglas, & Windhover, 1982).

Children sometimes become hearing-impaired as a result of illness in early childhood (e.g., meningitis) after they have learned spoken language. The object of early oral intervention for such adventitiously hearing-impaired children is to maintain their naturally acquired oral skills so that they can continue to speak and have the advantages of spoken language both for their education and later adult life. Children who become hearing-impaired after learning language have great advantages over their peers whose hearing impairment dates from birth or before spoken language has been acquired. The procedures used with adventitiously hearing-impaired children are aimed at developing the use of any residual hearing and reinforcing the use of existing speech skills so that articulatory coding abilities are preserved and expanded. However, if appropriate early intervention is not provided, most of the skills already acquired can deteriorate and be lost within the space of a few months (Binnie, Daniloff, & Buckingham, 1982). Such rapid loss of spoken language skills is more common in younger children than in older children but rare in adults.

Good spoken language skills afford hearing-impaired children many personal, social, and educational advantages and are an asset in many areas of employment in adult life. Accordingly, the development of speech reception and speech production skills is seen as highly desirable by most parents and by the vast majority of professionals regardless of the early intervention options they provide. There is general agreement that hearing-impaired children who have the potential ability to learn to speak and to understand speech should be given the opportunity to do so. Since the greatest emphasis on the acquisition of spoken language is to be found in oral programs, teacher/clinicians in such programs often recommend that all hearing-impaired children whose parents want their children to speak should first select an early oral intervention program. Their rationale is that individual children's potential for spoken language can best be determined in the course of diagnostic teaching in which every opportunity to speak and to understand speech is provided in the absence of competing means of communication. This view, which is held by all four of the contributors to this book, has been challenged on several counts. It is not our intention here to enter into a controversy over its validity. The arguments for and against oral intervention as the first option are far-reaching, and can only be resolved by research studies that directly and adequately address the many facets of this question. Research that has bearing on the matter has either not been undertaken, provides only indirect evidence, or is experimentally unsound and, on this account, is not reviewed.

SUMMARY

This chapter discusses oral options for hearing-impaired children, particularly in relation to early intervention. Hearing impairment can range from mild to total deafness and can be more severe for some (usually high-frequency) sounds than others. All types of hearing impairment can cause personal, social, and educational handicaps; and the more severe the hearing impairment, the more extensive the handicap is likely to be. Hearing impairment involves not only children who suffer it, but their parents and families. When parents and families take a very active role in the habilitation process it is more likely to succeed than when the task is left mainly to professionals. Professionals who offer oral options are usually either teachers of the deaf or speech–language pathologists, although some audiologists also work with hearing–impaired infants and their parents. Early intervention programs providing oral options are not available in some areas. Oral options emphasize the development of spoken language skills and the eventual integration of children into society at large. While many children succeed in acquiring high levels of spoken language, some do not. Four exemplary early oral programs are described in the following chapters.

REFERENCES

Bess, F. H., Freeman, B. A., & Sinclair, J. S. (1981). *Amplification in education.* Washington, DC: Alexander Graham Bell Association for the Deaf.

Binnie, C. A., Daniloff, R. G., & Buckingham, H. W. (1982). Phonetic disintegration in a five-year-old following sudden hearing loss. *Journal of Speech and Hearing Disorders, 47,* 181–189.

Bloom, L., & Lahey, M. (1978). *Language development and language disorders.* New York: Wiley.

Boothroyd, A. (1981). *Hearing impairments in young children.* Englewood Cliffs, NJ: Prentice–Hall.

Bromwich, R. (1981). *Working with parents and infants.* Baltimore: University Park Press.

Bronfenbrenner, U. (1975). Is early intervention effective? In M. Guttentag & F. Steuning (Eds.), *Handbook of education research* (Vol. 2). Beverly Hills, CA: Sage.

Catlin, F. I. (1978). Etiology and pathology of hearing loss in children. In F. N. Martin (Ed.), *Pediatric audiology* (pp. 3–112). Englewood Cliffs, NJ: Prentice-Hall.

Conrad, R. (1979). *The deaf schoolchild.* London: Harper & Row.

Cornett, R.O. (1967). Cued speech. *American Annals of the Deaf, 112,* 3-13.

Erber, N. (1982). *Auditory training.* Washington, DC: Alexander Graham Bell Association for the Deaf.

Ewing, A. W. G., & Ewing, E. C. (1971). *Hearing impaired children under five: A guide for parents and teachers.* Manchester, England: Manchester University Press.

Fraser, G. R. (1976). *The causes of profound deafness in children.* Baltimore: John Hopkins University Press.

Geers, A. E. (1983). Spoken language of deaf children. *Central Institute for the Deaf News Notes,* Fall, 1–2.

Jensema, C. J., & Trybus, R. J. (1978). *Communication patterns and educational achievements.* Washington, DC: Office of Demographic Studies, Gallaudet College, Series T, No. 2.

Karchmer, M. A., Milone, M. N., & Wolk, S. (1979). Educational significance of hearing loss at three levels of severity. *American Annals of the Deaf, 124,* 97–109.

Lane, H. S. (1976). The profoundly deaf: Has oral education succeeded? *Volta Review, 78,* 329–340.

Ling, D. (1976). *Speech and the hearing-impaired child: Theory and practice.* Washington, DC: Alexander Graham Bell Association for the Deaf.

Ling, D., & Nienhuys, T. G. (1983). The deaf child: habilitation with and without a cochlear implant. *Annals of Otology, Rhinology, and Laryngology, 92,* 593–598.

Luterman, D. (1979). *Counseling parents of hearing impaired children.* Boston: Little, Brown.

Markides, A. (1983). *The speech of hearing-impaired children.* Manchester, England: Manchester University Press.

Mulholland, A. M. (Ed.). (1981). *Oral education today and tomorrow.* Washington, DC: Alexander Graham Bell Association for the Deaf.

Nicholls, G. H. (1979). *Cued speech and the reception of spoken language.* Washington, DC: Office of Cued Speech, Gallaudet College.

Nix, G. W. (1975). Total communication: A review of the studies offered in its support. *Volta Review, 77,* 470–494.

Proctor, A., & Goldstein, M. H. (1983). Development of lexical comprehension in a profoundly deaf child using a wearable vibrotactile communication aid. *Language Speech and Hearing Services in Schools, 14,* 138–149.

Shontz, F. (1967). Reaction to crisis. *Volta Review, 69,* 405–411.

Stone, P. (1983). Auditory learning in a school setting. *Volta Review, 85,* 7-13.

Stubbins, J. (1982). *The clinical attitude in rehabilitation: A cross cultural view.* New York: World Rehabilitation Fund Inc., Monograph 16.

Truax, R. R. (1978). Reading and language. In R. R. Kretschmer & L. W. Kretschmer (Eds.), *Language development and intervention with the hearing impaired.* Baltimore: University Park Press.

Vaughan, P. (Ed.). (1981). *Learning to listen: A book by mothers for mothers of hearing-impaired children.* Toronto: Beaufort Books.

Zeitlin, S., du Verglas, G., & Windhover, R. (1982). *Basic competencies for personnel in early intervention programs.* Seattle, WA: Westar (Westar Series paper 14).

2
THE HELEN BEEBE SPEECH AND HEARING CENTER

Helen H. Beebe
Helen R. Pearson
Mary Eager Koch

Basic to the philosophy of the unisensory approach is that minimal amounts of residual hearing can be capitalized upon to aid in the development of speech and language with which the hearing world can be comfortable. With appropriate amplification and training it is possible for most children to learn to process language auditorally. If, after diagnostic therapy by a skilled teacher/clinician, it is found that a child cannot reach his or her potential through auditory–verbal teaching, alternatives must be considered. Our philosophy is that every hearing-impaired child should be given that opportunity to learn to listen.

To facilitate reading this chapter, children are referred to in the masculine gender and therapists in the feminine.

PRESENT STATE OF THE CENTER

The Helen Beebe Speech and Hearing Center, Easton, Pennsylvania, has been in existence for more than 40 years. Helen Beebe began working in the middle 1940s as a one-person private practice, and today the Center's staff consists of four therapists, two interns, and two administrative staff. In addition, there is a part-time occupational therapist and a part-time psychologist.

Beebe opened the practice as a general speech and voice clinic. Gradually, as the word of her success using the unisensory philosophy

The authors express appreciation to each and every member of the staff for their contributions to this chapter in the forms of support, constructive criticism, and proofreading. Special credit goes to Doris Bader for her patience in typing the manuscript.

spread, profoundly deaf clients were seen. Today, the Center is still run as a general practice, serving all ages with all types of communication problems. At the present time, approximately two thirds of the clients are hearing-impaired children and the remaining one third are seen for other reasons (i.e., delayed language, articulation, stuttering, voice problems).

Easton, Pennsylvania, is located in the foothills of the Pocono Mountains along the Delaware River and is rich in history and tradition. Its proximity to both New York and Philadelphia provides easy access to a widespread population for commuting to the Center. The Center is situated on the main street of a lovely residential area known as "College Hill" because it is where Lafayette College's spreading campus overlooks the city of Easton.

The present building which houses the Center is the product of years of hopes and dreams. The Center has been growing in clients, staff, and outreach, necessitating a consolidation of bulging and makeshift quarters. An old brick residence was purchased and a capital drive was successfully promoted to cover the cost of renovations. The main entrance opens to a foyer; there is a waiting room to one side with an access hall to the offices of the clinical director and executive director where clients are directed for their initial interviews. On the other side of the foyer are three threapy rooms, each with its own one-way window and intercom.

The second floor is also divided. The area to the left is the administrative office–secretarial suite and a board room where the videotape library is housed. A spacious third floor provides space for a research center and facilities for sensory integration.

The right side of the second floor is the Larry Jarret House apartment, a fully equipped two-bedroom, large living room, kitchen-and-bathroom housing facility with a separate outside entrance.

There are plans to enclose a porch at the rear of the building for full audiological services in the future. At the present time, there are limited audiological services at the Helen Beebe Speech and Hearing Center. The present equipment consists of a portable audiometer, impedance bridge, and hearing aid test set.

There is a small backyard and garage with an off-street parking area. The tree lined street is mainly residential with small businesses as well as conveniences common to areas surrounding a college campus. There is a bank branch, drug store, florist, grocery store, laundromat, and several restaurants. Next door is a luncheonette which is used by almost all of the clients. The owners, Harriet and Jake, know the families and follow the children's progress.

The Beebe Center is presently governed by a board of directors. The board had developed from a parents' group and was originally composed of parents of the clients. The purpose and thrust of the board has changed through the years, and the current composition of the board is parents of present clients, parents of former clients, professional and business persons from the community, and interested friends. The board meets monthly with the administrative staff, and special committees meet regularly to promote the welfare of the Center.

There has been an outreach into the community through a membership drive and the response was generous and enthusiastic. Members of the staff speak to service clubs, lecture to classes in colleges and universities, and participate in workshops throughout the United States. The videotapes, which show various aspects of the program, have been an effective way of demonstrating the quality of communication that is possible for many children in a unisensory setting.

The Center receives requests for workshops or conferences, which the staff fills when possible. Inquiries from parents and searches for information by professionals are answered individually with the Center's brochure and appropriate literature.

Pennsylvania State University began sending graduate students for practicums in the unisensory approach in 1976; later, Temple University, McGill University, and Smith College–Clarke School sent students to spend 4 to 10 weeks to be exposed to the unisensory philosophy. Some of these students have gone on for further training in this area.

A more formal intern program was established in 1970. This program is 1 year in length. The main requirement is a master's degree in the area of communication disorders (speech pathology, audiology, deaf education). Experience is immaterial; it is provided through on-the-job training. (One intern who had had 3 years of experience teaching in a school for the deaf made the remark that she had spent the first few weeks "unlearning.") The program entails a good deal of observation of therapy sessions, taking over therapy under supervision, parent guidance and, at the completion of 1 year, the competence to carry a caseload. There are required readings as well as lectures and discussions about educational philosophies. The purpose of the program is to strengthen the present staff and to make unisensory therapy available to areas where needed.

The Helen Beebe Speech and Hearing Center had its inception in 1944. The practice began in a two-room rented basement. In 1955, Beebe built a one-story office, later expanded to provide two additional treatment rooms. The practice included the treatment of speech, voice, and hearing disorders. Although Beebe had been an oral teacher of the deaf, trained at Clarke School, she was eager to put into practice the techniques she had learned during the period 1942 to 1944 from Emil Froeschels, MD, her instructor in speech–voice pathology. Her first cases, which included stuttering, cleft palate, delayed speech, brain damage, and functional voice disorders were indeed challenging. Then, in 1945, she was consulted about a 15-month-old child, Mardee, whose hearing was questioned. Indeed, it turned out that the only evidence of the existence of minimal residual hearing was obtained through Emil Froeschels' Direct Tone Introduction Test, using Urbantschitsch whistles (Froeschels & Beebe, 1946). Later it was discovered that the mother had Rubella during pregnancy. Thus, Beebe had the first opportunity to put into practice the theory she had learned from Froeschels, which had originated with Victor Urbantschitsch in Vienna (Urbantschitsch, 1895). Namely, if even very small remnants of hearing are stimulated early enough and sufficiently, spontaneous speech might develop. Language could be processed through amplified hearing. The child might acquire oral communication adequate to permit him to be educated with hearing peers. Max Goldstein (1939) had also learned the so called acoustic method from Urbantschitsch and had tried to introduce it in St. Louis. This method was not practical until after World War II when wearable hearing aids were made available.

Without any of the modern refinements of audiology, Mardee was fitted with a powerful hearing aid so large that the cell batteries were carried in a jacket on her back. Her parents were instructed in home training in order to stimulate her amplified hearing all her waking hours. Spontaneous speech emerged about a year after she received the hearing aid—a miracle to a teacher of the deaf who had experienced only synthetic speech development. And, in contrast to that "oral method," as speech/language developed, there were no attempts to correct articulation—only encouragement to imitate a natural speech melody. Gradually, oral communication adequate to cope with the hearing world was achieved and educators were initiated into accepting a "deaf" (only deaf without a hearing aid) child into the classroom. At that time, there were no special services, not even a speech therapist, in public schools.

Through disc recording, Mardee was presented as a case demonstration at a meeting of the International Association of Logopedics and Phoniatrics (IALP) in Amsterdam in 1950. (Soundfilm, Six Children, 1965, Vienna; 1980 videotape, ICAVC, Washington.) Mardee, a university graduate, has been described in the literature (Beebe, 1953; Crannell, 1948).

In 1947, Beebe trained an assistant, Antoinette Goffredo, who became invaluable as the practice grew. For 3 years, Beebe also had a speech clinic in Easton Hospital, and she and "Guffy" maintained both settings. However, Beebe had to give up the hospital clinic when she agreed to go to New York 3 days a week to work as Dr. Froeschels' assistant in his private practice, as well as in his clinic at Mt. Sinai Hospital. This affiliation was invaluable to Beebe, not only as a learning experience, but also as a source of expert medical consultation when needed for her private cases. Beebe had the opportunity to work with some other cases in the late 1940s to early 1950s (Beebe, 1953). However, it was not until the rubella epidemic of 1964–1965 that the caseload included a number of hearing-impaired children. The closest audiological services were in Philadelphia. The director of audiology at St. Christopher's Hospital had first-hand knowledge of Beebe's work. She consented to Beebe's request in 1964 to try using a hearing aid on a 5-month-old "rubella baby," although there was no objective evidence that he had any residual hearing. The baby, David, had been referred to Beebe by the family physician who was acquainted with several of Beebe's cases.

By this time, Beebe had proven through experience that even small amounts of residual hearing, when stimulated sufficiently through amplification, could lead to spontaneous speech development. She was also able to demonstrate to David's apprehensive parents an ongoing case who had already achieved a satisfactory quality of oral communication. Five-month-old David's mother observed the nine-year-old girl and concluded bravely, "If she can do it, David can do it." With this kind of determination and motivation on the part of a parent, the battle is won.

In the early years of Beebe's practice, there was a negative sort of motivation. If the child did not succeed in such an auditory program, he would have no choice but to enter a residential school for the deaf at age 4.

At the time David was first seen at the Center in 1964, Beebe had not had the opportunity to treat infants under 6 months of age in formal therapy. He was a local child so his mother received instruction by means of the telephone or visited the Center to observe, to report, and to receive suggestions. (His mother was so conscientious that one day she phoned almost in a panic to say she was afraid David was lip reading.) David was almost 2 years old when he came to the

Center for regular therapy twice a week for 1 hour. He had been fitted with a powerful aid using a Y cord.

At age 5, David's Y cord was exchanged for two, really binaural, aids directly after Beebe visited Pollack in Denver in 1969. Until that time, Beebe had not had the opportunity to observe other programs using a so-called unisensory approach. She concluded that the major difference between Pollack's clients and her clients was that most of Pollack's clients had binaural fittings (Pollack, 1970). The rationale for monaural fittings 20 years earlier must have been that infants could not have managed the bulk of two body aids.

From that time on, binaural fittings were recommended. (With few exceptions, the older cases adjusted to using two aids.) Audiologists were not always enthusiastic about recommending two aids, but when parents learned of the advantages of binaural versus monaural aids, parents won out. If the argument for neglecting the poorer ear arose, Beebe insisted that ear could be stimulated with special exercises and eventually be an asset in binaural listening. A number of families with hearing-impaired children of a variety of etiologies had found their way to Beebe during the 1950s. In 1960, a parents' group was organized by George Fellendorf who had moved to Easton so that his daughter could receive therapy. This group was comprised of families from the Lehigh Valley. In 1970, they financed the first intern to be trained specifically in the unisensory approach.

The Larry Jarret Foundation was started in 1972 in memory of Larry Jarret, one of Beebe's hearing-impaired children who had been killed in an accident. The Jarret family felt that the Lehigh Valley parents' group had lost its impetus to promote the unisensory approach and hoped that the foundation could underwrite more interns and generally spread the philosophy so that more children could have the opportunity to profit from such an approach. A governing board was established and money-making projects, in addition to an appeal for grants, were initiated. However, this was on a voluntary basis until 1977 when a secretary and Larry Jarret House coordinator were acquired through CETA funds and an administrative director was hired.

The Larry Jarret Foundation had been financing the rental of the Larry Jarret House from 1975, and since 1978, another building which housed the secretary, administrative director, and sensory integration facility. There has never been support from state or federal sources, only donations from private sources, service clubs, and foundation grants. Since 1978, when Mrs. Beebe donated the building and practice, client fees have also been included in the budget.

In 1981, a capital fund drive was initiated in order to buy and renovate a building for the purpose of consolidating the clinic and two rental buildings. At the time, it was decided to name the nonprofit organization the Helen Beebe Speech and Hearing Center and to retain the Larry Jarret House as the name of the apartment with a separate entrance. The new building has been in use since May 1982.

A grant-in-aid program was initiated in 1981. No client is turned away for lack of funds. An effort is made to help clients obtain insurance coverage. A scholarship endowment fund for both therapy and related costs has been instituted.

PHILOSOPHY

Simultaneous clinical work by others in the field produced a more widespread awareness of the importance of early detection of hearing loss and of the possibility of capitalizing on stimulation of even minimal residual hearing. In addition to Pollack, there was the work of Whetnall and Fry (1964) in England and Griffiths (1974) in California.

Sometimes it seems we are working to overcome the prejudice of centuries, namely, that a deaf child has to grow up mute. Almost a century ago, Urbantschitsch in Austria and Goldstein in the United States were working against the same prejudice. Teachers of the deaf then, and tragically some of them now, are indoctrinated with ideas of unwarranted limitations placed upon the child with impaired hearing. Boothroyd (in Stark, 1974) states, "The development of communication follows a natural law; what does not work will be dropped and what does work will be accepted and survive. The motivation of the child to adapt to the language of the larger community is reduced as the community adapts to his language" (p. 148). Furth (also in Stark, 1974) states, "As long as the deaf child is treated as deficient in concept formation, and as long as the teaching of language is considered a means of overcoming this deficiency, his motivation for language learning will be poor. We must accept the deaf child as he is and not explicitly nor implicitly convey to him the image that he is deficient or failing" (p. 151).

Informed parents sought an auditory approach and were willing to travel great distances to give their hearing-impaired children the benefit of this type of training, therefore, the hearing-impaired cases at the clinic now came from a much broader geographic area, even from abroad, and also comprised a much larger proportion of the overall caseload. Frequently the suggestion has been made that the Center limit its clients to hearing-impaired, but Beebe has maintained (and the staff agrees) that there are great advantages to being involved with the speech–language problems of children who hear normally. The hearing-impaired child may well have problems in speech–language development which are unrelated to his hearing deficit (Figure 2-1).

All clients at the Beebe Center are seen on a one-to-one basis. Children are seen without their parents, although in recent years parents may observe therapy through one-way windows. The last part of the session is used to confer with and to advise the parent about home therapy. Teachers and other concerned professionals may also confer and observe therapy. Parents are given the opportunity to meet, informally or formally, with other parents. Particularly with the hearing-impaired child, the lessons serve to demonstrate not only what should be done, but what the expectation level should be in home training.

Therapy has to be on a one-to-one basis because our training of the hearing-impaired child is geared to follow the speech and language development of the hearing child. At whatever age the child is aided and training is begun, one must "zero in" on the child's intellect and personality which have been conditioned by his soundless world. A child of superior intelligence deprived of normal hearing is apt to organize his world to his satisfaction without making the effort to use oral communication. Another child may be satisfied to remain in the stage of echolalia or telegraphic speech. Chronological age, hearing age, psychological types, and many other factors, for instance sensory integration, in addition to the primary condition of impaired hearing, may have to be taken into consideration when planning a habilitation program. Individual therapy seems the only effective means of monitoring and implementing these various factors.

The Center advocates team teaching in the sense that a child is seen by more than one therapist. There are several advantages to this procedure. After treating the child for several sessions, a review and discussion of problems observed by the therapists involved adds perspective to subsequent treatment of the child or advice to the parents. Also, the child, whether hearing impaired or not, must learn to communicate orally with the community at large.

The following qualifications have been established as requisites for a parent-centered auditory program:

Acceptance of a commitment to the unisensory philosophy that profoundly deaf children are able to learn language through hearing;

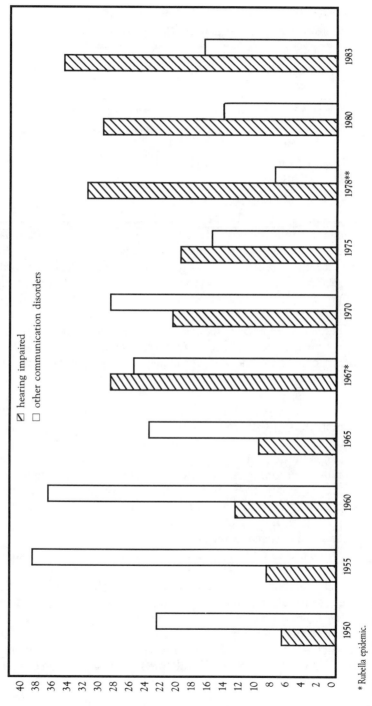

FIGURE 2-1. Client distribution at the Helen Beebe Speech and Hearing Center.

☑ hearing impaired
☐ other communication disorders

* Rubella epidemic.

** Increase in Larry Jarret House cases.

Appropriate binaural amplification during all waking moments;

Controlled behavioral management; establishing firm guidelines for behavioral management and establishing the child's responsibility for appropriate behavior;

Intensive intervention: one-to-one therapy for demonstration of teaching techniques;

Full family involvement;

Educational and social environment with hearing peers;

Acceptance of the hearing-impaired child as a person and respect for his right to develop his fullest potential;

High expectation for performance and achievement.

GOALS FOR THE PROGRAM

The aims of the program at the Helen Beebe Speech and Hearing Center are to incorporate these requisites in the goals for staff, parents, and children. The high achievements of any individual at the Center are due to a unified effort of therapist, parent, and child working together. The unisensory approach could not succeed without all three responding to the challenges of teaching, learning, and living the philosophy.

The staff members are required to function efficiently in many areas. Since the Center provides a team-teaching approach, each staff person is expected to be knowledgeable about every aspect of the Center's services, although each member is encouraged to develop her area of expertise.

A major responsibility of each staff member at the Center is demonstration teaching. Primarily it is done so that the family is challenged to carry through at home. At the same time, it serves as a demonstration for interns, practicum students, and visiting professionals. Counseling the families is an important and ongoing aspect of family contact. Parents constantly need to be informed and encouraged. In addition, interaction with other staff members is important for sharing ideas and thereby helping the clients. Each staff person is challenged to keep abreast of new trends and research through the literature and to be enlightened through conferences and related courses.

Staff members have a responsibility to be aware of outreach through the intern training program, serving as a practicum site, and encouraging visits from other professionals. School personnel serving the Center's clients are invited to visit and confer and conversely to request a visit from the staff when appropriate. Occasionally, a member of the staff will accompany a family for an audiological assessment. As well as giving support to the family, the staff member can become familiar with audiological services in the area and the audiologist can learn firsthand about the philosophy of the Center.

Participation in workshops and seminars and lectures to the public through service clubs, parents' organizations, and church groups serve as outreach channels. Staff members are also encouraged to publish articles and to maintain communication with other professionals and agencies. Efficient record keeping, testing, and videotaping are ongoing projects; in order to provide effective data for research purposes, all aspects of the child's profile must be documented.

The parents have a responsibility to understand the unisensory philosophy. They need to be knowledgeable about their child's hearing loss and the implications. They must monitor the hearing aids regularly. Most importantly, they need to know normal language development and expect the same from their child. If there are no siblings, the parents should use neighborhood children as models and/or visit play centers, nursery schools.

Parents need to be aware of their counseling needs and to seek help from professionals. Other parents can be a source of help and, conversely, a good supportive parent group can provide a service for parents of newly identified cases. The informal waiting room atmosphere can be conducive to exchanges of experiences. Talking with those who have been through the experiences one is facing can be the best source of information and support.

Parents (primarily the mother in most cases) need to be aware of the home dynamics and encourage family members to provide the best learning environment for the child. Demonstrating to siblings, grandparents, and close neighborhood friends the expectations for performance is the surest way to achieve success. Effective parenting skills are important to set the stage for learning. Hearing-impaired children have the same needs from parents as any other child: guidance, acceptance, approval, and love.

The main goal for children is to process language through their hearing, to order their world with natural languages, to achieve linguistic competency. Using their hearing to the maximum will in most cases ensure acquisition of receptive language in a natural manner and, with encouragement, expressive language can also follow a normal developmental model.

Good attending behavior is necessary to set the scene for optimum learning and from that point developing the use of amplified residual hearing to the maximum is the goal. Listening with good auditory attention should be extended to causal listening in the ideal learning environment.

Responses are encouraged and expected. The child's efforts are accepted and language is elicited without pressure for accurate articulation. As a hearing child needs to store up speech sounds and spoken language before expressive speech emerges, so does the hearing-impaired child *from the time of amplification with training.*

The children are placed with hearing peers from nursery school on in order to be exposed to the language of their peers. Social skills are developed through home, neighborhood, and educational setting. The same limits and expectations are placed on the hearing-impaired children, and they are usually able to cope with unfamiliar situations without too much difficulty. The emphasis on attending behavior at times makes them better candidates for the regular educational setting than their hearing peers.

ENROLLMENT PROCEDURES

The children seen at the Helen Beebe Speech and Hearing Center are referred by a variety of sources. Some are referred by physicians, others by audiologists. But, in many instances, the medical schools and training institutions for audiology do not give adequate information about all of the options available. Other professionals and individuals working in centers and programs where the reputation of the Helen Beebe Speech and Hearing Center is known have sent cases to the Center. However, to date, the major source of referrals is word-of-mouth. A convinced parent whose child is making good progress can be an enthusiastic advocate of the program.

Many times parents have had to search long and hard before discovering the availability of an auditory approach to educating their hearing-impaired child. They have been limited by professionals who are not fully informed of all the alternatives. Informed parents with all the options clearly and objectively defined should have the privilege of making the choice for their child.

At the initial appointment, the child is assessed informally using a variety of therapy materials to check auditory responses and communication skills. The therapists meet with the parents, review past records, discuss the rationale for the philosophy at the Center, and stress the need for parent participation, which is necessary for developing speech and language in an auditory approach.

The parents are given an opportunity to meet and confer with several staff members, and also to meet parents whose children are having therapy. They may also view videotapes which demonstrate therapy techniques and show children at various stages of language development. Most importantly, there is an opportunity to meet children in the program and to interact with them.

There are no specific criteria for selection of clients. The ideal is early detection *and* amplification *and* training. However, therapy is initiated as soon as possible after identification, no matter how old the child is. It must be pointed out that older children entering the program can be taught to listen and to hear, but their gains may be less significant that those who are initiated early. The hearing level is not a selection factor, for the therapists at the Center feel that opportunities for the child should not be limited on the basis of an audiogram.

At times, children with multiple handicaps are seen and can be taught using this philosophy if the hearing impairment is the major factor interfering with communication.

A schedule is set up for diagnostic therapy. Children are usually seen twice a week for hourly sessions and the parents are expected to follow through at home with direction from the Center. There are conferences with the families and annual reevaluations to monitor progress. Comprehensive reports are written periodically. These can be shared with other centers where the child has been evaluated and with the regular school when appropriate.

PARENT GUIDANCE

Families come to the Beebe Center with a variety of backgrounds and experiences. Some are referred to the Center directly following the initial diagnosis of hearing loss. Others have begun treatment and/or guidance at other centers. Many have received conflicting views regarding hearing loss and communication potential. Whatever the initial experience may have been, all families are given specific and practical guidelines so that they may begin effective auditory intervention at home.

The parent program at the Beebe Center is as highly individualized as each child's therapy. There is no schedule of instruction or guidance. As the staff–parent relationship builds through weekly interactions before or after the child's lesson, an awareness develops of the parents' needs, their strengths and weaknesses, concerns, skills, and understanding. Time is taken, as necessary, to meet these needs.

At first, parents as well as professionals are shocked by the idea that in order to force the child to attain his maximal use of residual hearing, we eliminate lip reading cues. This is a crucial departure from traditional oral or aural–oral teaching which from the beginning presents speech–language in multisensory fashion. Given a choice, the child would certainly use his unimpaired sense, sight, rather than the weaker sense, hearing. Yes, he would probably acquire receptive and some expressive language more quickly in the beginning, but he would do no more than perceive sound through the aid. He would certainly not learn to process language auditorally nor achieve his *full* potential in oral communication. Croft (1977) states that we are turning a four-sensed child into a five-sensed child. Parents and therapists working with the child are expected to cover their mouths or to avoid having the child visually focus on the lips during speech–language stimulation, whether during a lesson or incidental learning. Many of the children never make a point of searching for lip reading cues. However, they all naturally learn to lip read in the course of exposure to school and other social situations. We are well aware that individual amplification is limited as to distance hearing so that hearing has to be supplemented with seeing in a classroom situation. Auditory trainers may be prescribed for classroom use.

Once a child has achieved maximal use of his residual (amplified) hearing, therapy sessions might be, at least partially, multisensory. Parents and therapists must, however, continue to guard against a deterioration of listening skills. One of the obvious examples of diminished listening skill is likely to take place when hearing aids are off for periods of time when children are swimming.

PROCEDURES

The parent education and guidance program includes instruction on hearing and hearing loss. Most parents arrive at the Beebe Center with their child's most recent audiogram. When asked if the audiogram has been explained to them, most reply, "not really." In fact, for many the only message the parent has perceived from the audiologist's evaluation is that their child is "deaf."

Presenting the audiogram in clear, concise terms can help alleviate many of the parents' misconceptions about hearing loss (and "deafness"). At the Beebe Center audiograms are discussed in terms of what the child can hear and not what he cannot hear.

Terminology is explained in simple, concise terms. The parent's hearing is tested on a portable audiometer to demonstrate how thresholds are established. Having experienced the concentration necessary, the parents can more easily understand the difficulty in establishing accurate thresholds in young children.

An explanation of the basic acoustics of speech is included. The phonemes of Ling's five sound test /a, u, i, ʃ, s/ are plotted on an audiogram along with the overall speech range or "speech banana." If the parents have understood the audiogram to this point, they will see that the speech range is inaudible (unaided) to a severely or profoundly hearing-impaired child. The basic function of hearing aids (gain) is then explained and an aided audiogram is plotted. The parents are encouraged to focus on the aided thresholds, understanding that this is a more significant representation of the child's hearing. The hearing aids are the child's ears and there is no reason for him ever to be without them (Figure 2-2).

A parents' educated observations are a valuable source of information in assessing a child's hearing. At the Beebe Center, parents are encouraged to keep a diary of their child's responses to sound as well as emerging receptive and expressive vocabulary and language. In addition to its value audiologically, the diary can serve as a source of encouragement when parents feel despondent about their child's progress.

Parents are expected to check their child's hearing aids at least once a day. (Checks should be done more often with very young, active children.) After the therapist (or audiologist) has determined that the hearing aid is in proper working order, a hearing aid check is demonstrated to the parent (Appendix 2-A). The parent is then observed practicing the check to be sure that it is done correctly. Although therapists at the Center do periodic checks (both listening and acoustic analyses with the Center's Phonix Box), it is primarily the parents' responsibility to ensure that the hearing aid is in optimal working order.

The parent education and guidance program also includes direct observation and/or videotapes of other children in therapy. Watching profoundly hearing-impaired children maximizing their residual hearing is often the most effective encouragement to a beginning parent. Parents new to the program are encouraged to observe other hearing-impaired children informally and in therapy. In addition, they have the opportunity to interact with other parents who share a common experience.

The Beebe Center has an extensive library of videotapes which are available to the parents and visitors; some tapes can be rented (Appendix 2-B). Tapes show techniques used in therapy, parents teaching their children, progress of children, and sensory integration.

FIGURE 2-2. Hypothetical audiogram showing the speech range, main components of the five sounds [u, a, i, ʃ, s] spoken at 2 yd (see Ling & Ling, 1978), aided audiogram (□), unaided audiogram (left ear x), degrees of hearing loss, and intensities of common sounds.

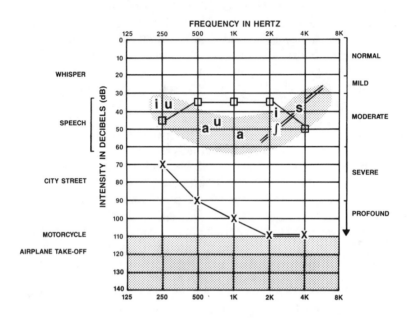

Instruction and Guidance on Topics Related to Hearing Loss

In order to effectively adapt and implement the formal therapy goals at home, the parents need to develop a basic understanding of a variety of topics related to hearing loss and child development. Parent training at the Beebe Center includes instruction and guidance in the basic principles of the unisensory philosophy; the audiogram; hearing and hearing loss; hearing aids; auditory, language, and speech development; behavior management; and guidelines for both formal and informal lessons at home. Most topics are introduced in the context of the child's biweekly lessons at the Center. During the lesson the therapist working with the child may make brief comments to the parent who is watching from the observation room. Ten minutes are reserved at the end of the child's lesson to discuss the lesson with the parent present, and to give suggestions for follow-up at home.

Appointments are scheduled, as needed, to address specific concern of either the parent or the staff.

General parent meetings are held at the Center three to four times annually. These meetings include presentations on a variety of issues related to hearing loss. Parents are often called upon to participate in panel or small group discussions. For many parents who live up to 100 miles from Easton, the parent meetings, seasonal parties, and picnics provide a valuable opportunity to meet with other parents from the Center.

DEMONSTRATION LESSONS: FORMAL AND INFORMAL

As previously discussed, observation of the child's lesson is an important part of the parents' program. Specific activities and techniques of auditory and communication development, instructional strategies, and behavior management are demonstrated. Parents are expected to follow through with a daily lesson at home. Whereas parents may get ideas from the lesson observed at the Center, they are cautioned from the very beginning to avoid using the identical activities and materials at home. Variety, versatility, and innovation are encouraged.

It is important that the parent develop the skills to apply goals of formal therapy to informal situations. This skill may not come naturally and may need to be demonstrated to the parent. A therapist may take a parent and child to the grocery store, dairy farm, or neighborhood luncheonette and show the parent how to capitalize on listening and language opportunities. Making cookies or play dough, sorting laundry, putting away groceries, are all activities with rich language potential. This potential is demonstrated to the parent to facilitate its carry-over into their own daily routines.

PARENT LESSONS

Implementing teaching goals and strategies at home may be difficult for a new parent. To aid them in the development of the necessary skills, parents occasionally give formal lessons at the Center. A staff therapist observes the lesson, which is usually a half hour in length. The remaining half hour is spent discussing the lesson. The therapist presents the parents with a list of specific observations, emphasizing both strengths and weaknesses, and suggestions of how the parent can be more effective in working with the child. In the beginning, many parents are reluctant to be observed giving lessons, but most find it a very positive, constructive experience. The parent lesson also enables the staff to identify problem areas which might otherwise remain undetected.

PARENT GUIDELINES FOR FORMAL AND INFORMAL LESSONS

When a child starts therapy at the Beebe Center, parents are expected to also begin daily lessons at home. In addition to these lessons, parents are expected to "teach" language throughout the day. Not all parents are natural teachers, but as parents of a hearing-impaired child, they must learn. The success of their child depends upon their ability to effectively adapt the strategies and goals of formal therapy to their child's daily life.

In the beginning, parents are given specific instructions such as procedures for daily hearing aid check, keeping the hearing aids on during all waking hours, eliminating gestures and other visual cues, covering their mouth when talking to the child, beginning a daily experience book, and talking to the child in a clear voice in short, simple phrases. The goal is that parents be able to utilize whatever materials are on hand, whether formal "learning materials" (Appendix 2-C) or the materials of daily life—the contents of the refrigerator, the child's clothing, objects found on a nature walk, animals at the farm, to develop language. Materials are the least important factor in developing the parents' effectiveness with their child. What is more important is that the parents understand the components of auditory–verbal communication and how to develop them.

THE COMPONENTS OF AUDITORY–VERBAL COMMUNICATION

Parents are encouraged, from the beginning, to observe normal hearing children their own child's age. This experience provides them (as well as their hearing-impaired child) with models of normal language development. It is in this context that the components of auditory–verbal communication are discussed with the parents.

Using demonstration, instruction, and related articles and books, parents are familiarized with normal language and speech development. Parents often tend to use only language that they are sure the child will understand. They need coaching in how to "be natural" while speaking at a language level which is slightly above that of the child's and to expose the child to new grammatical structures, vocabulary, and concepts.

The basic auditory skill areas (detection, discrimination, comprehension, memory, etc.) are presented to parents through demonstration and discussion so that they can incorporate these skills into formal and informal interactions. As in all areas, parents are given guidance in how to constantly raise their expectation level for the child's auditory development.

Emphasis is not placed on precise articulation in the early stages of expressive language development. As the child develops confidence in his ability to express himself orally, the expectations for speech are raised. Specific communication guidelines include the following:

1. Whenever possible, avoid visual cues (lip reading, gestures, contextual cues, etc.).
2. When talking to your child, cover your mouth, talk from beside or behind the child. Do not allow lip reading.
3. Speak naturally and clearly. Do not overarticulate.
4. Do not speak too loudly.
5. Avoid repeating too much. (Otherwise the child will expect repetition and not learn to listen the first time.)
6. Provide silences for processing what has been said. Do not talk constantly.
7. Be natural. Expect a response and provide time for that response.
8. Present the auditory message before the visual. (Talk about an object or picture before you show it to the child.)
9. Do not respond to your child's demands unless he has given his best language/speech effort.
10. Do not limit yourself to predictable language.
11. Address the child using language that is slightly above his functional language level.

MANAGEMENT

At the Beebe Center, training the parents to use behavior management strategies effectively and consistently is an important part of the treatment program. Many parents share the concern of being unable to "control" their child. This often stems from the parents' inability to overcome their feeling of pity for the child. They are hesitant to make demands because they feel that it is unfair to a child who "cannot hear." They may pay lip service to maintaining expectations but are, in fact, catering to their child. Some parents may say, "It's not my nature to be strict." It must *become* their nature. And in order for that to occur, parents often need specific guidelines in developing effective behavior management.

Parents observe behavior management in their child's lessons at the Center. However, unless they understand the principles of management, they may not be able to apply effective strategies at home. Therefore, parents are given general and specific guidelines in the context of both formal and informal interactions. As in all areas of parent skill development, the parents are observed working with their child and are given suggestions on how to most effectively utilize these strategies.

Parents are referred to a variety of texts on parenting, behavior management, and so on (see additional reading list). They are often encouraged to enroll in a parent effectiveness training class.

MANAGEMENT GUIDELINES
A. Provide Appropriate Enriching Language Experiences

A stimulating environment is important in developing a child's desire to communicate. Parents are given guidelines on how to make even the most mundane activity full of language potential. Breakfast, lunch, and dinner become language "lessons." Sorting laundry is an early lesson in categorizing. Grocery shopping can become a "scavenger hunt." The possibilities for language stimulation are limitless, but parents need guidance in identifying and maximizing language opportunities. The goal is to enable parents to capitalize on the language and listening "potential" in all of their hearing-impaired child's daily experiences.

1. Choose activities that are interesting to the child.
2. Vary activities and materials as much as possible. Too much repetition may cause a child to lose interest, making learning difficult.
3. Use "intrigue" to stimulate child's curiosity (Appendix 2-D).
4. Finish an activity before the child tires of it. (Otherwise the child may not be interested when you bring out the materials again.)
5. Eliminate distractions:
   • Table should be clear except for materials being used at that time.
   • Child should not face a visually distracting area of the room.
   • Choose a quiet area for lessons.
   • Siblings should not be allowed to interrupt (unless they are cooperatively involved in the lesson.)
6. End on a positive note (success). The child will want to come back for more.
7. Make learning fun. If you enjoy the lesson, your child will too.

B. Establish Appropriate Expectations

To overcome the low expectations that have been associated with persons with profound hearing losses, parents need to witness hearing-impaired individuals of all ages achieving their potential. The conviction that profoundly "deaf" children are able to learn language through hearing (requisite Number 1) may come slowly but it is paramount in establishing "high expectation for performance and achievement" (the last requisite).

The goal for every hearing-impaired child is that he become an independent communicating adult. Parents are encouraged to keep that objective in mind when establishing appropriate expectations for their child. Guidelines for continually raising expectation levels are provided in the context of the child's lessons at the Center as well as through observation of the parents' interaction with the child whether in the waiting room or while the parent is giving a lesson. Expectations are different for every child, but the "golden rules" are:

Do not accept less than the child is capable of producing.

Once a skill has been achieved, raise the level of expectation and performance.

C. Reinforce Success

The key to effective behavior management is providing a child with consistent reinforcement of appropriate behaviors. If the environment is stimulating and expectations are clear, a child will usually respond positively. When those responses occur, the parent should reinforce the child with a smile, a hug, or some sort of tangible reinforcer. In facilitating communication as well as overall development, the effective use of positive reinforcement will tend to increase the behavior that precedes it.

Reinforcement (both tangible and social) is demonstrated regularly in the child's lessons at the Beebe Center. Many parents need assistance in recognizing what behavior to reinforce and how to most effectively reinforce that behavior:

Provide opportunities for success.

Recognize appropriate behavior.

Reinforce immediately so that the child associates appropriate behavior with reinforcement.

Reinforce small steps.

Gradually increase the level of expectation necessary to receive reinforcement.

Vary reinforcers (Appendix 2-E).

D. Establish and Maintain Appropriate Consequences for Inappropriate Behavior

Parents often need support as well as demonstration on how to establish and maintain appropriate consequences for inappropriate behavior. They are hesitant to discipline their child, feeling that "he will not understand." Parents must realize that consistent, objective intervention in a hearing-impaired child's developing behavior patterns is essential, even more than with a hearing child.

If a child exhibits an inappropriate behavior it is important to make it clear to the child that it is unacceptable. If the child persists and the behavior is repeated, consequences must be defined ("time out" in the corner, going to his room, etc.). On the third "offense," the consequences must be followed through.

THE LARRY JARRET HOUSE—A PROGRAM FOR PARENTS

The Larry Jarret House is not a simulated home environment. For 5 days it *is* the home for visiting families. This fully equipped two-bedroom apartment provides an ideal setting for teaching families how to effectively implement the goals observed in formal therapy into their daily lives. While the child receives daily individual therapy, the parents receive guidance and instruction in developing their own skills in maximizing language opportunities for their hearing-impaired child.

The week begins at 9 AM on Monday morning. The family is introduced to the staff, and then the child is taken into a therapy room for his first lesson. The parents observe the lesson through a one-way mirror. The Larry Jarret House coordinator/therapist also observes this lesson, familiarizing herself with the child's abilities. The parents then receive a schedule for the week. The usual schedule includes:

Daily
One hour of individual therapy at the clinic.
One hour of therapy, guidance, and instruction at the Larry Jarret House.
One hour discussion and/or demonstration with a participant in the Center's Teaching Family Program.
Scheduled observations of hearing-impaired children's lessons at the clinic.

Other

A discussion with the Center's consulting psychologist.
An evaluation for sensory integration by the Center's occupational therapist.
A conference with the staff at the end of the week.

DAILY INDIVIDUAL THERAPY

The hearing-impaired child is seen every morning for an hour of individual therapy. The goals of these sessions are to assess and develop the child's level of auditory and communication abilities as well as to demonstrate to the parents strategies that they can use in working with their child at home.

THERAPY, GUIDANCE, AND INSTRUCTION AT THE LARRY JARRET HOUSE

The content of the sessions at the Larry Jarret House is adapted to meet the individual needs of the family. The first session is usually aimed at identifying the primary concerns of the child and family and establishing a schedule for the week which will meet these needs. Subsequent sessions usually include discussion and instruction on topics related to hearing loss (i.e., the audiogram, hearing aids), demonstration of both formal and informal home lessons, and observation and discussion of parent lessons. The emphasis is on developing the parents' competence, creativity, and confidence in working with their child.

TEACHING FAMILY PROGRAM

The Beebe Center's Teaching Family Program is made up of "veterans" of the program: mothers, fathers, and older children (high school age and above). Based on the particular needs of the Larry Jarret House family, participants of the Teaching Family Program are selected to meet individually with the family. The format of these sessions is left to the discretion of the teaching parent. Sessions may include demonstration lessons or activities with the child, discussion with the parents, an outing to a local park, farm, or restaurant. Whatever the activity, the Teaching Family Program provides the Larry Jarret House family the opportunity to share their concerns with people who have had a similar experience. This program offers the parents a necessary source of support and inspiration.

OBSERVATIONS OF OTHER HEARING-IMPAIRED CHILDREN IN THERAPY

In addition to viewing videotapes available at the Larry Jarret House, resident parents are encouraged to observe other hearing-impaired children in lessons at the Center. Seeing is believing. High expectations are more easily established if parents are given the opportunity to observe profoundly hearing-impaired children at various stages of development reaching their potential. These observations also provide visiting families with an opportunity to meet informally with other parents of hearing-impaired children.

CONSULTING PSYCHOLOGIST

Toward the beginning of the week at the Larry Jarret House, parents meet with the staff's consulting psychologist. This provides parents with the opportunity to discuss their feelings, their adjustment to their child's hearing loss, and many other factors that may have an effect on their relationship with their child. The psychologist also provides the Center's staff with additional insight on the dynamics of the family's interactions.

SENSORY INTEGRATION EVALUATION

In order to most effectively develop communication skills, the hearing-impaired child must be treated as a whole person, a product of the interaction of all the senses. The Beebe Center's staff occupational therapist conducts an evaluation for sensory integration which includes the tactile, kinesthetic, vestibular, and proprioceptive senses. When sensory deficits are discovered, an exercise program is prescribed for the parents to follow at home. The findings of the sensory integration evaluation contribute a great deal to the total habilitation program of the hearing-impaired child.

PARENT–STAFF CONFERENCE

At the end of the week, the Larry Jarret House parents meet with the staff of the Beebe Center to discuss the child's abilities and progress. The staff provides the parents with suggestions on how to proceed with the child's program at home. The conference is followed up by a summary report which includes background, communication skills, observations, and recommendations.

A week at the Larry Jarret House is intensive for the parents as well as the child. However, not all areas can be covered in the 5-day period. Therefore, many families come to the Larry Jarret House annually, others come two or three times a year. Families who receive therapy weekly also stay at the Larry Jarret House for what they refer to as "a shot in the arm." Regardless of the age of the child or his level of achievement, the Larry Jarret House program can revitalize the parents' conviction, and enhance their commitment to teaching their child to listen and communicate.

TEACHING STRATEGIES

Once a child is accepted into the program, therapy sessions are begun immediately. Meanwhile, the parents have been given a background of information as to goals and philosophy. The first sessions are, of course, geared to establishing rapport between therapist and child, and toward acceptance of diagnostic therapy in general.

The first efforts are directed to alerting the child to sound. Whether banging a door, blowing a whistle, mooing like a cow, dropping an object on the floor, or saying, "up, up, up" as we lead the child to a chair, the therapist, mother, or anyone helping the child learns to point to his hear, calling attention to the sound, in an effort to make it meaningful to him. Toys one can spin, pull, or push; and boats, cars, airplanes with related sound effects are presented and manipulated so that the child through hearing alone (therapist's mouth not visible) can identify the toys. Switching roles is used from the beginning to give the child the opportunity to vocalize a meaningful sound. The sounds (language) used in therapy must be applied appropriately in the child's general environment.

The therapist goes into initial sessions prepared with an abundant variety of materials, mechanical toys, toy animals, pop beads, puzzles, picture books, puppets. The watchword is to "listen." Assuming that the child hears, his attention is held as long as possible with one activity. Having in mind the goal that the child is to process language through auditory channels, the therapist offers appropriate natural language while presenting the materials. Care must be taken to give the child time to process (receive) what is being said. The brain is being trained to process what is perceived by the hearing mechanism. One of the rules that should be demonstrated is not to start an activity that cannot be finished even if it has to be speeded up. For instance, when looking at a book, turn *each* page—reach the end. As attention span lengthens, the therapist will need fewer activities. This is a good criterion of progress.

Actually, the first part of every session is a "conversational" period using the experience book of daily entries prepared by the parent. The child at first may assume a very passive role, even disinterested, but gradually becomes involved and chatters away until the day when the therapist might be "put down" in this fashion: "Ben, what did you do yesterday?" Ben replied, "You can read it there." At every stage of development, without fail, these books are a great source of language learning. The experience book at the Helen Beebe Speech and Hearing Center is more than a book of the child's experiences; it is living language depicted through daily occurrences. The events need not be momentous or catastrophic. A broken shoe lace, a trip to the grocery store, a pet's birthday, all present opportunities for framing everyday events in language. The books contain drawings which depict everyday happenings. They must be stick figures (and the children know who all those sticks represent) or they may be lifelike artistic masterpieces. Mothers say, "I can't draw," but they do. The books are enhanced by birthday invitations, ticket stubs, candy wrappers, and snapshots; but the important thing is that the event depicted lends itself to language extension. The captions which accompany the picture, scene, or sequence generally use language which is not within the child's grasp. A narrative, a description, or an explanation which incorporates new vocabulary and/or concepts will encourage language growth, and the child is held responsible for the new vocabulary.

Language is enhanced through the experience books; a single experience can promote expansion of language. The child can be encouraged to help choose the event to be depicted and help put the language to it. As the experiences broaden, so will the concepts— from concrete to abstract.

The children take pride in their books and share them with many persons in their environment—family and friends. Their books are dog-eared and mended with tape or tied together. One child at the Center is currently working on book number 20. As we review the books together at the Center, at times unhappy events are recounted—a broken vase, a fall and stitches, a punishment. But more often the children "page ahead" to talk about happy events—birthday parties, the first snow. The books serve as a means to open communication for the quiet ones. These are truly a child's *own* book of experiences (Pearson, 1983).

Therapists must keep in mind the normal sequence of language development and be alert to identify and fill in the gaps for each child. Babbling, which may have been short-lived for the hearing-impaired child, has been stimulated and encouraged. Parents learn that while they must "teach" language in a natural way, they may call attention to key words or phrases by using firm intonation, always imbedding new vocabulary in varying contexts. For example, "*Open* the door. *Open* your eyes. *Open* the book. *Squeeze* the orange. *Squeeze* Mommy's hand."

Infants do need to learn that things have names; therefore, as cognitive skills develop, a check must be kept on vocabulary as well as syntax. For this purpose, parents are given word lists: *Language Thesaurus* (Ling & Ling, 1977), *Curriculum Guide* (Northcott, 1977).

The therapist must constantly introduce action words and function words. It helps her to have drawings (stick figures provided by parents will do) and matrix cards incorporating colors, shapes, numbers, and spatial relations. These cards can be homemade. Another activity using what we call a "direction box" can be started by saying something predictable such as "put the spoon in the cup" but at a higher level something less predictable, such as "put the spoon in your pocket." The next step would be to give dual directions. Hiding tiny objects under plastic eggs, three or four at a time, and asking the child to find them by description can be easy or made more difficult by lengthening the description. All of these activities are done receptively for a time until the child can fill the "teacher role" expressively. Again, he should be rewarded for even minimal attempts at playing teacher, that is, vocalization with perhaps the right number of syllables or with proper inflection.

In the first lessons, as the child is asked to listen and to identify through hearing the names of things, people, and actions, he is also presented with opportunities to develop fine discrimination of phonemes. A set of "face pictures," stylized drawings representing phonemes, are presented one at a time, alerting the child to the sound before showing him the picture. It is not important at this point that the child imitate or approximate the sounds. Three or four of the pictures are then placed before the child, perhaps with a token on each, and he is asked to discriminate the sound spoken by the therapist. This can be done also at an increased distance and/or in a softer voice. Ling's five-sound test can be incorporated into this exercise. Eventually, the child may assume the therapist's role, but should he be a too visually oriented type, and try to form a sound by exaggerating the shape of the mouth drawn in the picture, the pictures are withdrawn. In any event, the therapist will have demonstrated to the parents how to stimulate the hearing and to elicit babbling by offering all kinds of syllable play at varying distances from the microphone (body aids held in hand).

Normally, expressive language emerges only after the child has heard for approximately a year. Therefore, we must keep in mind, as expressed by Pollack (1970), the child's hearing age. Language "falls into" a hearing child's ears. If we are to capitalize on residual hearing, parent and therapist must structure a child's life so that he depends upon and develops confidence in what he hears. The child is learning to listen, to discriminate, to repeat, and to understand that speech is a tool with which he can handle his environment.

Any attempt at vocalization should be rewarded so that the child experiences a positive response. As soon as an opportunity arises, help the child learn that he can manipulate his world with vocalization, and give him the language with the most mileage—up, pick me up, open the door, I want a cookie, more milk." Listen for the speech melody, repeat the phrase. Later look for longer phrases and better articulation.

As cognition develops, lessons progress from discriminating to identifying, for instance, names of animals rather than animal sounds; cars, boats, airplanes, rather than the sound effects. Then, objects may be recognized by description: something to ride in, something to eat, a big blue car, a small yellow plane. This sort of exercise can progress to a very high level using long descriptions and more mature language. Uncluttered picture books are used to focus the child's attention while the therapist (parent) introduces not only object naming, but question forms— "How many? Let's count. What color? Whose dog? Where are they going? What happened? Do you have a _2_? What is your favorite? Do you like? No, I don't." Keep the child alert to variety, change the subject, help him to do deductive thinking. A 5-year-old might be ready to work with language involved in geographic context—city, county, seashore, mountains; professions, workers. At kindergarten level he should be able to follow directions using matrix or crayons involving shapes, colors, size. Other drawing directions might entail phrases, such as "draw the cat under the tree and put a bird on the house with the yellow roof." Remember to switch roles, giving the child a chance to use newly acquired language. The game "go fish" is played with many sets of cards, most of them made from stickers found in card shops. These can be identified by very simple modifiers such as a black bird versus birds of other colors, or by a much longer description such as a cat with a blue bow and a dog with floppy ears versus a cat with a ball and a dog with short ears.

Sequence stories of increasing complexity may be used for a variety of goals. For example, a boy has a new bike, falls off, runs to mother for a Band-aid. This can involve listening, logical thinking, deduction (place one card face down), speech, language. These series can grow in length and complexity. Eventually, without illustration, the child can be asked to give directions for making things as simple as play dough up to building a dog house.

Short stories such as those found in *Listen My Children* or *Aesop's Fables* may be read to the child, checking for content with just one or two questions at the end. Croker, Jones, and Pratt (1936) books, although not used in the original format, are a good source of progressive language development.

Story books are used for entertainment just as they would be with a hearing child. Texts may be edited and the contents dramatized to make up for the language which could be meaningless until receptive language has progressed. However, what we call story modeling is a very important strategy used for a number of specific purposes; auditory memory span, acquisition of language (vocabulary as well as prosodic features), refinement of articulation. The child is asked to repeat after the therapist one phrase at a time. The therapist must be aware of which of these objectives to keep in mind when asking the child to model. Obviously, if the goal is to extend the flow of expressive speech with appropriate prosody one would not call undue attention to articulation. On the other hand, just as we sometimes do with a hearing child who needs speech therapy, we might introduce a newly acquired sound into the flow of speech by encouraging the child to incorporate the sound into story modeling.

As the child progresses through elementary school, the therapist has an overall goal of maintaining auditory skills (by this time the child by interactions with peers, teachers, neighbors, etc., has become multisensory and has acquired lip reading, so is apt to neglect audition), filling language gaps, and refining articulation. This can be made an enjoyable experience for both child and therapist by using the following materials and games: children's magazines, such as Highlights, Cricket, World, Your Big Backyard, idioms, crossword puzzles, memory games, twenty questions, hangman. Riddles and jokes are very important sources, for they involve words with double meanings—subtleties not easily picked up by the hearing-impaired person. Nursery rhymes provide the rhythm and repetition of nonsense sounds which hearing children love to repeat. Nursery songs are used so that parents can encourage their children to sing!

All children should be given the opportunity to develop telephone listening skills. At the Beebe Center, these skills are established using the interoffice phone with simple discrimination and comprehension games or activities (Appendix 2-F).

The experience book, which is a form of daily diary or current events, gradually incorporates broader areas of news. Special interests such as sports, space ships, theatricals, may direct interest to newspaper accounts. One family started a newspaper book which motivated their 8-year-old son to search for clippings of interest to him—a great source of language acquisition.

The older children are challenged on a higher level. Although formal tutoring is not a procedure at the Center, the extension of concepts currently presented at school serve as a reinforcement and force the language exchange to a high level. Crossword puzzles, listening to stories on tape, telling jokes, and using idioms are areas in which the older children are involved.

The children continue therapy well into their school years to monitor progress. Some of the older children (and/or parents) have sought help from the Center on their own to refine their speech and sharpen their auditory skills. Two of the children this past year wanted to be ready for college. The postgraduates keep in touch, and many have offered their services to the Center to enhance the family's experience and to ensure the perpetuation of the unisensory philosophy.

EVALUATION PROCEDURES

An evaluation of the scope of services at the Helen Beebe Speech and Hearing Center and the impact on the lives of the families whom we serve can best be addressed by assessing the role of the staff, the effectiveness of the parent role, and the involvement of the children.

With the growth of the Center, and the increased number of professionals dealing with each case, certain areas of expertise needed to be defined. Qualities essential to effective teaching were formulated. Staff members (clinical and administrative) were asked to rate themselves in each category. The list continues to serve as a periodic reminder for permanent staff members and a rating scale for interns and practicum students.

Personality: Sense of humor, rapport with clients, parents, staff.

Teaching Competence: Lessons planned, effective use of materials, knowledge of unisensory philosophy, background of case.

Therapy Management: Control of behavior, parent counseling, high expectations, teach individually, carry through plans/targets.

Professional Competence: Continuing education, knowledge, application, adherence to policy, records/reports, continuing self-evaluation, maturity, response to criticism.

Professional Relationship: Interaction with staff and other professionals, respect, good listener.

The atmosphere among staff members is open and frank, and each individual is encouraged to give supportive feedback. It creates a caring environment in which each member grows and matures in a teamwork effort.

Formal staff meetings are held weekly and more frequently on an informal basis. Since the team-teaching approach prevails, each staff person is well informed about each case. In general, one therapist follows a case regularly with other clinicians seeing the client at intervals. Everyone is familiar with every case through observation and discussion. This provides some continuity for the child and identifies the therapist-in-charge for the parents. The rotating therapist practice provides the versatility the child needs for learning to interact with different persons and is good preparation for dealing with the world at large. Each clinician brings her own area of expertise to the therapy setting. The child benefits. Case discussions in staff meetings incorporate different views of case management. Again, the child is the beneficiary.

Staff meetings are planning times when areas of responsibility are delineated to avoid repetition of tasks and overlapping duties. Progress in the assigned areas is reported to keep the entire staff informed about each aspect of the Center's functioning. New and innovative ideas are encouraged and discussed.

Parent effectiveness is evaluated periodically in an informal fashion. The child's progress is usually related to an effective parent and under the guidance of the therapist, the goal is for the parents to shoulder a great deal of responsibility for their child's natural language development. It is a major commitment and the cases in which the children come closest to reaching their potential have parents who are willing to take on the challenge of creating an optimum language learning atmosphere. For some parents, this aspect of teaching is natural; other parents require more guidance and demonstration. The parents are asked to do demonstration teaching as requested by the clinician if she perceives that progress has slowed, or by the parents if they want reassurance that their expectations for performance are high enough. Both therapist and parent lessons are discussed in relation to the child's progress and prognosis.

Conferences are held whenever necessary for therapist or parent, but yearly conferences are held with each family to evaluate the child's progress, to review the formal testing, and to evaluate the home/therapy teaching. Parents and therapists share views on progress, lack of progress, and both positive and negative factors in the child's environment. The school situation is evaluated and therapists help the parents find the best placement and support for the child. Ultimately, it is the parents' decision as to the appropriate educational setting and the therapist guides the parents by making them aware of all factors related to the optimum setting for that child. The parents are responsible for contact with the school and familiarizing themselves with the services available for their child. The Center offers support in conferences with the schools as needed.

Since each child is treated as an individual, the criterion for success for each child is individual. A case in which appropriate responses are noted immediately might progress more rapidly than a case in which there are several months of effort before responses are noted. But this is not always true. Each child is on his own time frame and periodic evaluation is necessary to ensure that progress is present and steady.

There are growth spurts, apparent regressions, and plateaus in the acquisition of language. It is essential that the clinician capitalize on the growth period, encourage more stimulation when there are plateaus, and ascertain the cause of backsliding (i.e., when there is a spurt in expressive language, the articulation may temporarily deteriorate). The therapist must be alert to the weekly progress and/or regression relative to the child's potential.

The child's language development is compared to normal language development at every level. The auditory approach to language acquisition is the most demanding of the educational options for child, parent, and therapist. It is expected that there be a lag in language learning, but we expect the gap to close and the child to be able to reach a language level both receptively and expressively on a par with his hearing peers. In order to monitor this progress, several formal tests are administered.

CHILDREN'S LANGUAGE EVALUATION

The *Preschool Language Scale* (Zimmerman, Steiner, & Pond, 1979) is given to define the areas of strengths and deficiencies. Two tests of receptive language are administered: the *Peabody Picture Vocabulary Test* (Dunn, 1959), alternating Forms a and b; and the *Test of Auditory Comprehension of Language* (Carrow, 1973). Two tests of expressive language are administered: the *Structured Photographic Language Test* (Werner & Kreshek, 1974) and the *Carrow Elicited Language Inventory* (Carrow, 1973). This test battery is administered yearly but at times some are administered more often for special circumstances such as a question about school placement or a spurt in language development. A language sample is taken periodically to identify emerging vocabulary and linguistic structures.

The children in the program are given standardized achievement tests in the regular schools. Some children may require individual administration of these tests. The Center uses *The Peabody Individual Achievement Test* (Dunn & Markwardt, 1970) to have an overview of the child's scholastic achievement.

Audiotaping and videotaping are used periodically to measure each child's progress. Tapes are heard/seen by the therapist and parent to aid in identifying deficiencies and to compare to the child's base line performance. At times, parents are taped with their children to aid in correcting teaching techniques. Both parent and therapist can benefit from actually seeing the teaching strengths and weaknesses on tape of which they might be unaware, or to see emerging responses which they might have otherwise overlooked.

Other supportive services are provided by the Helen Beebe Speech and Hearing Center. One is an informal discussion with our psychologist. The services of our psychologist are available on a need basis to any of the Center families at the Center. This is a routine appointment in the week at the Larry Jarret House.

Another service is an evaluation of sensory integration by our staff occupational therapist, D. Maloney (1983). She states,

"When the children are seen, the vestibular, proprioceptive, tactile or touch, and visual systems are evaluated. Deficits in the vestibular or balance system are often found in children whose hearing impairment has been the result of a virus or infection. Commonly, rubella and meningitis attack this system since the receptors are located in the inner ear. Children with severe deficits in the vestibular system that are untreated are often slow in language development. These deficits can affect visual perception as the child must maintain good balance of the head and trunk in order to focus on objects at home or in school."

"Tactile deficits are often found in the children who have good language but poor articulation, i.e., the hearing-impaired child whose receptive language is good, who is trying hard to communicate verbally, but whose speech is unintelligible to the unclued listener. Often, the child who has tactile defensiveness is hyperactive which makes his attention span short and his activity level high. This affects the child's behavior to the degree that he or she is labeled as "difficult," "hyper-active,"or "undisciplined." These babies are not quiet and cuddly. Often parents will report problems at a very early age, but deficits are often undetected or pushed aside when the routine visit to the doctor occurs." (Maloney, 1983).

A sensory integration evaluation is given routinely to the child in the Larry Jarret House. Every child seen regularly in the program is also given an evaluation and some are seen regularly for therapy. Several others are given a home program to follow with a reevaluation at a later date. The *Miller Assessment for Preschoolers* is used as part of the evaluation when appropriate. Dramatic improvement has been observed in some of the children receiving sensory integration therapy concurrent with speech–language therapy at the Center.

Medical referrals and follow-up are made where appropriate. Audiological assessments are made elsewhere. Parents in the program are used to seek the best audiological evaluation possible for their child. Several centers are familiar with the work of the Helen Beebe Speech and Hearing Center and are skilled at testing young children. The aided and unaided audiograms are valuable as a point of departure in therapy. Although we do not limit the expectation for performance on the basis of an audiogram, if a child's performance is lagging, we might advise the family to have a reevaluation or to have a test done elsewhere. With the sophistication of hearing aid technology, there is no reason why every child should not have the optimum fitting for his hearing loss.

At the present time, all of the preschool children at the Helen Beebe Speech and Hearing Center, 2 years old and above, are in a regular public or private nursery school setting. With a regular school setting, ongoing therapy, and good parent support, much can be accomplished. However, even with the best conditions, there are a few children for whom an auditory approach alone is not appropriate. We feel with a good trial period the groundwork is laid for language learning in those children for whom an alternate approach seems indicated. The first option would be a resource room, then a self-contained classroom in the child's school district with a traditional oral approach. Should no oral class be available, another recommendation might be a residential oral school, with the possibility of mainstreaming at a later date.

Most of the school-aged children being seen at this time are in a regular school setting with the services of the school speech or hearing therapist. The therapist's role is to enhance language learning by capitalizing on the language of the classroom and teaching vocabulary for some of the more difficult subjects. Two of our clients have a special placement in a public school; one is partially integrated from a resource room, and the other is in a traditional oral classroom. Both children have additional handicaps. All of the children (including these two) are functioning at grade level.

Many of the children seen at the Center start elementary school a year late. For some, an additional year of nursery school or kindergarten will give a broader language base to effectively communicate in the school setting. It is our belief that this added preparation time gives a child a better start socially, emotionally, and educationally as long as he continues to be challenged to achieve. Other children may be above age level in one or more of these areas; for these children a program should be selected to further develop present skills and give support for areas that may be deficient. These decisions are made by the parents with support from the Center. Placements are made individually, for each child's progress is based on his own developmental time frame.

CASE DESCRIPTIONS

"In my opinion, the most important thing Beebe has done for me, is that she made me and my parents believe that there was little I couldn't do....She has given me a world of opportunities....Most of all, she gave me the freedom of choice....The degree of my success will no longer be dictated by my handicap" (Davis, 1983).

The following children have achieved varying degrees of success in reaching their own individual potential. Their backgrounds are diverse, their communication skills vary. The goal for these children is the same, that they become independent adults with the ability to choose their future from all the options available to individuals with normal hearing.

John

John began wearing hearing aids consistently at Age 4. At that time, his only means of communication was gestures and a few formal signs. Learning was especially difficult, for his profound hearing loss was compounded with sensory integration problems. John had received virtually no therapy or education, and he had no family.

At age 4 John was adopted. John was fortunate. His new parents were not only loving and supportive, they were also convinced that John could learn to talk. Professionals whom they met in their early months with John tried to convince them that they were wrong. Oral programs refused him admission. John's mother pleaded for a chance. Six months was all she asked for. Reluctantly, a large center for hearing-impaired persons accepted him. In the first year of biweekly therapy, John developed an expressive vocabulary of over 600 words. He had realized that things had names and wanted to know them all.

When John was 5 his parents heard about the Helen Beebe Speech and Hearing Center. They visited the Center and met some of the children. Although John had been receiving auditory training, his parents felt that he could make better use of his hearing and that his speech would improve if given the opportunity to receive unisensory therapy. John began therapy at the Beebe Center at Age 5½ and has continued weekly since that time. Now, Aged 11, he is an expressive, insatiably curious fourth grader. John is a truly auditory child. His speech has natural melody and his vocabulary is extensive, placing him on a par with his hearing peers.

John has his own unique set of strengths and weaknesses. He has had difficulty with a regular school placement, and has been placed in a special class; however, John's limitations have not been a result of his hearing loss.

Tommy

Tommy, aged 7 has a moderate-to-severe hearing loss which was diagnosed when he was 3½ years old. He came to the Helen Beebe Speech and Hearing Center shortly after being fitted with hearing aids and has been receiving biweekly unisensory therapy since that time. Tommy, presently in first grade, also receives hearing and speech therapy from the school therapists.

Tommy's parents are committed to the unisensory philosophy and maintain high expectations for his achievement. They devote much of their time to the work of the Center and to supporting other parents of hearing-impaired children. Tommy has made progress. However, considering the extent of his residual hearing and committed, creative parents, Tommy does not seem to be reaching his oral communication potential. He is able to make his needs known, but uses improper word order and habitually imprecise articulation.

Neither Tommy nor John received early amplification or training. Both began therapy at Age 4. Both are now attending regular schools and receiving supportive services in addition to weekly therapy at the Beebe Center. Both have parents who are committed to the unisensory philosophy. John is an inquisitive, articulate child. Tommy, however, is content to let others communicate for him.

The basic difference between John and Tommy is their parents' interpretation of "high expectations." Although both children's parents were clever and creative in working with their children, John's parents focused on the goal of raising an independent, communicating adult and never deviated from that path. Tommy's parents focused on the individual steps, losing sight of the goal of raising not only a communicating, but also independent, adult.

Jill

At Age 18 months, Jill was diagnosed as having a severe-to-profound hearing loss. Her parents were told that she would never learn to speak. The family was referred to a local center for hearing-impaired children and Jill began to learn to sign. Jill attended a total communication preschool for one year. During this time, her parents became increasingly skeptical about the professionals' prognosis for their daughter and they began to search for alternatives. Through a business contact, they learned of the Helen Beebe Speech and Hearing Center and made an appointment to visit the Center and for Jill to receive an evaluation. Observing hearing-impaired children at the Beebe Center was all Jill's parents needed to confirm their feelings. If the observed children could learn to listen and communicate, Jill could too. But unisensory therapy was not available in their area. They felt that the only solution was to move to the Easton area. Jill's father found a job in a neighboring city, the family moved, and at Age 2½ Jill's unisensory therapy began.

Jill is now almost 5 years old and is able to carry on an intelligible conversation using phrases of five words or more. She is outgoing and her natural language includes colloquial expressions that she has picked up from her nursery school friends.

Debbie

Debbie first came to the Helen Beebe Speech and Hearing Center at Age 12 months. Her parents moved to the Easton area because unisensory therapy was unavailable near their home. Soon after therapy began, Debbie indicated an awareness of speech and environmental sounds at all frequencies. Therapists were encouraged about her potential and shared their feelings with her parents. Although resistant and strong willed, Debbie's listening and receptive skills developed steadily. From the beginning, however, there was concern that Debbie did not vary her spontaneous vocalizations. Because of inadequate expressive skills, she began to rely on gestures to communicate. Finding these inadequate, she became increasingly frustrated. Her behavior became aggressive. When Debbie was 3, her parents, very discouraged with her progress, decided to stop unisensory therapy. They enrolled her in an oral preschool with five other hearing-impaired children. There Debbie received individual multisensory therapy as well as group instruction. After a year, her expressive skills had not improved and her gestural system had become more pronounced. Debbie was taken out of the oral program and returned to the Beebe Center.

Debbie and Jill's parents so strongly believed in the unisensory philosophy that they left their home towns and moved to the Easton area so that their children could receive therapy at the Beebe Center. Both children exhibited excellent auditory potential early. Both were strong willed and often resistant to demands placed on them at home as well as in therapy. Initial expectations were high. However, it seemed that Debbie's parents tended to falter in their initial conviction. They questioned her hearing. They blamed themselves for her lack of progress saying that they were not able to follow through at home. Debbie became more resistant. Her parents became frustrated and temporarily gave up. Jill's parents, on the other hand, maintained their conviction. With love, discipline, and dedicated effort they persisted in constantly raising their expectations for Jill as a whole child. Jill responded and is fulfilling their expectations and, consequently, is also fulfilling her own potential.

John and Jill (and David) each came to the Helen Beebe Speech and Hearing Center with different backgrounds, unique personalities, and with their own strengths and weaknesses. But, as David so aptly stated, their "degree of success is no longer dictated by their handicap."

The goal for each child at the Helen Beebe Speech and Hearing Center is that they be given the opportunity to fulfill their own unique potential. That potential may or may not include academic success. What is important is that the child become an independent adult able to communicate comfortably with the world at large. In order for the hearing-impaired child to succeed, the parents and staff must not lose sight of that goal.

Jill's mother shared a story which illustrated the conviction necessary to achieve that goal. Two children were asked if they could walk a straight line to a tree several yards away. The first replied "sure" and started on his way. He watched his feet closely to be sure that they pointed straight ahead. Occasionally he glanced up at the tree then continued looking at his feet. When he reached the tree, he looked back at his path. It wound back and forth. The second child said, "I can walk a straight line," and with that he fixed his eyes on the tree and set off. Not once did he look down to monitor his path. When he reached the tree and looked back, his path was straight.

Jill, John, and David each had parents who had an unwavering conviction that their child would reach his potential. Each had setbacks and times of despair, but they maintained their focus. They sought the education, support, and guidance they needed from professionals as well as other parents of hearing-impaired children. They made their commitment and adapted their lives to meet that challenge.

One can never say that the success or failure of a hearing-impaired child is entirely due to any one factor. The children described illustrate that factors such as late detection and amplification, degree of loss, and initial treatment can be overcome if there is proper therapy and guidance and a total commitment to achieving auditory–verbal communication and independence. Therapy alone will not accomplish these goals. The parents must be able to effectively interpret and apply these goals and strategies to their daily lives. Parents need to accept the commitment, make the necessary sacrifices, and maintain the conviction that their child will fulfill his own unique potential. A parent who loses sight of that goal will flounder and the child will suffer. Although even the most dedicated parents may confront insurmountable problems, most parents who believe that hearing loss does not need to limit their child's potential, will succeed and their child will then have a world of opportunity and the freedom of choice and they will know there is little they cannot do.

PLACEMENT OF GRADUATES

Many of the cases who came for therapy over a 40-year period discontinued therapy at the Center for various reasons and at various stages of development. However, the goal of having the hearing-impaired child educated with hearing peers and of attaining his full potential has been exemplified many times with the early cases, among whom are a lawyer, a social worker, a medical technician, a purchasing agent, a hairdresser. Some obtained jobs after a high school education. Some have their own businesses. The important achievement is not so much the job level as the quality of communication which helped them to fit comfortably into a hearing world.

Among the 1964–1965 rubella generation, several are in universities, others in businesses or community colleges. These are the children whose families stayed with the program. Some cases, who lived at too great a distance to come regularly, came for periodic consultations and managed to find clinicians who came to the clinic to learn how to give appropriate help.

There are others who for a variety of reasons discontinued. If it was decided by mutual consent that a child could not achieve sufficient language skill to cope with regular school, our training stood him in good stead for entering a traditional program. In fact, it was found in several cases observed after they entered a self-contained class or traditional oral program, that they compared very favorably with classmates and tended to have more fluent speech and language than other students enrolled in the alternate program.

When clientele started coming from a wider geographic area, decisions about placement in alternative programs had to be adjusted to what might be available in respective school districts. The first choice when seeking an alternative might have been a self-contained day class. There were none of these classes in some of the locales, so a residential oral school might have been the placement of choice, at least for a while. In several instances, although parents were reluctant to send their child away from home, this turned out to be a very acceptable choice mutually agreed upon by parents and the Center.

Before Public Law 94-142 came into effect, our hearing-impaired children had to depend upon the policy of the local school district and the public relations established by parents and the Center staff. The law turned out to be a mixed blessing, but in most cases it was really advantageous to have hearing therapists and/or resource teachers available in the schools. We were more than ready to cooperate with this sort of staff, and parents could relax a little, realizing they did not have to do the whole job of informing school personnel and obtaining therapists and tutors.

In retrospect, one could say that many of the children whose parents could not see the program through would have had a better chance had they been given the sort of support that PL 94-142 provided.

Financial support, as well as support from educators, was also missing some years ago and, unfortunately, is still not available to all of those who need it. Investment in hearing aids, batteries, repairs, as well as in therapy and in transportation, can be overwhelming.

In the less tangible areas, our parent education and support, which is a very important part of our program, has become stronger and more enlightened as a result of experience and additional staffing. There are always parents who are willing, capable, and caring; who, given adequate help, will extend themselves to keep their child in the hearing world.

We try not to mislead our parents by encouraging wishful thinking. We do think their hearing-impaired children should have the chance of auditory–verbal education as the first option.

SUMMARY

The Helen Beebe Speech and Hearing Center is known throughout the world for teaching deaf children using the unisensory philosophy. Therapists and educators visit the Center from different areas of the United States and from other countries. Both professionals and parents seeking placement for their children are shown videotapes and meet the children after therapy. Various philosophies are discussed with members of the staff. The comment most frequently heard from the visitors is that the expectation level is higher at this Center than anywhere else they have visited.

Some professionals who have not been exposed to the unisensory philosophy in their background, have difficulty in accepting this program as a viable option for parents. It is hoped that this philosophy will become known to, and understood by, all professionals so that it will be considered when the various alternatives are offered to parents.

Although there is a rationale for each philosophy adhered to in teaching deaf children, the pros and cons must be weighed. In some alternative approaches, the children are prepared to become part of a smaller society. Our rationale is that hearing-impaired individuals should be given the opportunity to be a part of the hearing society in which they can interact and communicate comfortably. These are normal people and the expectation is that there will be normalcy in every facet of life. Parents who doubt their own ability to carry their part of the responsibility, do learn to be effective teachers.

The parents' task is crucial in establishing control and assuming a teacher role. They need to get on with the job of teaching their child and not be testing, for this casts doubt on their belief in themselves and in the child's ability to learn. Timing is a crucial aspect of interaction. A parent who does not have an innate sense of how long to wait or when to intervene needs to be shown through demonstration and critique. Normal child development is the model for growth, language, and behavior. By setting firm limits and teaching naturally, the expectations will exceed the limits set by others.

The language surrounding the child is continually on a high level. Rather than merely reinforcing the child's language and expecting further growth through casual listening, parents must always be alert to giving their child more sophisticated language. At some time, it is conceivable that a child who is trained auditorally would be a casual listener; but until that time the parent must structure the environment so that it is a continual auditory learning experience.

As expressive language emerges, it is encouraged, perhaps consisting mainly of melody at first, and refined after a period of time. The conversational level is important from the beginning, initially consisting of good attending behavior from the child, then expecting a response and finally initiating conversation. Following the topic at hand without the limitations of a structured plan will maintain a high interest level. In conclusion, the key words for success in an auditory program can be summed up as follows:

Initiate effective parent involvement;
Expect good behavioral management;
Teach, do not just test;
Build on success;
Never accept less than the child's best performance;
Challenge above the child's level;
Provide versatility;
Have high expectations.

REFERENCES

Beebe, H. (1953). *A guide to help the severely hard of hearing child.* New York: Karger.

Carrow, E. (1973). *Carrow Elicited Language Inventory.* Hingham, MA: Teaching Resources Corporation.

Carrow, E. (1973). *Test for Auditory Comprehension of Language.* Hingham, MA: Teaching Resources Corp.

Crannell, M. (1948). Parents talk it over. *Volta Review, 50,* 642.

Croft, J. C. (1977, October 8). *No longer deaf: A dilemma of classification.* Paper presented at Workshop for Parents, United Parents of Hearing Impaired, Louisiana.

Croker, G., Jones, M. K., & Pratt, M. E. (1936). *Language stories and drills:* Book III. Brattleboro, VT: The Vermont Publishing Company (available through A. G. Bell).

Davis, D. (1983). Speech presented at Easton Area High School, Easton, PA.

Dunn, L. M. (1959). *Peabody Picture Vocabulary Test.* Circle Pines, MN: American Guidance Service.

Dunn, L. M., & Markwardt, F. C. (1970). *Peabody Individual Achievement Test.* Circle Pines, MN: American Guidance Service.

Froeschels, E., & Beebe, H. (1946). Testing the hearing of newborn infants. *Archives of Otolaryngology, 44,* 710–714.

Goldstein, M. (1939). *The acoustic method.* St. Louis: Laryngoscope Press.

Griffiths, C. (Ed.) (1974). *Proceedings of the international conference on auditory techniques.* Springfield, IL: Thomas.

Ling, D., & Ling, A. (1977). *Basic vocabulary and language thesaurus for hearing-impaired children.* Washington, DC: The Alexander Graham Bell Association for the Deaf.

Ling, D., & Ling, A. H. (1978). *Aural habilitation: The foundations of verbal learning.* Washington, DC: The Alexander Graham Bell Association.

Maloney, D. L. (1983). The Beebe Center's sensory integration program. *The Listening Post.* Easton, PA: Helen Beebe Speech and Hearing Center.

Northcott, W. H. (Ed.) (1977). *Curriculum guide: Hearing-impaired children (0–3) years and their parents.* Washington, DC: Alexander Graham Bell Association for the Deaf.

Pearson, H. R. (1983). Where is your book? *The Listening Post.* Easton, PA: Helen Beebe Speech and Hearing Center.

Pollack, D. (1970). *Educational audiology for the limited hearing infant.* Springfield, IL: Thomas.

Public Law 94-142, the Education for All Handicapped Children Act, passed by Congress and signed into law in November 1975.

Stark, R. E. (Ed.) (1974). *Sensory capabilities of hearing-impaired children.* Baltimore: University Park Press.

Urbantschitsch, V. (1982). [Auditory training for deaf mutism and acquired deafness.] (S. R. Silverman, trans.). Washington, DC: Alexander Graham Bell Association for the Deaf.

Werner, E. O., & Kreshek, J. D. (1974). *Structured photographic language test.* Sandwich, IL: Janelle Publications.

Whetnall, E., & Fry, D. B. (1964). *The deaf child.* London: Heinmann Medical Books.

Zimmerman, I. L., Steiner, V. G., & Pond, E. P. (1979). *Preschool language scale.* Columbus: Merrill.

ADDITIONAL READINGS

Auditory approach conference (1973, December 1). *The Volta Review, 76,* 82–83.

Ayres, A. J. (1979). *Sensory integration and the child.* Los Angeles: Western Psychological Services.

Beebe, H. (1982). When parents suspect their child is deaf. *Hearing Rehabilitation Quarterly, 4,* 4–7.

Bitter, G. B. (Ed.). (1978). *Parents in action: A handbook of experiences with their hearing-impaired children.* Washington, DC: Alexander Graham Bell Association for the Deaf.

Boothroyd, A. (1982). *Hearing impairments in young children.* Englewood Cliffs, NJ: Prentice–Hall.

Davis, J. M., & Hardick, E. J. (1981). *Rehabilitative audiology for children and adults.* New York: Wiley.

Erber, N. (1982). *Auditory training.* Washington, DC: Alexander Graham Bell Association for the Deaf.

Griffiths, C. (1967). *Conquering childhood deafness.* New York: Exposition Press.

Knickerbocker, B. M. (1980). *A holistic approach to the treatment of learning disorders.* Thorofare, NJ: Charles B. Slack.

Knox, L. (1980). *Parents are people too.* Englewood Cliffs, NJ: Prentice–Hall.

Kretschmer, R., & Kretschmer, L. (1978). *Language development and intervention with the hearing impaired.* Baltimore: University Park Press.

Ling, A. H. (1977). *Schedules of development in audition, speech, language, communication.* Washington, DC: Alexander Graham Bell Association for the Deaf.

Ling, D. (1976). *Speech and the hearing-impaired child: Theory and Practice.* Washington, DC: Alexander Graham Bell Association for the Deaf.

Ling, D., & Ling, A. H. (1978). *Aural habilitation.* Washington, DC: Alexander Graham Bell Association for the Deaf.

Lowell, E., & Stoner, M. (1970). *Play it by ear.* Los Angeles: John Tracy Clinic.

Murphy, A. T. (Ed.). (1979). *The families of hearing-impaired children.* Washington, DC: Alexander Graham Bell Association for the Deaf, Monograph.

Nix, G. W. (Ed.). (1976). *Mainstream education for hearing-impaired children and youth.* Washington, DC: Alexander Graham Bell Association for the Deaf.

Scott, D. (1979). *Keep on learning to listen.* Toronto: Voice for Hearing-Impaired Children.

Scott, D., & Ho, N. (1979). *Join in learning to listen.* Toronto: Voice for Hearing-Impaired Children.

Vaughan, P. (Ed.). (1981). *Learning to listen.* Don Mills, Ontario: General Publishing Co.

Volta Review, (1973). *75*(6).

CHILDREN'S PUBLICATIONS

Auslin, M. S. (1978). *Raining cats and dogs.* Beaverton, OR: Dormac.

Auslin, M. S. (1979). *Hold your horses: A workbook of idioms.* Beaverton, OR: Dormac.

Barbe, W. B. (Ed.). *Highlights for Children.* Columbus, OH.

Carus, M. (Ed.). *Cricket.* LaSalle, IL: Open Court Publishing Co.

National Geographic World. Washington, DC.

Ranger Rick's Nature Magazine. Washington, DC: National Wildlife Federation.

Your Big Backyard. Washington, DC: National Wildlife Federation.

APPENDIX 2-A
Procedure for Body Hearing Aid Check

1. Check volume setting to see where the child has been wearing it.

2. Check to see if the aid is clean. The microphone can be cleaned carefully with the brush on a typewriter eraser.

3. Check receiver for cracks because these can cause feedback.

4. Check earmold for wax, cracks, and the fit on the receiver. Clean earmold with mild, soapy water and pipe cleaner if it is dirty. Make sure the earmold is dry before attaching it to the receiver.

5. Check the battery compartment for corrosion. Clean contacts with the typewriter eraser. Check battery with battery tester.

Now you are ready to listen to the hearing aid. Turn the aid on and set at a low volume setting (No. 1, 2). Make sure the switch is on "M" for microphone and the tone control is where the child wears it. Snap the receiver into the center part of the stethoscope and then put it in your ears. Now set the volume at a comfortable level while talking into the aid.

1. Check the cord by twisting it between your fingers while listening to the aid. If there is a break in the cord, it will sound scratchy or go on and off. There are two weak points in the cord: at either end. Wiggle the connections gently to see if they are good.

2. Check the sound of the aid. Try to listen at the same volume setting. The sound should be clear with little static noise. Say *oo, ah, ee, sh, s* into the aid. These sounds should sound the same every time you check the aids. If they sound different, notify your child's therapist or hearing aid dealer as to the nature of the problem.

3. If the child has feedback problems, try to identify the cause. Don't just turn the aid down.

   a. Check earmold for wax.

   b. Remove earmold from receiver, cover hole in receiver, and hold it close to the microphone. There should be no feedback with the volume on full. If there is, check the receiver for cracks.

   c. If there is no feedback with the receiver, try the same procedure as "b" with the earmold attached. Make sure you cover the hole in the earmold.

   d. If there is no feedback from the receiver and earmold, put it in the child's ear snugly. Turn volume to the setting required by the child and check for feedback.

4. Check your child's response while he is wearing the aids. Get to know how the child hears. Use the five sounds: *oo, ah, ee, sh, s* to evaluate how well the child responds to sound and try to know at what distance the child responds to these sounds.

Procedure for Ear Level Hearing Aid Check

1. Check volume setting to see where the child has been wearing it.

2. Check earmold for wax and cracks or loose tubing. Wash earmold in mild soapy water and dry tubing by blowing through it before attaching it to the hearing aid.

3. Check tubing for holes or cracks; replace if necessary.

4. Check the battery with a tester; clean the terminals if necessary.

5. Check sound of the aid with stethoscope. Listen to the five sounds: *oo, ah, ee, sh, s* to make sure there is no static or distortion. Only by listening every day will you be able to detect changes in the aid's performance.

6. Feedback problems: Don't turn the aid down—try to find out why it is whistling.

    a. First check earmold for wax.

    b. Cover hole in earmold, turn aid on full. There should be no feedback at his normal volume setting.

7. Check the child's response to sound. Use the five sounds: *oo, ah, ee, sh, s* and determine whether or not he is listening well and know the distances at which he responds to the five sounds.

APPENDIX 2-B
Videotapes

DEMONSTRATION TAPES—1973: Six of the first children (Ages 3–7 and update, 1979, Ages 8–13) fitted with binaural amplification demonstrate their use of audition in the therapy situation. (20 minutes)

MANAGER'S CHAT—1974: A made-for-television interview with Helen Beebe and two of her pupils. The interview covers the philosophy and rationale of the unisensory method. (30 minutes)

DEMONSTRATION AND TECHNIQUES TAPE (with printed audiograms)—1980: Several of the children (Ages 3–6) at the Helen Beebe Speech and Hearing Center at various stages of therapy. (10 minutes)

LEARNING BY LISTENING—These tapes were originally developed specifically for teachers of the deaf to demonstrate and present the rationale of unisensory therapy techniques. Through use, the tapes have also proven to be effective for parents and others interested in unisensory techniques.

APPENDIX 2-C
Suggested Materials for Getting Started

Doll furniture
Family (small dolls)
Cars, boats, planes, trains, etc.
Small plastic animals (pets, farm, zoo)
Puzzles with simple pictures
Books with simple pictures and clear story line
"Action" pictures

Wind-up toys (a great attention getter)
Stacking blocks or rings
Plastic food (fruits, vegetables, mini groceries)
Box of "junk"
      Boxes (small), buttons, paper clip, pencil, spoon, fork, cup, pictures, string, whistle,
      ball, small toys, old jewelry—ANYTHING and EVERYTHING!
Tape recorder and tapes
Paper (plain, lined, colored)
Crayons and pencils
"Pop-up" toys
Plastic beads
"Playdough" and an assortment of cookie cutters
Puppets
Small blackboard and chalk
Doll house
Flash cards with simple pictures (good to have duplicate sets for pairs activities)
Camera (Polaroid if possible) to take pictures of familiar places, people, and special events—
      (and not-so-special events too!)
Small set of drawers filled with miscellaneous small objects and miniatures.
Simple gameboards
Simple "Lotto" games
Musical toys
Your Imagination!

APPENDIX 2-D
Suggestions for Motivation

Gather a wide collection of "motivators" to create intrigue.

- Suprise Box—Use a large cardboard box. Cut holes in sides, front and back. Make objects
  "pop up" (after you have talked about them).
      Use "mailbox" slot in back of box. Have child "deposit" the correct picture.

      Have pictures pop through slot in the top of box.

- Cups, small boxes, barrel, coffee cans, etc.

      Hide objects in three of the above.

- Windows—Put pictures behind windows (doors) made of lightweight cardboard. Leave top
  open to slide pictures in.

- Containers—It always adds interest if you "hide" your materials.

      Talk about them before you bring them out. Make it mysterious.

baskets	coffee cans
boxes	Tupperware
bags: colorful ones	pillowcases

    Hiding things in your hands is the simplest!

APPENDIX 2-E
Suggestions for Reinforcers

Gather a bunch of reinforcers, as wide a variety as possible. Vary them OFTEN (overuse destroys interest). *Simply taking away reinforcer has more effect than saying "no."*

- *Tangible reinforcers*

M & M's	grapes	Keep small containers of these
raisins	cookie crumbs	on hand so you can use them
cereal		when necessary.

- *Marbles in a jar—Put water in a jar (with food color or sudsy water for variety).*

  Draw a line on the jar. Tell the child to see if he can fill the jar to the line.

  Drop a marble in the jar for each correct response.

- *Mechanical banks—These fascinate children. Find as many different ones as you can, though they are often hard to find.*

  Have a container of coins.

  Put a penny (coin) on each picture, under each object, under pictures.

  When child makes correct choice, he puts penny in bank.

- *Puzzles—*

  Dump out pieces of a simple puzzle.

  Each time child makes correct choice in (any) activity he puts a piece in the puzzle.

  Activity ends when puzzle is complete.

- *Surprise (Treat) Box—*

  Select a small box to be used in every lesson.

  Gather a variety of "treats."

candy	"gift certificates" (that you make yourself)
gum	for an ice cream cone
stickers	for a hamburger at McDonald's
small toys	to make popcorn at home
funny picture	for a toy that the child wants
whatever!	

  Put a treat in the box *before* the lesson. DO NOT show it to the child.

  Explain that if the child "works hard" he will get what is in the box.

  When (if) the child's attention wanders or he misbehaves, just tap the box as a reminder.

  DO NOT give the child the treat if the lesson has not been good or he will know it does not matter how he behaves—he will still get the treat.

- Tower of blocks—

  Colored blocks

  After correct response, child puts block on tower.

  Activity ends when tower is completed. (Choose an appropriate number of blocks for the activity. Do not have too many.)

APPENDIX 2-F
Suggested Activities for Development of Telephone Skills

I. *CLOSED SET*

    A. *Card pairs* (playing cards, Old Maid—any matching set)

        1. Caller has one set—receiver has second set.

        2. Place receiver's card out on a table.

        3. Caller gives word or phrase for card.

        4. Receiver puts card called in a pile.

        5. CHECK—when call is finished; see if they are in correct order.

    B. *Directions*

        1. Have a page with simple shapes, letters, objects.

        2. Caller tells receiver to draw a circle, triangle, around, under, beside shape, object, letter.

    C. *Questions*

        1. Make a duplicate list of common questions and/or phrases.

                When will you be home?
                I won't be home until...
                This is Mrs. _____ , Maggie. Mom...

          a. Caller reads question/phrase and numbers them as he reads.

          b. Receiver numbers questions/phrases as he hears them.

          c. Check to see that numbers correspond.

        2. Make a duplicate set of questions. (Eventually do this activity without a list.)

          a. Caller reads question.

          b. Receiver answers question.

    D. *Role Playing*

        1. Make up hypothetical situations on index cards (two sets).

        2. Choose one card.

        3. Carry on a conversation with predictable questions.

II. *MESSAGES*

    Practice taking messages (with friends and family). Include the following information:

        NAME
        PHONE NUMBER
        WHO THE CALL IS FOR
        MESSAGE

    and appropriate responses.

3
AN EARLY AUDITORY–ORAL INTERVENTION PROGRAM

Gillian Clezy

AN EARLY ORAL HABILITATION PROGRAM
History and Philosophy of Program

This particular program is one section of the "in-house" clinical facility provided for college students training as speech pathologists in the State of Victoria, Australia. It is therefore important to appreciate that this is not an overall educational program for the hearing impaired, it is one in which all facets of human communication and interaction are dealt with, particularly in relation to hearing, language, and speech development. These factors cannot, of course, be separated from all those encompassed when talking of "early childhood development" and therefore include cognitive and learning processes. However, direct consideration is not given to classroom subjects, strategies, behaviors, or achievements. Management is essentially on an individual basis.

The program started in 1976 when the entire audiology/aural rehabilitation course for speech pathologists was reorganized. Details of the program and its philosophy are given in Healey (1982). The current theoretical knowledge and extensive practical experience of the students is an essential strength of the clinical work. The students do not work in this program until the fourth and final year of their training. They have by then received 100 clock hours in basic linguistic theory, 170 clock hours in the theory of child language development and its disorders, and a total of 144 clock hours in audiology/acoustics and aural rehabilitation. Listing hours in this manner does not necessarily suggest instant "adequacy," but the students have also had some clinical experience with children with a variety of developmental speech and language disorders, and basic experience in screening audiometry and hearing testing. This work is part of the first 3 years of training which also includes all other areas of speech pathology, many of the behavioral sciences, and clinical training in specific etiologies such as voice and fluency.

Staffing

The program for hearing-impaired children is supervised by one speech pathologist who is also a lecturer in aural rehabilitation. She has 25 years of experience in that field. This person, or a second, experienced, speech pathologist, is present for every child's session. The program runs throughout the year for three mornings a week only; but since its start some 78 children have attended and 43 are currently enrolled. The program can call upon three audiologists, one of whom is always available as a support person while the clinical sessions are running. A full backup audiological service is provided on site. This offers not only assessment, but surveillance of the children attending. The hearing aids are checked at every session, spares provided, and such services as impedance profiles on children with suspected or known conductive overlay are given. The immediacy and accessibility of this service is its outstanding advantage. This audiological service is also incorporated into the training of the speech pathologists, as explained in Healey (1982).

The primary diagnostic agency and hearing aid supplier is the National Acoustic Laboratory of Australia which has many branches throughout the State and country and to which all children suspected of hearing loss are referred. Apart from speech pathologists and audiologists, the services of psychologists are readily available and there is close liaison with all the services for the hearing impaired provided by the Education Department of Victoria.

The trained staff are very much involved with all the program's detail and are present for at least part of every session, frequently working with the child and family members. They are therefore the persons with whom the family relate most closely and consistently over a long period of time. The college students have 10-week placements in this program, and, often two are allotted to one family for that time. Each student may assist with three families in one morning. Some of the families attend weekly at the start of their association with this service, others far less frequently. During the Institute's vacation periods the supervisory staff continues to work with those families who might be disadvantaged by a long break from attendance.

Having described the role of the professionals, however, a misleading picture may develop, for it is not really they who are seen as the prime agents for the child's habilitation but rather it is the mother, father, or some designated caregiver as described by Clezy (1979). The communication dyad or partnership is seen as critical to the child's developing optimum auditory, speech, language, and communication skills. Therefore, a significant person in the child's life is always present and becomes part of all *evaluation* and *management*. This person implements all the work under the clinician's guidance. The clinician's role is observational, and essentially passive as far as the child is concerned, although intervention takes place to demonstrate or model a particular recommended behavior or strategy.

Population and Funding

The Institute is funded by the Federal Government of Australia and children attend from throughout the State of Victoria and even further afield. However, the program primarily serves the greater metropolitan area of the city of Melbourne (population just under 3 million). Those who come from farther afield have normally done so by their own choice and are seeking an alternative to the services available to them in their home district. The families pay only a nominal fee. This is not for services but for materials used. Many are generous with donations which help subsidize the running of an extremely expensive program. This is not the only service available to young hearing-impaired children in the area. There are four others, of which some offer facilities for play groups, kindergarten, or alternative means of communication such as Total Communication (TC) or Cued Speech (Cornett, 1967). A few families choose to attend two agencies. Their prime reason for attending Lincoln Institute is the very close involvement of the family, the demonstrations and support given the parents, and the intensive one-to-one facilities for speech and language training through a naturalistic interactive approach. This service is also seen as a long-term support program for the family which can, in fact, continue regardless of the child's school placement and age and even beyond the educational years. The program is not, as far as the children are concerned, part of the educational system of Victoria. This is seen as an advantage, as the service is not governed by any of the bureaucratic controls inherent in large systems or departments.

Facilities

At present sessions are conducted in two small, informal rooms furnished with tables and chairs and equipped for all ages and sizes. The rooms are divided by an observation area. Video and audio recording equipment is built in, and there is a sophisticated audiological suite next door. Shortly a "kitchen-cum-family-living-room," with all appropriate furnishings, will be added, in an endeavor to develop a more naturalistic environment. The acoustics of the environment have been given maximum attention.

Referrals

This service is known to the body within the state primarily responsible for the educational placement of all hearing-impaired children. The body is called the Ascertainment Committee; its role and composition are discussed in greater detail later. Public information is generated through the distribution of leaflets upon request, but *publicity* is not sought. The greatest number of referrals are made through the parents. One tells another, and those seeking this approach apply for admission. By using the families as agents of therapy, a very great number of children can attend at relatively infrequent intervals; but there are, of course, those whose needs dictate a greater rate of supervision even after the initial period of training. Every attempt is made to avoid having a waiting list so that immediate attention is given to the children's and the families' needs. This is achieved by encouraging parents to assume, to the greatest extent possible, the responsibility of handling their children and by the natural process of reduced demands as the child acquires increased auditory/oral communication skills.

Initially this program was developed to help children immediately upon diagnosis of hearing loss, through the early critical years until language and speech had developed. The program was intended to help children with severe to profound hearing losses. The anticipation, therefore, was that the children would be between approximately 6 or 7 months to perhaps 10 years of age. Subsequently a new demand was made upon the resource. Parents of children already placed in total communication classes or much more structured classroom oral environments began requesting assistance. The consensus seemed to be that although their children were receiving assistance, they (the parents), were not, and their understanding of speech, hearing, language, and communication was extremely limited. These families are now also accepted into the program, but it means that the children are divided into two main types and categorized as children needing either *developmental* or *remedial* treatment. Their management differs greatly as does that of each child due to individual differences. Lincoln Institute also offers a further facility to adults who are manual adult communicators without intelligible speech or those with limited language who wish to improve their skills. In general it is interesting to note that many of the children in the developmental group who are acquiring, or have acquired, near normal language and speech skills are in fact more profoundly deaf than many of those who need remedial help. They are fortunate in that they are now benefitting from recent advances in hearing aid technology, the boom in our knowledge of language, acoustics, and speech acquisition; and the fact that they are learning through their own experiences in a naturalistic environment with their families to assist, just as normally hearing children do.

Hearing Aids

Many of the children attending, particularly those in the developmental category, are fitted with radio-frequency (FM) hearing aids at a very young age. This is often the recommendation of this particular program. The philosophy behind this has been developed more from behavioral than acoustic criteria, although of course very careful audiological assessment is undergone and aided thresholds compared. Results have been gratifying, and many of the children show a pattern of auditory development which is quite marked in that they acquire a greater recordable frequency range over a period of some years (see Appendix 3-A). This does not, of course, mean that it can be assumed that the hearing per se has improved. It could also be the child's listening skills or test aptitude. However, whichever it is, the acquisition is apparently quicker and greater in those using an FM aid, although it is also evident among all those children making maximum use of their residual audition, whatever their aiding. Perhaps it is the constancy of input afforded by the FM aid which apparently accelerates this process. It is common for a child to start attending with an unaided audiogram of 90db at 250Hz and 100db at 750Hz and to find that some 3 years later they are responding to these frequencies in the range of 75–85db (unaided) and to 2000KHz at 85db. With correct aiding this is a "revolution" in terms of speech potential. The Institute has a number of FM aids, and therefore children can undergo prolonged trial periods. The constancy of input, signal-to-noise ratio, the convenience to the speaker (parent) who cannot always be at 3 ft distance from a manically mobile toddler, and the freedom of the child to explore, but still be within conversational range, are seen as the great advantages of the FM system. This aid costs well over 1,000 dollars in Australia, but it is felt that the parents should at least be advised of its existence and have the opportunity to experience its apparent advantages and cosmetic disadvantages. Only then with this information and that obtained from audiological assessment can parents and audiologists make an informed decision about the child's aiding. With kindergarten aged children it is frequently the child who, along with the parents and audiologist, appears to make the "choice" between the acoustically equally appropriate FM system, postauricular, or body-worn aids. The child often selects the aid preferred when a choice is put before him.

Bulk and cosmetic factors do not seem to be important factors to an auditorily conscious hearing-impaired child struggling to acquire language. Careful counseling is given especially in relation to economic factors and if the family would like the device, but cannot afford one, long-term loan is arranged or finance sought through philanthropic agencies. It is, however, surprising how nearly all parents budget for this perceived advantage for their child over and above a new kitchen gadget, TV recorder, or some other appliance. Certainly, the short-term pain of a heavy expense of money and effort is seen by most to be superior to the long-term drain in support needed by an inadequately habilitated child.

Program Objectives

The overall philosophy of the program is that profoundly hearing-impaired children should have complete language, prosodically normal and intelligible if not perfect speech, and be able to achieve their potential integrated within normal society, provided there are ancillary support services during the educational years. It is accepted that this will require a great deal of motivation on the part of the parents, that, without help, others in the family might suffer, and therefore the family must be seen as a whole. Despite this philosophy which also believes that it is the right of all children to receive what is *natural* and *normal* in the first instance, it is acknowledged that there are some children who may need augmented or alternative systems at a *later* stage. However, without trying what is natural and normal first and *diagnosing as one manages,* only arbitrary decisions can be made about which compensatory system should be selected, particularly in terms of the sense modalities used and the child's learning and overall *communicative* strategies. Historically, such decisions have only been made on the grounds of what the system itself is *supposed* to provide, the wishes of the parent (often made from an uninformed base), the audiogram (often immature), and psychometric tests. We cannot assume that a child will or will not achieve particular skills. We can only try and see. To try means to give that child every possible assistance to learn what is *normal*. If we first practice any alternative communication system with children, we will in turn develop deviancy and we will inevitably program their cortical functioning to accommodate that deviancy. Therefore, it is the philosophy of the program to take all that we know about normal childhood development and normal mother–child interaction in the prelingual and critical years and incorporate this into our diagnosis and management. Management is therefore never finite and static, there is no "fixed" program. We need to be able to incorporate, for example, the wealth of information we have recently acquired on pragmatics from Dore (1974) and Halliday (1975); and on prosodics from Crystal (1981) and Garnica (1977) into other aspects of our language program.

Management of the younger children follows a developmental hierarchy for *both* members of the dyad, *but* allows for delays, which are protracted in some cases. Stages and not ages are seen as critical and, in general, parents are advised and counseled about the fact that there may be a delay of a year or two in initial school placement, in order to allow for prerequisite language development.

For children in the remedial population, we generally adopt a slightly different philosophy, and our remedial work tends to be more experimental in nature. These children are less able to use their residual hearing and to process acoustic patterns linguistically as do most younger children. Many children in our remedial group have never experienced what is normal and natural, and have therefore not acquired even the most basic of normal communication skills. Turn taking and the use of referential cue are examples of such absent skills. These children and their families come because they "want to learn to talk and understand." Many have only the rudiments of our language and it is asyntactic. Our philosophy is to go right back to the beginning, to the earliest of communication skills, and by working with the mother–child dyad, introduce what is natural and normal in a developmental hierarchy, while taking into account their many other skills and advanced cognition. Normal spoken language skills are usually difficult and sometimes impossible to achieve with late starters or those who have long been exposed to alternative means of communication, but many children and adults respond well if their motivation is high. Often the family had, for years, also been mute in all interactions with their hearing-impaired child. They need more help than the child himself. In this there are many parallels to second-language learning, a process which is often used as an example to help the family conceptualize the tasks involved.

There is one great advantage to this program, whether developmental or remedial. The candidates come by choice. They are frequently highly motivated and have sought out the program because they believe in their children's potential and their need to communicate naturally. Thus, they are self-selected, and the oral/TC/cuing/manual issues have already been decided by them. Some of the remedial children's families are overly optimistic and have to be counseled toward *realistic* goals in terms of objective data. Frequently they have visited other programs and made many inquiries. The significant people in the child's environment, the family and extended families, usually all want to be involved. They believe it is their role to help the child acquire speech and language just as it was with their hearing children. There are families from all walks of life and all socioeconomic backgrounds. They only have one thing in common: *motivation*. It is the program's task to enhance, utilize, shape, and reinforce that motivation into productive behaviors untrammeled by damaging anxieties and maladaptive communicative strategies.

Enrollment Procedures

As previously mentioned, the initial body to whom all deaf children in the State are referred is the Ascertainment Committee which comprises an otologist, medical practitioners, psychologists, teachers of the deaf, and speech pathologists. This committee advises the parents at all stages of the child's education, and strongly recommends specific placements and modes of communication. Normal kindergarten or school with a peripatetic teacher of the deaf may be recommended. Conversely, residential schooling, total communication, or cued speech may be urged. Decisions are reached only when all available data from contact personnel have been received. When a child is first referred to this committee the family is counseled about the many options available to them and the program under discussion is mentioned and relevant literature handed to the parents. Frequently referrals to this program come from this source. Referrals are also received from the National Acoustic Laboratories, otologists, schools, other teachers/clinicians, or, as mentioned earlier, from the parents themselves. There are no selection criteria as far as age, hearing levels, or family factors are concerned. However, it is always recommended that a care giver be involved and hitherto this has always been acceded to. Children with moderate loss very rarely attend. It is a facility for children with severe or profound impairment of hearing, speech, and/or language. Children with multiple deficits are not excluded and many such children attend.

Predominantly the model subscribed to is one in which the child learns in the manner outlined by Piaget in Ginsberg and Opper (1979). The child is the "experiencer" and "experimenter," and some of this experimenting is, when necessary, facilitated by using strategies similar to those outlined in Lund and Duchan (1983) in relation to language development and all its elements. Finally when facilitation is not enough a direct teaching mode is employed to help the child overcome specific areas of difficulty. These strategies, therefore, must involve the most significant person in the child's life, and it is that person's strategies which are observed, qualified, quantified, and frequently modified to match the current objective data on the mother's role in the acquisition of language. The entire program is dyad centered.

Treatment Procedures
Assessment for Treatment: Goals

Once a child has been enrolled, all the relevant case history and audiological data is collected from other support agencies. The data is studied prior to the first visit, for it is the usual policy not to have a formal "case-history" session on the first occasion, and the rationale for this is explained to the parents who have already been to numerous agencies and more often than not have reached the stage in postdiagnostic trauma when they are wanting to "get on with it and do something" for their child rather than have to answer endless questions. The first visit is therefore frequently very informal and carried out by the senior clinician, although the students may be in attendance and often engage the child in play while the parents converse with the clinician. That conversation is used by the clinician to try to ascertain the following:

1. The stage of postdiagnostic trauma the parents have reached;
2. The attitudes of both parents in relation to each other, the child, and the child's hearing levels;
3. The apparent needs of the parents;
4. The state of the parents' knowledge and the level of information they have already received in relation to the audiogram, the aids, hearing levels, and their relevance for speech and language acquisition and development in general;
5. The state of parental anxiety levels (because this will immediately be relevant to their potential performance as "agents" in therapy);
6. The family etiology;
7. The stage of habilitation already reached particularly in relation to the fitting and the acceptance of the first hearing aids;
8. Previous parenting strategies.

Relevant counseling, whether affective or informational, will only be given at this stage if overtly sought by the parents. Every effort is made not to bombard the family with information at a time when they may not be receptive to it. However, when information or support is sought, it is given. Parents are encouraged to see the child in the most positive, favorable light, as able to respond to their child-rearing strategies. The parents, initially at least, know far more about the child as an individual than the clinician, and appreciate that before therapy can commence the clinician will need to find a base from which to start. The parents are told that in order to get to know the child the clinician would like to watch the parent interacting with him or her. Sometimes the parents are given the option to join in the play with the clinician and the child, and the clinician then gradually withdraws. Alternately, they may be asked if they would like to play immediately, or during the next session. They decide. It is rare for a parent to defer. The majority seems anxious to demonstrate either the child's skills or their difficulties in general. Frequently parents comment that it is nice to be the one involved with the child, because often they feel the child in a "testing" situation has not achieved his potential because of the lack of opportunity to build up a relationship with the relevant professional. Right from this initial session there are comments such as "it is *so good* to be involved," "it makes me feel *so good,*" or "that's the first time I've had to *do* something."

Sometimes the parents are indeed surprised at the level of involvement expected in the first session. This strategy of intense initial involvement for observer purposes may be too threatening for some parents. The skill of the clinician is the all important variable here. It is no more difficult for a parent, with high-level skills and reasoning powers, to participate in a first observer session than it is for a child to run the gauntlet of a test session. The clinician should be able to reduce the anxiety of child and parent to a level at which they can function in a representative manner. If this is impossible, some time will need to be spent in alleviating the anxiety and the occasion may have to be deferred while preparatory conditioning takes place. The philosophy is also that the parents will have far greater ability to elicit the *representative* skills of their child, and will initially know more about their child than the clinician. This knowledge and ability should be tapped immediately.

The overall aim of the first session is to observe how the child and significant person or parent are communicating. Nonverbal and verbal skills are observed and assessed. How parents and children reinforce each other is seen as critical, and whether or not their interaction is a suitable basis for rehabilitation strategies has to be judged. How, if necessary, it may be modified has to be decided. Initially, random observations are made; but a sample of controlled observations in which as many variables as possible are qualified and quantified is also taken. It is critical to reiterate that both members of the dyad are evaluated. The diagnostic procedure used is that of the Lincoln Interactive Profile which is described in detail by Clezy (1984). At the end of the observation session the parents are always asked if they feel that the interactions were representative of the normal home-based behaviors, and their comments are taken into account.

Behaviors to be Assessed

The behaviors to be observed and assessed are described below. They are recorded in a special manner using the Lincoln Interactive Profile, which is described later in the chapter. All the behaviors described are looked at whatever the age of the presenting child, for it is important to realize that many of the "earliest" skills in developmental terms are absent in the oldest children's or in the parents' communication strategies.

Reinforcement is the first aspect of behavior to be scrutinized. Dale (1976) supports the works of many as he discusses the notion that motivational rather than selective reinforcement is crucial to language learning. Clezy (1979) referred to the works of Kahan, Jersild, Ironside, and May in stressing the need for *diagnosing* and *remediating* anxiety levels through looking at the symptomatic behaviors brought about by inappropriate levels of anxiety which produce Kahan's (1971) interdependent state of "contagion" between mother and child. Clezy (1979) argued if the mother is neurotically anxious and becomes critical, negative, and/or bossy then the child is withdrawn and lacking in motivation; the child's resultant lack of performance would only increase the mother's natural anxiety and serve as a stimulant to her inappropriate behaviors. These behaviors may well have developed initially only because of her naturally anxious reaction to the diagnosis of deafness, and latently she may well possess all the skills mentioned in the literature as crucial in the mother of a language-learning child. Brown (1977) has outlined the importance of the affection content in the prosodic, tactile, and linguistic elements of "motherese" (the way mothers talk). With these factors in mind it is important to observe whether the mother is motivationally reinforcing her child. Does she reward his *effort* rather than focus upon the "wrong" results? Does she use affectionate prosody? Does she touch gently or demandingly? Does she smile or frown? These factors are the basis for healthy communication and are therefore observed and actually scored for statistical purposes, and in relation to the need for a therapeutic baseline.

Gaze patterns and the common referent are the next aspects to be observed and recorded. The population under discussion has one common feature whatever the presenting age, namely lack of language. To build that language, referential cues are essential. These are the objects, activities, and relationship which are described by the ongoing language. Bloom and Lahey (1978), Brown (1977), Bruner (1976), Muma (1981), and Nelson (1978) have all identified this essential ingredient to communication, yet how do we actually diagnose and see if it is used by our communication dyads? We need to see if the mother follows the infant's gaze before she makes a comment on a current happening, or if the infant's gaze follows her pointing finger or glance if she is initiating the interaction. In the older, manual, child we need to see if he knows how to match his utterances to the referential cue or whether the mother uses such cues. It is frequently apparent that many such children have not had their language learning based on the referential cue. It has not been the deep structure or generative base from which they have worked. They have learned their language by rote or imitation and not in a generative manner. Cognition and language have not been matched. If by chance the child is able to use some language, does he have the correct original semantic or syntactic referent? The older remedial child frequently suggests by his performance that whole stages of normal interactive developmental communicative strategies have somehow been ignored or altered completely. For example, let us take the area of supraseg-mentals. How often are naming tasks reduced to one word? In normal development the final lexical item or object may contain two or three words, the significant one being stressed to allow for the appropriate information to be filtered by the child. The meaning of the "big *blue* car" being entirely different from the "*big* blue car." Deaf children needing remedial help have often been patently prevented from developing such a distinctive prosodic grammar. Initially, in communication, it is the situational circumstances which help to generate the language. To quote Bloom and Lahey (1978, p. 573), "The facilitator's task is to provide experiences that clearly demonstrate certain concepts while providing the linguistic forms that code these concepts at a time when the child is attending to both." Simply put, there is no language-learning base if the child is gazing at his own toes wriggling in the air while the mother is talking about the yellow teddy whose name she wants her child to recognize. She either needs to follow the child's gaze, or interest him sufficiently by her strategies to alter his gaze to her referent. The mother of a deaf child who believes that he or she should watch her lips or her hands cuing or signing detracts from the appropriate reference. The referential cue will not be ignored, by an auditory–oral child. It will be used as in normal and natural language acquisition and the *rate* of learning and communication will not be altered. The auditory–oral child can simultaneously process the auditory and visual stimuli. The gaze patterns and deictic (pointing) strategies of each member of the dyad should be evaluated and if necessary modified to establish the use of the common referent. Information along this line is collected in the first observer session. The observations are then qualified and quantified.

Turn taking and listener versus speaker strategies are next analyzed during this initial session (see Duncan, 1972; Stern, 1974). We determine whether the gaze of both members of the dyad meet as they change conversational turns. This is charted and analyzed even if the "conversation" is at a babbling level, or if the child is preverbal and responding with an action rather than an utterance. Does the hearing-impaired child look or even glance at the speaker, and remain quiet while that speaker is talking? Similarly, does the listener attend to the child's vocalizations and then respond? Are the vocalizations understood? Are they passed off as meaningless, left unreinforced, uninterpreted, or unanswered? Can the hearing-impaired child recognize who is speaking to him and localize? Does the hearing-impaired child follow the conversation of others with his gaze when he is not part of that conversation? Such questions have to be answered, for these skills are some of the earliest to develop in normal communication. All of this can be observed and scored while the child is at play with his parents.

Prosodic and pragmatic analysis of the interaction is important at this early stage of observation. Does the mother use a greater *prosodic range,* as described by Garnica (1977), than she would when talking to adults, or is her range flat and unvarying? Is she using the parameters of *tone,* (intonation) *tone unit* (clause boundaries) and *tonicity,* (stress), as described by Crystal (1981), appropriately and at a phonologic level. Are the tone units too short and the tonic markers inappropriate? Is the child developing these naturally and normally? Crystal (1981) suggests a developmental hierarchy for prosodic skills; are these being followed? Are there rising, falling, and compound patterns? How does the child use his prosodic skills pragmatically? Does he use his voice to greet, initiate, make a statement, ask a question, or portray his emotions as described in Ling (1976)? Although our knowledge is in its infancy in these areas there is much that we should observe and diagnose and establish before concentrating too discretely on language per se. At this stage it is interesting to comment on how bizarre the prosodic patterns often are in those on *both* sides of the dyad who enroll for remedial help.

Language sampling is undertaken in accordance with the theory behind the clinical practice that dictates that normal, natural "motherese" or mother's language should be adhered to and should follow the broad outlines suggested by the overview in Snow and

Ferguson (1977). Consequently, aspects such as repeated utterances, reduced length of utterance, and syntactic balance must all be analyzed and measured against what is normal in relation to the child's stage of development. If, for example, an overuse of imperatives or yes/no type questions is scored in the mother, this needs to be modified. Later, strategies such as prompting, modeling, and expanding are scored. The number and types of questions versus designative statements will be counted and the eliciting grammar analyzed to see if it may be limiting the child's utterances or thoughts. For example, the child who is always asked "What is it" will have great trouble in expressing anything other than a noun-based grammar. We know from the work of Cheskin (1982; Clezy, Brown, & Moore, 1983; Cross, Johnson-Morris, & Neinhuys, 1980; Gregory, Mogford, & Bishop, 1979) that mothers' speech to hearing-impaired children varies considerably from the norm. It is assumed, therefore, that this practice will endanger the child's linguistic development unless it is modified to approach the norm as far as we are able to understand it.

These observation sessions are therefore critical in the initial stages of management and are used to develop the professional–parent relationship. They also help to establish parental control and participation from the very earliest stages. The importance of participation cannot be stressed too highly; it is *not* mere observation. Right from the earliest sessions, no home practice is given, or strategy suggested until the clinician has actually monitored that strategy being carried through by parent and child together. One of the philosophies of the program is that too often parents are told rather than shown what to do. They then go home with high motivation, but fail in their attempts for a variety of reasons. Their failure depresses their motivation and increases their anxiety over the child's performance. A valuable learning opportunity is lost. Parents who are left unguided by demonstration may fail, for example, for some of the following reasons:

1. Lack of understanding of what the child *can* hear rather than what he cannot hear;
2. Inappropriate modeling;
3. Ineffective reinforcement in relation to the target strategy and ongoing motivation;
4. Unrealistically compound goals;
5. Failure to recognize fatigue or boredom;
6. Didactic teaching rather than interaction;
7. Incorrect sequencing of target behaviors; for example, emphasis on phonetic before pragmatic, prosodic, or linguistic competence;
8. Inability to upgrade and accept their child's utterances through their own interpretative skills;

9. Lack of understanding of the order of normal linguistic development;
10. Inadequate use of the situational cue.

Parents cannot be expected to achieve without support, yet with appropriate support their skills will often surpass those of the teacher/clinician. Their need will motivate them and their child's success will stimulate further effort provided all goals are realistically set and rewarded by the clinician.

Management Procedures

Now that a general description has been given as to how a baseline for intervention is reached, the specifics of management are addressed. It is important to reiterate that at the beginning of every therapy session the child's hearing aids and hearing status for the day are checked by the administration of the Ling (1976) five-sound test. We then look at communicative skills in a developmental heirarchy and attend to both members of the dyad.

Reinforcement strategies are the first behaviors to receive attention at whatever age the child presents. This is because reinforcement substantially affects learning rate and cognitive tempo (Clezy, 1979; Muma, 1981). Reinforcement is the ingredient of interchange that renders interaction mutually satisfying. Parents frequently need to reduce anxiety and to learn various possible motivational strategies. Smiles, caresses, gentle and varied prosodic range are all encouraged and demonstrated. Reinforcers are developed which show an appropriate *response* to the child's behaviors. Parents are *shown*, not *told* what to do. If the infant gazes at an object, the parent is shown how to respond (if they do not do so already). If the infant babbles, the parent is again shown how to respond and reply. The infants' achievements are pointed out to the parents: "Look, he is looking at you when you vocalize; He is following your play strategies." Whatever the child achieves the parents are shown how to respond. At this early stage they are shown how to follow the child's lead rather than try to dictate where and how his interests should be held. Of course, they may also initiate activities. The goal is to reduce constraints rather than impose them.

In older children receiving remedial help, the reinforcement is carefully monitored until a mutually motivating interaction is achieved. This may take a long while because parents by now have the attitude that language is taught, and a pass/fail dichotomy is often unconsciously adhered to. This is a legacy of the formal classroom-based strategy. The approach that an error may just be an experiment, a trial, or even an approximation, is often a new concept to be absorbed. Again, realistic goals need to be set.

It is often at the earliest stage in working with children who need remedial help that parents have to be encouraged to vocalize at all times. Many have remained mute or have only mouthed when the child has looked at them. It is a whole new experience for them to talk to their child as the child is engaged in an activity. Gradually they acquire the concept that only if language is uttered can it be heard and processed. When such parents do start talking it is often in single words with a terrific fear of using flowing language "because their child will not understand all those words." It is then explained and demonstrated that mothers of infants use full syntax (Phillips, 1973). Parents come to understand the need for speaking in syntactically complete utterances when they see that, if they were learning a second language in another country, they would have access to the "whole." They could then set their own rate of extraction according to their own rate of learning. Often, at this stage, simple strategies have to be used to demonstrate to the parents that the child can in fact hear at all. The Ling (1976) five-sound test is a useful basic example. Given that the child can detect a range of speech patterns, it has to be demonstrated that hearing-impaired children should not *always* be expected to respond in a visible manner. The parents are counseled that the first response to their strategies may be vocalization. The child's response to the care givers is the best form of reinforcement available to them.

By introducing strategies that are alien to the parents of older children, they may be made to feel guilty at the enormity of the differences from their previous practices. We can thankfully "blame" the advance in our knowledge for these changes in the approach and therefore not cast blame on the parent or other systems. It is often *not* their deafness which is at the base of childrens' problems but rather the manner and order in which they were taught. Many normal developmental behaviors can be acquired by hearing-impaired children and then later extinguished by maladaptive teaching practices. Abnormalities in gaze, turn-taking vocalization, absence of normal prosody, and rate of utterance in our remedial population, are evidence that such behaviors have received reinforcement.

It is critical in the treatment sessions to make sure that the development of all the sense modalities is being fostered and reinforced. Some dyads seem to be more visually in tune. Those, perhaps, ignore maximum use of audition. There are those who are so keen to use audition that normal use of vision and touch are ignored; for example, the initial following of gaze patterns for establishing the common referent. Whatever the behavior required, the therapist models it for the parent and requires the parent to model it back before going home to practice and generalize. The clinician reinforces the parent when the behaviors are achieved. If the suggested strategies appear to be difficult then home practice is contraindicated.

Frequently, more than one discrete behavior is modeled and reinforced. The management package for the parent to take home might encompass prosodic patterns, child reinforcement techniques, gaze and pointing patterns to establish the common referent with accompanying spoken language, and affection content.

Visitors often attend this program and it is somewhat frustrating to be told by such visitors and allied professionals "Oh but you have such good parents, and no behavioral problems with your children!" While agreeing that all the parents are motivated, it is the belief of the writer that it is the extra care in the initial stages which has helped the parents tap their optimum reserves. Many have started with devastatingly inappropriate behaviors, some have admitted to hating their children to the extent of wishing to kill them. Some have physically abused their children; others have ignored them. Many are manipulated beyond belief by their children. In almost all instances a longitudinal survey of their interactive profiles illustrates how their reinforcement has changed them for the better (see under Evaluation).

Among the children there appears to be the normal range of hyperactive, aggressive, negative manipulative, or bored individuals. Language and speech training that has its base in communication will inevitably fail while such personality traits exist. Fortunately for us, however, the need for improvement in a relationship is often so great that the response to therapy is almost immediate. How rewarding it is to have a parent of five children come in only some 2 weeks after the start of therapy and say "You know I'm trying this positive approach with the other four as well. It works. We are all so much happier! I've even tried it with my husband!" Naturally there will be breakdowns, but a behavior baseline has been established to which the parent can consciously return when interactions are breaking down. They, too, must then be rewarded by the clinician for their achievement. It is gratifying when a parent says "I come not only because it helps my child, but because it makes *me* feel good." Is that something the parent of a hearing-impaired child often experiences? We doubt it. They also feel they have a goal which is specific and realistic, or a substage which is not just that apparently unobtainable "speech and language" but may be one small achievable step in that direction.

The mutual reinforcement and the manner in which it is implemented is therefore the all important base from which we begin. At this stage touch must be remembered as critical, for so often our hearing-impaired children are on the receiving end of digs, prods, and nudges to gain their attention. This hardly fits in with the strokes advocated by Brown (1977).

Turn-taking skills—gaze and vocalization are skills which can usually be developed fairly easily in children whether they require developmental or remedial help. If we experiment by passing an object from one person to another among a group of adults, eye contact is invariably made between donor and recipient, and the object glanced at in turn. The latter, of course, is the "common referent." As the object is passed, a comment is frequently made in turn first by donor and then by recipient. Modeling this behavior is useful for facilitating these basic skills where they do not exist, and there are many such dyads in which they need to be developed. This strategy also indicates the importance, even the necessity, of having more than just the child and teacher in at the therapy session. There are a number of reasons for this: One cannot demonstrate turns between a pair as well as in a triad, or a small group, where an informed person is able to model a natural behavior for the hearing-impaired member. Modeling is a part of facilitating without forcing a child and is a practice to which all children are exposed in their natural and normal environments. Small groups are particularly valuable where language is concerned; one only has to think of the variety of personal pronouns which can be generated by a group, or restricted if only two of the same sex are present. Turn taking can be encouraged in the course of many activities. For example, with the infant we can take rings off a stick as we pass it around, with an older child we can pass a die, or play a game, and with an adolescent mute we can pass cups of tea or coffee or deal playing cards slowly. All such activities can serve to develop the required behaviors.

Turn taking is essential in the initial stages of the Ling (1976) speech system. In developing syllable, word, sentence, or discourse production we again work in triads, or even more, with mother, father, clinician, and child. Not only is the clinician modeling a pattern for the child to reproduce, which encourages turns, but the teacher models for the mother or vice versa. The latter is then instructed to make intermittent errors which the child is trained to detect. This ensures that the child not only monitors interactions in which he is involved, but those involving other speakers as well. He is expected to be able to monitor the conversation of others—both through audition and through vision. This he must do from the earliest stages of development, as does the hearing infant when he is interested. To create that interest requires the use of a wide prosodic range, as described by Garnica (1977). Some children who need remedial work have long since lost interest in any conversation which does not involve their own form of compensating communication, whatever that may be. Facilitation of verbal interaction may be achieved by slowing the rate of conversational turns to allow for appropriate gaze and vocalization patterns to develop.

Some readers may think that too much emphasis is being placed on such basic skills. Yet imagine how they can help one work on personal pronouns in a contextual manner. The pronoun used is dependent upon whom one is looking at. For example, the clinician gives the child a teddy and asks the mother "Who did I give that to?" If the mother is looking at the clinician when she answers she should reply, "To her" or "You gave it to her." If the mother is looking at the child she will say, "To you" or "She gave it to you." The surface structure of the language has to be generated from the deep structure or the action. If a child has failed to develop normal turn-taking skills, his ability to analyze and utilize language appropriately at a later time will obviously be impaired.

With both the therapeutic strategies already described it is important to stress that "stage" of development rather than age, audition, or IQ of the individual is the basis of therapy.

The use of deixis (pointing) and deictic terms (this, that, here, there) by both members of the dyad draws attention to *the common referent;* that is, the object or activity which is the subject of comment. Language and speech impairment can be largely overcome by the listener if he knows the subject under discussion and can therefore better interpret the speaker's intent. Focusing attention on the common referent is a skill used by all parents in the language-critical years of their children. So it is with our hearing-impaired dyads. The two minds must be focused on one subject for any meaningful inter-action or conversation to take place. When assessing this skill, it is surprising to see, and score, how often two minds are apparently at polar extremes. This is particularly so when the unimpaired partner is trying to teach or lead the impaired partner to too great an extent. To develop the use of the common referent we explain the model for the parent. We use pointing or glancing as we name, question, or describe. We also follow the child's gaze or pointing as he vocalizes and then we expand on his chatter. Meaning is thus given to utterance and the utterance is consequently understood.

The utterance is the basic unit of verbal expression. The phrase "/ɔ/ /i/ /u/ /ʌ/" ("aw ih oo uh"), can be interpreted if one looks at or points to a *big blue truck*. It would be extremely hard to follow such an approximation on a busy highway if no gaze or finger indicated the object referred to.

The most exciting stage in interactive therapy is when the parent begins to understand the child's utterances—or the child understands what is said by the parents. Critics will then say, "But the child is attending to the situational cue." That, however, as a first step, is in itself a great achievement, a perfectly natural and normal stage of development, and one through which all children must pass. If sound is consistently matched to that cue, the basis of language is either being received or expressed.

To establish the use of the common referent many activities, matched to the cognitive development of the child, are used in therapy. The activities involve the child in many differing roles and interactive situations. The activities may be cooking, model making, structured turn-taking games, or role-playing, but most are concrete at first with a strong dependence on situational cues. Quite often the child is given the teacher's role or parent's role and immediately adapts pragmatically and prosodically to that role. The choice of activities should also be based on the child's development as a whole and take into account strengths and weaknesses in all areas. Books and pictures are avoided, particularly with the remedial population, because often tenses or even verbs are not understood. A picture of a child hopping does not show the movement or whether he *is* hopping or *has* hopped. Throughout this time the mother is encouraged to match exactly what she is saying to what the child is doing.

Prosodics and pragmatics are the main bases of early verbal interaction and development. It is these elements of his language which, if natural and normal, should portray what he is really saying. Such discrete terms should not, however, suggest to the reader that each of these areas is being discretely worked upon. Language is either generated from the activity, modeled, or elicited informally throughout, with appropriate use of prosodic information and a variety in function. The parents' attention is drawn to these elements in the framework of a healthy, communicative environment. Stress is given to the fact that, in therapy, these areas cannot be separated, although in our analysis and evaluation discrete observations can and must be made and then qualified and quantified.

Diagnostic observations as described above will have already established at which level language intervention should begin. Is there a limited "functional" grammar? Is either member of the dyad prosodically limited or deviant? Necessary modifications will be explained and demonstrated to the parent and their replication or adaptation then monitored. For example, it may be necessary to point out that although a child's voice level is inappropriate and too deep, he is, in fact, using the intonation contours to match the meaning. The use of appropriate tone boundaries (Crystal, 1981) matched to clause boundaries will often need to be demonstrated to the parents of those children in the remedial program. Many of these parents communicate with tone boundaries marking every syllable. Likewise their use of tonicity (stress) may not allow for appropriate semantic and grammatic discrimination on the part of the child. For example, "the *big* blue car" means the big, as opposed to the little, car; but the big *blue* car means the blue versus the red. Similarly, "*You*/went to school," means something utterly different from "You went/to *school*." It is only the stress and tone unit (boundary) which allows the child to make the significant distinctions. It is *not* the words.

If the pattern of prosody is diagnosed as normal and appropriate it is not even mentioned in therapy, although care is taken to watch that the parents of the auditory–oral children do not fall into bad habits. The less said, however, the less there is to confuse. It is no use working on syntax if these prosodic prerequisites are not established. If there *is* a break down in prosody, the clinician *must* know what is wrong. Is it the stress, the boundaries, or the rises and falls in inflection?

Children under remediation may need some kinesthetic input (tapping) as well as audition to help with this element. Also these children cannot be expected to have a varied pragmatic grammar, that is, to *use* their voices to mean different things if the situations in which they find themselves do not promote such variation. A child's voice will not convey excitement if he is bored. With auditory–oral children this is not usually a problem. The introduction of this *use* however is often quite bizarre and alarming to the parent of a child under remediation. The first sounds of the child who begins to demand, greet, and show his emotions with his voice can be demoralizing for a parent used to a mute and slient being! With appropriate explanations such stages in vocal development become rewarding. It is important to facilitate parents' interpretations of these levels of function. There is nothing more rewarding than when a small silent or "just vocalizing" auditory–oral child begins to nod or shake his head in response to a question. It means he has *heard* the prosodic form of question versus statement. Often the situation will then allow his total comprehension of that question. At this stage, therefore, not only must the parents be helped with their balanced use of prosodics and pragmatics, but also with their interpretation of the child's use. Each skill needs to be demonstrated by the clinician where possible, and the resultant modification scored, to see if the therapeutic strategy suggested has or has not worked.

Establishing all these skills *must* be done while all are engaged in a joint activity appropriate to the age level and interests of the child. Whether hair-dressing or manicuring with teen-aged girls, making mobiles with tots, or playing chess with informed young adults, the actual language strategies can be as simple or advanced as required. The activity can frequently be manipulated appropriately to achieve the required linguistic result (Lund & Duchan, 1983).

The syntax program aims at achieving a balanced grammar according to the information outlined in Snow and Ferguson (1977). The "motherese" or mother language should contain approximately 40% questions, but that should break down to all forms of wh-questions, open-ended, and tag questions. There should apparently not be an overuse of imperatives (commands) and designators (statements). There should be much prompting and eliciting of present and past tenses backed by the appropriate activity. We need to cover the full range of nouns and adjectives. Very early on, conjunctions are important. The correct use of the earlier personal pronouns is established (Lund and Duchan, 1983) but always in the situationally appropriate context. Parents are shown, and then given the opportunity to practice, all the syntactic forms necessary at a receptive level, and are then encouraged to use the appropriate eliciting strategies, matched to the necessary environmental cue. Frequently this format is followed with the clinician eliciting the responses from the parent, so the child can experience receptively situationally correct language, without being pressured to perform himself. Techniques of eliciting from the child are introduced, but it is really the situation which is manipulated to promote the language despite the strict attention given to the syntax. Detailed description of some of the syntactic strategies used are given in Clezy (1979). Modeling of a required structure is sometimes used initially, particularly between clinician and parent, but it is soon dropped in favor of controlled eliciting to produce the required appropriate grammatic structure. Great care is given to demonstrating to the parent how the language must be matched to the situation. In language learning the parents' need to "hear the right response" from the child often outstrips the need to see if that utterance was situationally appropriate. This is often the case with grammatic markers. The parent who is fixated on eliciting "v + ing," that is, "Daddy's going," might need to be counseled against working on that structure after Daddy has long since *"gone."*

Let us now revert to some of the clinical activities mentioned earlier, and illustrate how they may be adapted or manipulated to achieve certain therapeutic goals.

First we have a profoundly hearing-impaired auditory–oral child who is nearly four but has only reached the Ling (1976) Stage 3 developmentally. That is, the child can use vowels and diphthongs to approximate words. The child is beginning to use these skills very well in the following situation which requires her to use terms and to match her "speech" to her needs and the situational cue. Her mother's understanding is also required.

The items for play are laid out in front of the little girl and some are duplicated. The names of some are given by the clinician and mother to the girl as they sort through together.

Clinician—(Normal prosody, slightly slow rate.)

> OK, yes that's the boy, and this (picking it up) is the girl. Whose hair shall we wash?

Girl—/ɜ/ (holds out "girl.")

Clinician—Hers? Great, it's nice long hair isn't it?

Girl—Nods (shows she has heard the question and responded), takes the doll and tips it upside down with its hair in the bowl. The shampoo is near the clinician, and the girl puts her hand out making a "request" vocalization with rising tone.

Clinician—"The shampoo? OK, do you want the pink (points), or the yellow?" (points).

Girl—/ɛə/ (yellow).

Clinician—Fine, I'll open it while you hold the baby.

Girl—Washes the doll's hair talking, soothing, and crooning. The jargon is phrased into tone contours, appropriately stressed and prosodically intelligible. The jargon "flows." Then the child looks at her mother who has the towels and comb beside her and says /i i æ/ (pointing).

Mother—Interprets this as "give me that" and says "please."

Girl—/i ʌm/. Note stops and spontaneous final consonant for "Mum"

Mother—Which? The towel or the comb?

Girl—/ə ɑʊwə/ (the towel, note the article *a*).

Mother—Passes the towel having completely understood her daughter's spoken request.

Next, by contrast, we have an auditory–oral 4-year-old with hearing levels of over 90 dB but who makes maximum use of residual audition. She has an informed parent to whom it is quickly explained that we shall try and use as many words such as *can, do, have, might, will won't,* and so on. (The emphasis of the session is on *auxiliary verbs.* These are italicized below.)

Clinician—*Can* you guess what we're *going* to do today? (Pulls out materials).

Child—/aɪ dənoʊ, mʌm wɔ'wɪ gənə du/? (I don't know Mum, what we gonna do?)

Mother—You guess darling, it looks like pasting *doesn't it?*

Child—Keeps working and sorting materials.

Clinician—"It *might* be pasting, it *might* be drawing or it *could* be..."

Child—/bʌpɪ'/ (puppets) aɪ noʊ, ə bɪ bʌpɪ; wi ə bʌpɪ bɪvɔ, dɪn wi mʌm, memba?/ (Puppet. I know, a big puppet. We (had) a puppet before, didn't we Mum. Remember?

Mother—Yes, darling I *can* remember. But I think it *might* be different this time *don't* you?

Child—(Impatient) /ɔ'ə wi gənə du dɪʊl/? (What are we going to do Gill?)

Clinician—We'll make mobiles like that one (pointing). *Do* you think you *can* Mum?

Child—/aɪ æn! aɪ æn! (I can, I can) and grabs scissors and materials—/wɛ ə gugɔ/? (Where's the glue gone?)

Obviously both parent and child have absorbed the fairly sophisticated strategy with great ease. The generalization to spontaneous language is almost instantaneous and words such as "might" and "would" are soon recorded.

In the case of this sample it cannot be assumed that the auxiliaries were introduced and taught in that one session, but rather that the child was being given an opportunity to *use* them in a situationally appropriate manner. Some might argue that by specifying particular syntactic forms on which to work the language process may become too formalized. This is not a formal program for language; nevertheless, the clinician should be sure that all necessary syntactic forms are covered. Such activities are often demonstrated with parents. However, everyday home-based activities are also used to help the parents appreciate that work does not have to be approached in such a formal manner. The parents very soon learn to adapt their skills to the ongoing home situation. It is, then, the normal everyday activities that generate the language. The reason for using special activities for clinical visits is to help the children to maintain motivation. They may attend at varying intervals for a period of 5 to 7 years, and exciting or interesting activities help maintain interest.

In the above sample some moderately advanced syntax is being used. Opportunity is given for all parents to appreciate, utilize, and facilitate all parts of syntax in a developmentally appropriate manner. Great care is needed, however, that this form of therapy does not become too ordered or too structured. Normal children do not learn language forms in a strict hierarchy. They do not learn one form and master it expressively before moving to another. Many forms are introduced together, depending upon the situation, so it must be with hearing-impaired children. We must, however, be sure that all forms are covered and that none is neglected.

Lexical development or vocabulary extension is also worked on. Once the child has acquired a basic grammar a great deal of work goes into vocabulary extension. The parents are shown how to introduce or elaborate their vocabulary even if the task in question is fairly basic. One of the greatest pitfalls here is that the parents may fall into the habit of testing for the new words they have introduced. There is, however, no real evidence in the literature that parents of normal children test for high-level vocabulary skills. The proposal or hypothesis for this part of the program is that if the children do not hear new words matched to the referent, they will not absorb them into their vocabulary. If, however, they do hear them, understand them, and have the opportunity to repeat them, they may well retain and at least understand them when they hear (or read) them again. It is also important to note that increasingly high levels of abstraction must be introduced. Gradually, language is used *without* the situation which it represents.

An example of such increased use of abstract language and vocabulary extension is provided below. In this case the child (again profoundly hearing impaired) is 7 years old. Bock and Mazzella (1983) found that "accent" as they called it, or stress, accelerated the learning of new information; so the teaching strategy is to provide slight stress on the "new" words. These are italicized in the sample below. Phonetic transcription is not necessary here to illustrate the point.

Clinician—Right. We'll make mobiles again today because you are so good at it. You're really *excellent*. Here are all the *utensils* we'll need, they're the things we'll need. Mum uses cooking *utensils* at home (abstraction) when she's make a *recipe*, don't you Mum?

Child—Mum made a cake at the weekend, didn't you Mum?

Clinician—Oh! did you Mum, what *utensils* did you need?

Mother—I used a bowl and the *electric* mixer and all the *ingredients* like flour, sugar, butter, etc.

all abstract

Clinician—Sounds delicious, now what *utensils* have we here?

Child—Scissors, brushes, lots of things. Ooh that's sharp. (shows comprehension).

Clinician—Right, and here we've got a *plan* or *design* but not really a *recipe* like we have for cooking. You look at the *plan* and see if you can understand it.

Child—Yup, you've got to draw this first.

Clinician—Mm, you do. You're drawing the *outline* and that thing you're using is a *template*. What is it?

Child—A *template*. We got these things at school.

This sample illustrates the manner in which one can go from the concrete (when the referent or object is there) to the abstract (when the object or happening is replaced by words only). This is a skill which needs to be developed as early as possible. It is an extremely difficult skill for anyone to master meaningfully unless they know about the child's recent experiences in detail. The informed parent finds it easy to relate to such experiences in the child's life. The clinician will only have minimal knowledge, so much of her abstraction may prove meaningless to the child. Skilled parents can abstract about time, place, manner, form, and consequence. They have the shared knowledge which makes the abstraction meaningful to the child. Similarly, in vocabulary extension practices it is really only the parent who knows what *is new* in relation to what is already learned and understood. It is only the parent who knows which of the young child's experiences can generate new and meaningful vocabulary and which will be useful rather than redundant. While the clinician can demonstrate these "arts" it is the parents who will have the ability to use them to the child's advantage. These are indeed strong arguments for using the parent as the agent for language therapy.

The Phonetic/Phonologic Element: Speech

This program uses the exact practices in diagnosis and evaluation as outlined in Ling (1976), with only a very few modifications or changes in emphasis. They are as follows:

1. The speech sessions usually incorporate three or four different speakers.
2. Parents are shown how to implement the techniques and very great care is taken with the ordering of subskills, modeling, prosody, and reinforcement.
3. Care is taken to monitor prosodic skills according to Crystal (1981) and to avoid introducing prosodic patterns which are not linguistically or developmentally appropriate. For example, we develop final, before initial, stress. The different prosodic parameters are *not* introduced discretely, but *are* evaluated separately (see under evaluation).
4. The parents quite frequently provide the material for the phonologic generalization of the drills. In other words, they provide words already familiar to and used by the child. Parents learn to adapt their strategies to elicit those words which are correctly produced. These words need not necessarily be nouns but the words which are *used* frequently. For example, *in, on, me*.
5. The entire Ling (1976) system is presented in a very simple form which parents can score and understand.

The above outline of treatment procedures does not allow for the detail in management necessary for each child. Individual differences are as important with this population as with any and *must*, of course, be catered to. The differences are not usually measured by hearing loss, age, background, or IQ, although such differences, of course, exist; but far more by *stage* of communicative development in relation to the normal acquisition of such skills.

Preparation for each session is carried out primarily by the students who are charged with the task of preparing a variety of cognitively appropriate activities. They must take into account individual cognitive, motor, and general learning skills, and behavioral anomalies and interests. Students are also required to plan the next stage of the Ling (1976) speech system in detail, and to identify the prerequisite subskills. Some overall goals are planned for the language session, in relation to the child's stage of development. For example, emphasis may be given to ordering of adjectives or irregular past tenses, but the specifics are *not* detailed. This is because the child's activities should generate the language. During the prelingual stage of the children's development much familiarization of the later language strategies is practiced with the parents. They use these skills, where appropriate, as the child plays.

The counseling part of each session involves any problem which may confront the parent at the time. These may include issues such as sibling rivalry, with the younger sister biting or scratching or teasing. In this case both children would automatically attend the session until the behavior had been modified by helping the parents improve their strategies and management of the problem. Another problem may be school placement, or mode of communication choice. This can be discussed fully with the parent, and then the Ascertainment Committee advised of the stance taken. It is the slowly developing auditory–oral child who presents the greatest problem to this program and counseling in relation to such cases, therefore, warrants some discussion. Counseling by various professionals may lead to difficulties because their views may clash or appear to clash. Parents may also have difficulty in sorting out whether the people concerned may be biased (have considered the issues and can support their views) or prejudiced (recommending something they have not thought through). Sometimes people's attitudes lead them to interpret given facts as expression of prejudice. In an emotion-charged field, these problems add to the overall confusion.

The severely hearing-impaired, and the great majority of our profoundly hearing-impaired auditory–oral children enrolled in our program from an early age, achieve integrated school placement with support services from teachers of the deaf. The older, remedial population tend to remain in their schools of origin with a very few moving from oral classes to normal school or from TC classes to oral classes. There is, however, a small number of profoundly hearing-impaired children, enrolled from an early age, who, for one reason or another, do not achieve sufficient language to cope in regular schools by the age of 5 or 6 years. These children may have been diagnosed later than most (over 2 years of age), may suffer compound disabilities, may (quite frequently) have a period of chronic middle ear dysfunction, in addition to profound sensorineural impairment, or may just be "slower" for reasons unknown. They have often achieved some speech and language acquisition. They vocalize freely and appropriately and use their skill to communicate and convey emotion. They have the basics of the suprasegmentals and apply these pragmatically and situationally appropriately. They have all the vowels, diphthongs, and some consonants which they match consistently and appropriately to a referent. They are not unduly frustrated, for the communication skills they use are understood by those around them. They can express themselves. The Victorian education system, however, does not allow for such linguistic delay, and pressure for placement at school age begins. Such children are invariably recommended for placement in total communication classes. This is often a devastating blow to the parents, and to the clinicians of this program. The child is slow, but is definitely achieving, in the *proper developmental hierarchy.* Hearing thresholds may even have improved (see Appendix 3-A). Once in the new program, however, the whole method of communication so painstakingly acquired is changed, and many of the skills which are natural and normal are extinguished. These problems have been identified and verified by evaluation. Counseling under this situation is a supremely difficult task; complete support for whatever decision is made by the parent is all that can be given along with a more "remedial" type program and an attempt at maintenance. This is hard for the children for at this age vision is still easier for them and peer models are strong. Parents are learning signs; their communication changes; prosody, voice, and rate change, and the referent is often ignored. This is all retrogressive, yet no guarantee could have been given that normal speech and language would eventually have been attained if this program had been followed exclusively. No guarantee could have been given that educational delay would not be damaging. Counseling in this situation involves as much information as possible and the use of videotapes to demonstrate individual differences in other children. It is the parents who have the agony of the decision, and it is one which rests with them forever.

This problem might be overcome if educational systems could allow for the fact that even a speech and language delay of 4 years may be inevitable for some children in this population. But *when* do we admit that compensation is required, and *how* do we avoid extinguishing valuable skills already acquired once we introduce an alternative system?

In the children requiring remediation the greatest problem encountered is lack of motivation. Sometimes motivation comes from the parents rather than the child or teenager. This problem fades as parents are counseled and as they see the children learn to talk, begin to use their hearing aids, and experience "success." At present there is quite a little group of teenagers all spurring one another to greater achievement in normal communication. This is rewarding. The second counseling problem to handle in this population is that of parent hostility and confusion. This is summed up in such phrases as "Why haven't I learned all this before?" "Why wasn't I told all this when my child could have learned to use it at the appropriate age?" "Why wasn't I told he did have some useful hearing?" "Why wasn't he encouraged to use his aids?" "Now I understand why he can't read!" "Why didn't he learn language before reading and writing?" "Why was I told to say only one or two words at a time?" It is important to answer such questions positively and to concentrate on the future rather than the past.

EVALUATION PROCEDURES

Regular evaluation of staff, parents, and children is an integral part of this program. A segment of every language and speech session is scored and a longitudinal profile of therapy emerges. The hypothesis behind the method employed is that clinicians should be able to specify exactly which therapeutic strategy produced a certain behavior. They should also be able to *score* whether the techniques they are applying are working. The rate of achievement is recorded. The data collected should be easy to evaluate for comparative purposes and long narrative descriptions avoided if possible. Time is always at a premium.

Although a number of tests are available, none seems to suit the overall purpose of this program in that they do not allow for both members of the dyad to be evaluated *together*. Yet this is critical as each person is mutually dependent. We have therefore developed our own evaluation procedure. At time of writing approximately 7 years of clinical trials have gone into developing the Lincoln Interactive Profile (Clezy, 1984). This profile was originally introduced as a means by which to score basic reinforcement schedules in mother–child interaction (Clezy, 1979). It has since been adapted to encompass nearly all the strategies mentioned under Treatment Procedures.

The profile now allows for complex observation of many behaviors in a naturalistic unstructured environment. Different items can be scored either sequentially or concurrently, depending on the skill of the transcriber. We need to acquire as complete a record as possible of *all* communicative behaviors. This method allows for quantification and qualification of verbal and nonverbal behaviors. Such factors as deixis, eye contact, reinforcement, pragmatics, and syntax can all be

FIGURE 3-1. The Lincoln Interactive Profile

Motivational Activity	M/T/S		●		
Appropriate Cue/Response	C/P	●		●	
Intervention	M/T/S		+ IMP		— WH
Inappropriate Cue/Response	C/P				
Negative Activity	M/T/S				—
Turn Event		1	2	3	4

KEY: M/T/S = Mother/Therapist/Spouse   IMP = Imperative
       C/P = Child/Patient   WH = Wh-question
       + = Deixis present   — = Deixis absent
                          ● = Response

recorded. Observers are free to chart any behavior in which they might be interested.

The Lincoln Interactive Profile

The Lincoln Interactive Profile has six categories as described below (Figure 3-1). Each row is allocated to a specific member of a communicative dyad. The dyad involved might be parent/child, clinician/child, student/parent, student/child, or clinician/student. In Figure 3-1 specific persons have already been allotted to each category, but each clinician is free to specify who is represented by each category. Factors and people's behaviors to be analysed should always be entered into a key as shown. Behaviors are charted on to the profile as an interaction takes place. This is seen as a great advantage over the more traditional method of taping and sampling for analysis at a later time. The six categories of the profile are as follows:

Intervention.

All those strategies, verbal and nonverbal which care givers use when communicating with a child, other than those categorized as reinforcers, are instances of intervention. These may be prompts, expansions, questions and statements, or just deixis (pointing).

Appropriate or Inappropriate Cue and Response.

Cues and responses are critical, for it must be remembered that quite frequently a child will either initiate an interaction or conversely follow a stimulus from the other member of the dyad. The appropriateness of the child's behavior is scored. This may be appropriateness either to the *situational* or *linguistic* cue. These two categories are also important when formal teaching strategies are being charted. Is the response appropriate to the cue? Does the child learn or not? How then is he reinforced?

Motivational Activity.

The motivational activity category is reserved for any behavior, verbal or nonverbal, which may be reinforcing.

Negative Activity.

Negative activity, the opposite of the above, whether a frown, a verbal negation, or any other form of undesirable behavior.

The Event.

For statistical purposes, occurrences need to be counted and one must define what the occurrence is. This system uses the *communication turn*, whether verbal or nonverbal. On the chart this is numbered and delineated by the transcriber with a vertical "bar line" similar to that used in music. By way of a very brief demonstration, the chart in Figure 3-1 represents the following interchange between a mother and nonverbal child.

Turn 1   The child tips some rings off a pyramid stick (appropriate to toy).

Turn 2   The mother says "Clever boy, that's right. Now put one back." (She points to ring and stick.)

Turn 3   The child puts a ring back.

Turn 4   Mother says "No, that's the little one, you need the big one first." Where is the big one?" (She no longer points.)

In this instance the clinician is interested in scoring the reinforcement, the use of questions and imperatives, and also deixis. Perhaps if this type of interchange were to be repeated a few more times the clinician would try to show the mother that the child's ability to put a ring back, for example, should not be negatively reinforced. He had, in fact, achieved what she had asked. In this particular program all effort is made to achieve results which encompass the top four lines. Many charts of mothers and children initially cover the bottom three until appropriate goals and reinforcement have been set.

Charting and evaluation takes place during every session. Only 2 or 3 mintues are necessary for each clinical strategy or observation session. Boone and Prescott (1972) found that if too much time was spent in evaluation, intervention suffered. Their studies also showed that short samples could be fully representative. Reliability is, of course, an issue here, and the many factors described by Taplin and Reid (1973) and Ramey, Farran, and Finklestein (1978) are critical. All charters should be aware of the pitfalls in observer reliability. Interrater reliability can be, and is, established among all observers in this particular program. A further reliability test for sole clinicians would be charting and then recharting of videotaped samples. However, the camera is often not a reliable "viewer" of both members of the dyad any more than is the charter.

By use of this procedure during short timed samples every session is analyzed. If the clinician is interested in the balance of the mother's grammar, noun phrases versus verb phrases could be superimposed upon overall interaction. Snow and Ferguson (1977), for example, suggest that a balance of 44% of questions of total content is normal in mother language. The number of questions can be counted and results then compared with this norm. If questions are absent, intervention can take place and ensuing results again counted and compared. The types of questions used should also receive attention. If just "what" were used constantly only a noun-based grammar would be elicited.

In a formal and structured therapy session, or for evaluation of the Ling (1976) speech teaching strategies, the chart is used in a similar manner (see Figure 3-2). Often speech is phonetically transcribed and prosodic information superimposed.

Event 5   The clinician smiled, remodeled the whole, saying "Now we'll do it all."

Event 6   The child succeeded.

From this very short chart we know that the child needed three trials to complete the target, but could achieve specific subskills each time. In this case the information was both segmental and suprasegmental. Such charting should give us an exact record of the strategies used by the teacher in relation to intervention and reinforcement. What does the mother do when her child is wrong? Can she help or does she confuse? Can she model correctly? The clinician in charge and the students need to be evaluated also. If the child is not achieving appropriate responses or appropriate subskills, obviously goals or teaching strategies must be reviewed, and then reevaluated. Longitudinal information can be collated in this manner, and clinical sessions compared over a period of time. The overall criteria for success

FIGURE 3-2. Profile of Formal Therapy Session Work on /f/ in final position and tone unit

Motivational Activity	M/T/S			●			
Appropriate Cue/Response	C/P		— ●				+ ●
Intervention	M/T/S	af/af af (two tone units)		●		●	
Inappropriate Cue/Response	C/P				+ ●		
Negative Activity	M/T/S						
Turn Event		1	2	3	4	5	6

Key: M/T/S = Mother/Therapist/Child   C/P = Child/Patient
     Response lines represent segmental   — = Tone Unit Incorrect
       factors   + = Tone Unit Correct
                            ● = Response

The example provided represents work on /f/ in final position and tone unit (prosodic contour-denoting clause) as described by Crystal (1981).

Event 1:   The clinician modeled the syllables in two tone units.

Event 2:   Child repeated the sounds, but with three equal syllables; that is, three tone units.

Event 3:   The clinician told the child the sound was right but there was also a tune to listen to and repeated the model.

Event 4:   The child produced the tone units and deleted the /f/.

are that the children should achieve and add more and more to their speech and language skills. It is also important to measure that the dyad does in fact benefit from the modifications to the mother's behaviors suggested by the clinicians. Here the profile is used to score "before" and "after" behaviors for comparison. Not only is it then possible to measure the mother's reshaped strategies, but also to see if the child responded as had been intended. Language samples of both dyad members are also taken approximately twice a year and these are analyzed grammatically (Crystal, Fletcher, & Garman, 1976). Phonetic transcriptions are done to ascertain how much of the speech work has generalized to the phonologic level of performance.

All assessment is in relation to hearing speech, language, and communicative interaction. Further evaluation such as psychometric assessment is arranged through the Ascertainment Committee with whom there is close cooperation. The children receive an audiological assessment once or twice a year from the National Acoustic Laboratories, but can receive assessment at any time from the in-house services already mentioned. If a child has a middle ear infection or some other medical or othodontic problem he is immediately referred to his general practitioner for ongoing advice and referral.

This program makes maximum use of all recording facilities, and each dyad is filmed on videotape as frequently as possible. Many other language and vocabulary tests are available for use as needed.

Recommendations can be made to the Ascertainment Committee with regard to the child's school placement. However, the staff on this program are not educationalists and therefore only assess the communicative abilities of the child. As can be seen, this is done in great detail. Members of the Ascertainment Committee come to observe the children to help with their evaluation. Classroom or peripatetic staff also observe. The clinician from this program observes the children in their educational environment. From these evaluations it is apparent that many of the childrens' communication performance varies considerably according to their environment, a point to be elaborated later in this chapter.

Case Descriptions

The program, like all others, has its successes, failures, moderate successes, and cases of particular interest. Despite all the evaluation described above, it is almost impossible to ascertain why children achieve at such differing levels, although one factor is certain, *hearing is not apparently the critical variable.* All the children described below have profound levels of loss. It seems that it is their ability to *use* their residual hearing, or the level at which they are *allowed* or *expected* to use it which is critical. Much of the discussion about these children is subjective in character for there is no way in which to measure the characteristics which are felt to be the cause of some of the individual differences.

The dyads described below are chosen as fairly typical of their group when classed as successes or failures, and this should be taken into account in relation to the overall figures given later.

For ease of description of the stages of spoken language the children have reached upon referral, and at later significant periods, the seven stages of development described in Ling (1976) are used. These are outlined below:

	Phonetic Level	Phonologic Level
Stage 1	Vocalizes freely on demand	Uses vocalizations to convey emotion
Stage 2	Basis of supresegmentals	Used to match specific situations
Stage 3	All vowels & dipthongs with control	Used to approximate words
Stage 4	Consonants (manner) with vowels	Some words clear with good voice
Stage 5	Consonants (manner & place) with vowels	More words clear with good voice
Stage 6	Consonants (manner, place, & voicing)	Most words clear with good voice
Stage 7	Initial and final blends	Intelligible speech with natural voice patterns

Successes

Subject S.B. was referred at the age of 3 years. Her diagnosis had been made at 1 year. She was already attending a kindergarten which caters to hearing-impaired children in an integrated environment. The parents brought her because they felt that they needed even more involvement in her speech and language training. At diagnosis and just afterward total communication had been recommended by the Ascertainment Committee because of her profound degree of loss. The parents had rejected this recommendation. The child was being fitted with an FM aid at the time of referral. She is the second of four children, one having been born in the second year of her attendance. At the time of referral the child vocalized with a high voice, but displayed excellent pragmatic use of these vocalizations, accompanied by normal gesture (Ling Stage 2). There was no intelligible speech, but she was obviously using her residual hearing and seemed to understand a great deal of what was said provided there was a contextual cue. She was extremely shy and inhibited. Analysis of the mother's language showed excellent prosodic content but a gross imbalance of grammar in the form of too many imperatives, and a noun-based format, particularly in eliciting. Some of the

FIGURE 3-3. Audiogram of S.B. (Aged 9 years.)

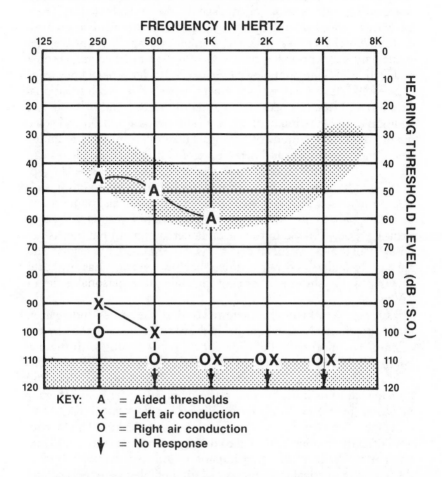

reinforcement was negative and corrective, and the teaching didactic, but the motivation was high and the mother quick to grasp whatever strategy was suggested. Speech teaching had not commenced.

For 6 years management has progressed as described. The greatest problem has been severe and recurring bouts of middle ear infection and illness. The child was able to start normal school at the normal age (this is rare), and is a very high academic achiever. She receives extra help from a visiting teacher. Her mother, who is a trained teacher, has remained the prime agent for her remediation throughout. The mother has achieved this while meeting her commitment to three other children and has constantly been aware of not "singling out" this particular child. As a result, all four have frequently attended sessions. The others are excellent "agents" too, as is the father. There have been periods when S.B. has only needed to attend once a month or less. All the child's syntax is normal and age appropriate, her vocabulary is exceptionally advanced, and she can, of course, abstract to a high level (Ling phonological Stages 6–7). Her general knowledge is excellent. As she learned to abstract she needed to watch situational cues less and less, has become a natural lip reader, and still uses her audition to the maximum. Her speech still needs attention and voice quality often lacks intensity. Strangers take a few minutes to adjust before they can understand her. At present all sounds and blends can be elicited, but the more complicated blends such as final /st/, /sp/ or /ts/, and /sks/ are extremely difficult for her in spontaneous speech at a normal rate. S.B. is a well-adjusted child but had some social problems, particularly when she changed school a year ago. She still wears her bulky FM aid in the classroom environment but prefers her postauricular aids on social occasions. She has so far accepted and apparently understood her deafness but just recently has begun to show signs that she is confronting the really deep personal issues of "Why me?"

R.O. was also three when referred and at the same kindergarten as the previous child, where he had only just been placed by his mother. The mother had already done a year's signing with the boy but had rejected that method of communication in favor of this program which she at least wanted to "try." The child was silent and therefore did not use a natural voice or prosodic range, so therapy had to begin at a much earlier baseline (Ling Prestage 1). R.O. is an only child. This dyad needed help in many more areas. The mother was critically anxious, admitted to hating the problems the child had brought to her life, was often impatient and negative with him to the extent of physical punishment. Marital problems also ensued and there has since been a divorce. Few of the mother's linguistic practices were stage appropriate, and the child showed little evidence of using his residual hearing. He was a very negative and behaviorally difficult child with strong ideas of his own, and deep frustration at his lack of communication. He gestured and signed a little to make himself understood. This mother's need dictated the speed with which she responded to help and guidance, and she is the arch success in this dyad. As a result of her changed practices and all her work with her child he, too, is in an age appropriate class in a normal school with ancillary help from a teacher of the deaf. He is now a supremely auditory child with excellent language and a high level of speech skills

FIGURE 3-4. Audiogram of R.O. (Aged 8 years.)

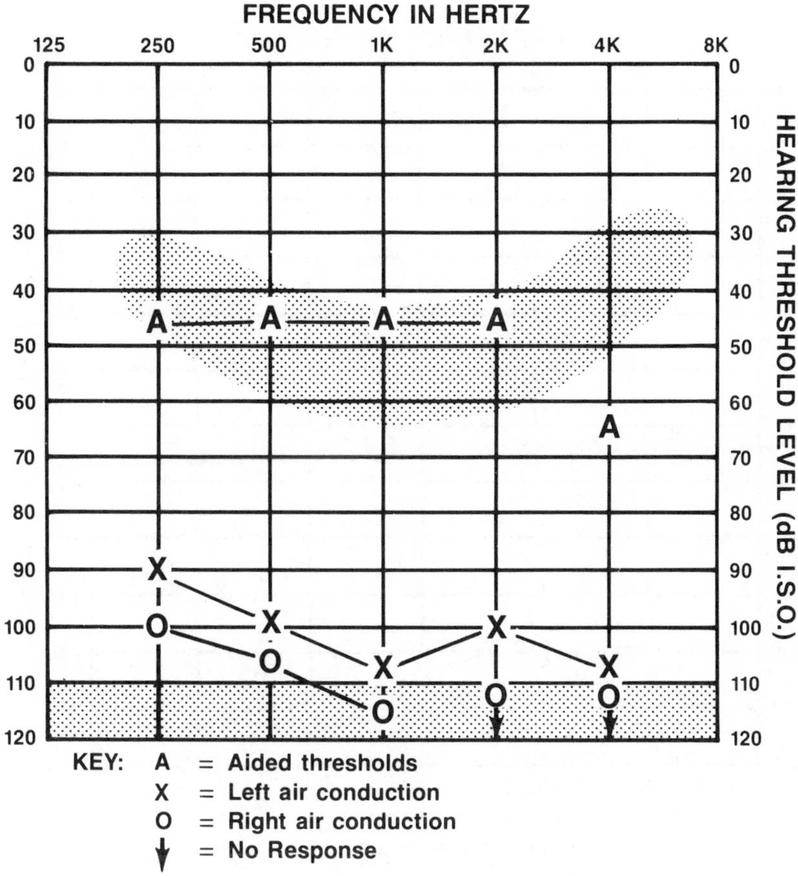

KEY: A = Aided thresholds
X = Left air conduction
O = Right air conduction
↓ = No Response

considering his profound loss (Ling Stages 6–7). At the time of the divorce his behavior was remarkably "even" and predictable (he was 7 years old), and he was able to discuss the issues fully with the counselors in the family court. Although speech work is continuing, few problems are anticipated, and the child seems socially well integrated at school.

K.L. was 14 years old when he was referred. He was an *entirely* manual communicator from a Total Communication school. He did not wear his hearing aids. Observation showed that all his family, although normally hearing, did not speak to him. They behaved as mute signers, who sometimes mouthed or used telegraphic utterances.

FIGURE 3-5. Audiogram of K.L. (Aged 16 years.)

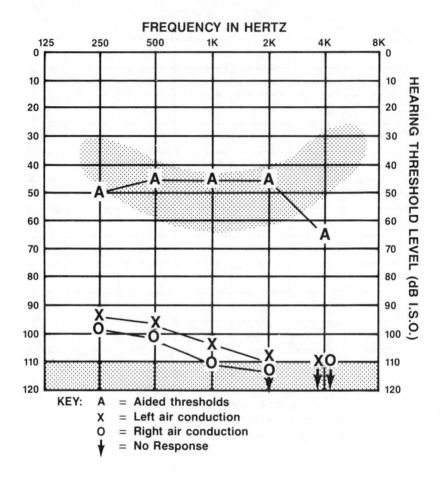

FREQUENCY IN HERTZ

KEY: A   =   Aided thresholds
       X   =   Left air conduction
       O   =   Right air conduction
       ↓   =   No Response

His written language was noun based and agrammatic with no idea of word ordering. He was dubbed a behavior problem at school. Although this child is a teenager, he is described here because the practices used in the last 2 years had to be introduced from the *earliest* of developmental levels; namely, vocalization, turn taking, and the use of the common referent for both members of the dyad (and all members of the family). First, everyone needed to start vocalizing, and it was very difficult for them to do so with normal prosody and normal language. It was impossible to allot one of the Ling stages to this boy at his time of referral; his performance was deviant because his concepts were patchy. There had apparently been no natural ordering, according to developmental criteria, in the acquisition of the skills he had. This child is now in a normal secondary technical school where he is advancing at an astonishing rate. His mother acts as an interpreter in academic subjects but not technical subjects. *He* has chosen to go to the school because his previous school did not have a secondary program. He is now at Ling Stage 5–6 in phonological development, and at the same stage with his phonetic development. However, the prosodic elements are still deviant in terms of all Crystal's (1981) parameters. They are improving slowly. K.L.'s use of residual audition is still minimal. In spite of this his language is no longer deviant. He has a complete grasp of the basic rules, although not the speed to apply them consistently in everyday speech. His speech is moderately intelligible despite the almost complete lack of prosodic skills. When he is abstracting he is difficult to follow, but he is becoming skilled at helping his listeners through clarification. He still uses signing as his first language. Spoken language appears to be at a level of a fairly fluent second-language speaker with a broad accent. His speech reading, which was nonexistent, is excellent, for he now has the language. This boy has a sophisticated and entirely appropriate sense of humor, he now socializes among the deaf *and* the hearing, and has friends among both societies. This case must be extremely rare, for the speed at which the change was implemented suggests there may have been latent skills which were unrealized and untapped. The boy has three brothers and all have attended at times. Mother, particularly, is highly motivated and was very very quick to learn. She is one of the mothers who deeply resents that she had to wait so long before she received the help which has undoubtedly been the basis for her son's achievement. She is not a highly educated woman, yet she has been one of the program's highest achievers, as has her son. This mother also wonders why she was not helped to appreciate how valuable the use of his residual hearing could have been. His prosodic inadequacy will always bear testament to this. All prosodic skills are within his hearing range, but he is now unable to process them. It is too late.

PROBLEMS

This bright little girl, E.H., with a highly motivated but critically anxious mother, first attended when she was 2 years old. She was fitted with an FM aid, and soon after began vocalizing and babbling with a normal voice. The program began. Interactive schedules were

FIGURE 3-6. Audiogram of E.H. (Now 6 years of age and no longer attending.)

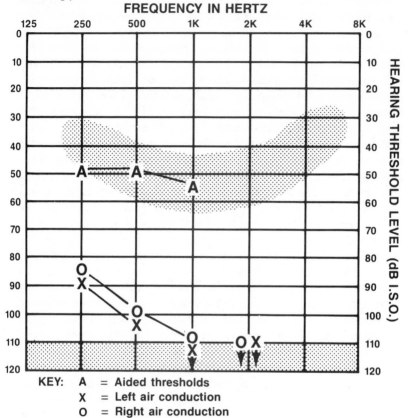

FREQUENCY IN HERTZ

KEY: A = Aided thresholds
        X = Left air conduction
        O = Right air conduction
        ↓ = No Response

modified to become more mutually reinforcing, and progress was excellent. A new baby arrived. The parents discussed other methods of communication and even residential school placement at the times when the child's behavior became difficult. However, progress seemed to be sufficient reward, and the child was beginning to match utterances to situations (Ling Stage 2–3), when the family had to move to an isolated area away from help. A year later they returned, without having attended in the interim, although it had been suggested. There had been long periods when the aid had broken down. Behavior was again a real problem, the mother was deeply depressed, and the child once again mute. (Ling Prestage 1). Scored interactions seemed maladaptive. Another baby was on the way. The mother and father started regular attendance once more and were very quick to reimplement their skills. The child gradually achieved original levels of performance and was matching utterances to situational cues, and using a good voice. Speech teaching was formally introduced and all vowels mastered along with distinctive features such as voiced/voiceless, continuous/stops, nasal/nonnasal. Several specific phonemes were mastered, some of which generalized to her speech. She was also beginning to lip read, which showed the existence of definite basic language skills. The child attended the integrated kindergarten system, but there it was felt that she was too far behind, and too deaf to achieve in that environment. Added to that, recommendations needed to be made for school placement and neither program could suggest that the child had sufficiently intelligible language for normal classroom placement at 5 years of age. Another year or two, however, might have made all the difference. With the parents' agreement and the recommendation of the Ascertainment Committee tthe child was transferred to a Total Communication setting and the mother began signing. At first they continued to attend our auditory–oral program. Analysis of the mother's speech, however, began to show marked changes in rate and prosody and some definite telegraphic utterances with poor syntax. The child picked up signing speedily, but her vocalizations diminished dramatically, and her mouthing increased. Turn-taking strategies changed and gesturing became very exaggerated. She began to match her own behaviors to those of her classroom peers. The family ceased to attend. Language and speech learning was no longer home centered, but classroom based. Given the child's high IQ (118), she would probably have achieved intelligible speech and language if she had continued, as all the basic skills had been acquired. She would also have been able to make up any educational delay caused by a necessarily late school placement. Likewise, it is also believed that she could at least have managed in an oral option. This child was never seen to be frustrated by her lack of communication, either in this program or on occasions when the child was observed in kindergarten. On scored observation there were very few occasions when she did not understand those talking to her. It is true she could not abstract at the age of 4 years, but the prerequisites for later abstraction were being achieved. During the final attendances the clinician saw many skills so painstakingly achieved being gradually extinguished. Normal or near normal speech and language were, by then, at risk.

The child had earlier used her residual hearing as was evidenced by her normal voice and use of prosody, but this was no longer evident and vision had taken over as the primary sensory modality for language.

In this case, long-term goals of inestimable advantage, such as normal language, achievement of academic potential, and adequate speech may have been sacrificed to meet the child's short-term needs, as perceived by professionals not involved in her teaching. These needs were age-appropriate school placement, quicker acquisition of a communicative strategy, albeit for a limited number of people, and classroom-based language and speech learning. Perhaps the most understandable of these short-term needs was the last. There were two demanding younger siblings in this family, there were financial worries, some marital stresses, and a shift-work routine all to be contended with. Both parents were extremely skilled and had managed to incorporate the necessary strategies into the everyday routine, but they felt the burden and underestimated their own contribution. They were led to believe that professionals would do better than parents, that more was needed than they were able to provide, and that one less child in the home would make the daily routine easier. There is some doubt as to whether a classroom routine, however skilled, will ever result in what can be achieved at home in a natural and normal environment.

DISCUSSION

This last case highlights many issues, the most important of which is the type of guidance needed when critical decisions have to be made. Although, fortunately, this particular situation has only occurred with four of the children throughout the years of the program, the need for immediate language and the decision about which school placement should be made are always the precipitating factors. This clinician believes above all that the auditory–oral children seen in the program have had the potential for intelligible speech and language, but not necessarily in the time allowed them, which is the preschool years. In the past, children seen in similar programs have begun to speak as late as 7 years but achieved in the end and subsequently compensated for the educational gap. There is, however, no guarantee which can possibly be given the parents when they are dealing with the "now" crisis of a nonverbal child. How to guide them is the dilemma.

It is hard for people, both parents and child, to maintain their normal speech, language, and interactive skills while they are learning signing and are inevitably slow. It is also difficult to use the referential cue naturally. Signs and speech appear to conflict when no previous experience of signs has been acquired and it is parents who have to learn sign who tend to leave the auditory–oral program when sign is introduced. It may not be so difficult to use one's normal speech, language, and interactive skills if one is already skilled in signing. In this case the care giver has only to learn to apply skills he already has. He does not have to learn a whole new system. The goals do not then seem polarized, because the "new" does not appear to be extinguishing already learned skills. It may often be that for those in need of remediation the new spoken skills extinguish the need for signing, but that is not an issue because language and speech is what this population come for, and the signing can still be used when required. It is these same factors which have led this clinician to believe that it is risky to have a parent learning to sign during the child's language developing years. It inevitably changes the normal, natural mother-language skills and patterns, particularly the prosodic and pragmatic level of performance which the child *can* hear.

When comparing the apparent "successes" and "failures" of our auditory–oral program, it can be established that hearing, or lack of it, is not the critical factor that many suggest. Nor are the skills achieved by the parents. There are many variables. Children achieve at different levels even when the skills of the parents are excellent. Only two parents associated with the program have ever failed to achieve high standards of work with their children. In each case, their children suffered a severe hearing loss but achieved the speech and language criteria of the program. However, they did have behavior problems.

If we compare successful and unsuccessful children we find no real pattern. Each of the two highly successful children had risk factors in their history. In this they were typical of others in the program. One had persistent periods of middle ear infection and the other the profound upset of his parents' broken marriage, yet each was a high achiever. Not one of the profoundly hearing-impaired children on the program has been without other such complications. The problem child had a year's break in management. This may have been a factor, yet other of our successful children have also had a similar break. One of the least successful children has had persistent middle ear problems, yet so have some of the successes. Both the youngest successful children attended the same excellent kindergarten with support facilities for hearing impairment, but so did the younger "failure." *All* of the least successful children had high IQs. All but two of the children have had highly motivated parents who achieved the goals set, some with difficulty, some with apparent ease. Indeed, the only common factor underlying success appears to be motivation, yet this does not bring success to all. One wonders if the least successful children have compounding neuropsychological disorders, but these do not appear to be obvious. It could be suggested that the changing parade of students affects some families more than others. This is not yet measurable but neither is it apparent when comparing "successes" with "failures."

Perhaps it is the "beliefs" of the parents and *all* those in the child's environment which are a critical factor. The rate of achievement of the children in relation to parents' concepts must also be critical. By far the strongest opinion held by society at large is that "very deaf people cannot and will never talk" and this opinion is battled constantly. The first sign of "difficulty" sometimes brings doubt, and if other professionals then voice their doubts the parents waver. There are, however, a few who never appear to waver at all despite the most incredible odds. Some professionals (not this one) even dub these parents stubborn, difficult "shopping arounders," neurotic, or unrealistic, yet it seems that they are the achievers. Their actual performance may not be any "better" than their slightly less convinced counterparts. All may be equally informed, and should have received equal amounts of information counseling, yet they "apply" this information or utilize it differently to reach their decisions. All may have comparable levels of achievement overall when working at their specific skills. Some may find reinforcement schedules difficult and others prosodic function, while still others have difficulty grappling with syntax and the referential cue. It could be that success or failure is in fact related to these detailed differences, but it will be years before it can be established which factors are relevant.

PLACEMENT OF CHILDREN

Management, in our program, continues regardless of the child's school placement, provided, that is, that the parents wish it and that goals are being realized. Some children have therefore been seen when they have been placed in (1) a play group, (2) a normal kindergarten, (3) an oral primary school for the hearing impaired, (4) a normal secondary school, or (5) total communication settings.

Others may have been in the ordinary school system throughout. Many attend private schools at considerable cost to the parents. This usually allows for smaller classes and a better acoustic environment.

Although management in this program is not dependent upon school placement, it is interesting to know what has happened to the children in relation to education. This must, in part, depend upon their speech and language skills. As previously mentioned, some 43 children are currently registered in the program (see Appendix 3-B). Of these, 21 are developing as auditory–oral children. Half of these would be classified as profoundly deaf and half very severely deaf. Twenty-two children remaining require remedial help and would also divide almost equally into the two hearing categories of severe and profound.

All the severely deaf auditory–oral children are in integrated school environments with speech and language within normal limits (Ling Stage 6–7). Of the *current* profoundly hearing-impaired children eight are in integrated environments with near normally progressing language skills, near normal prosodic and communicative skills, but with a range of speech deficits still to be attended to. The age range of these children is 2 to 16 years. The younger two are not yet in kindergarten. One child is in a total communication class. Of the children in remediation all but four are still in their original schools, although they may have progressed from kindergarten to primary, or from primary to secondary levels. However, although their educational placement may not have altered, this should not reflect upon their achievements, because most of these children are moderate newcomers to this program. Of the four who have already changed from their original school placement one has moved from total communiction to an oral school, two have moved from a total communication school to an "integrated" technical school, and one has gone from a total communication primary school to a private school. All four are achieving well, but the last is an exceptional performer educationally. None of the latter four has good speech.

Of the 35 children who are no longer on the program, 8 are "drop-outs." They came, they tried for a *short* period and then opted out. The reasons were not always given, but some who left had difficulty with time, distance, or family pressures. Two have already been mentioned earlier as having transferred to total communication and then leaving the program. Two more transferred to total communication school placement after a very short period of attendance, almost before management had started. These parents did not appear to have any doubts about signing or segregation, but accepted it as part of deafness. Of the remaining 25 all but 3 are severely deaf and at last contact were progressing normally through school, although some have been referred for extra help in local speech therapy clinics. The three profoundly deaf who have already left the program are now young adults, each at technical level of education and managing well in an integrated environment. Their speech is intelligible but not perfect.

One of the more important factors in the communication of all children is that they appear to perform as they are expected to perform. The children coming for remediation nearly all give evidence of this in their very first visit. If you ask them a question orally they may answer vocally and without a sign. The question may only require a one-word response, and there may be a strong contextual cue. Frequently, however, the parents' reaction to these spoken utterances make it obvious that they did not ever know that their child *could* vocalize, let alone understand or reply. If you do not expect a child to understand you and talk to you, and do not provide him with the means to do so, he will not do so.

SUMMARY

From the preceding discussion it can be seen that it is almost impossible to list the prerequisites for success or failure. Nevertheless, there are certain elements in our management to which we strictly adhere. These can be listed as follows, but are not in rank order.

For Success

1. Include the mother or care giver actively in both diagnosis and management;
2. Try FM hearing aids for the reasons outlined in the text;
3. Pay strict attention to reinforcement schedules, avoiding selectivity at the expense of motivation;
4. Follow normal and natural development stages;
5. Make sure the prerequisites are there for a proposed target behavior;
6. Diagnose along with remediation;
7. Evaluate constantly (every session);
8. Monitor aids and hearing constantly;
9. Listen to responses as part of a communicative "whole";
10. Have realistic goals based on related current theory and research findings;
11. Concentrate on and know exactly what a child can hear in relation to language prosody and speech and *know* aided audiogram.

Avoid
1. Compensatory and abnormal use of other sense modalities at the expense of audition;
2. Abnormal prosody, rate, and syntax in communication partners;
3. Didactic formal teaching;
4. Formal language programs;
5. Testing for performance away from situational context;
6. Too much early abstraction;
7. Any assumptions whatsoever about a child's prognosis.

Finally, if a family wishes for aural–oral skills for their child, and eventual integration, then it is doubted whether this can be achieved through classroom versus the normal and natural mother–child interchange. However, it is acknowledged that there are some children who for reasons unknown appear to be unable to achieve this despite maximum assistance. Then it is to be hoped that there will always be an adequate system for them to turn to which will maintain the normal skills they have already acquired, rather than extinguish them as is so often the case. If such children come from families who had hoped for integration, wise counseling is needed to help them through their change of goals. Some families automatically accept signing as the lot of the deaf, and society has much to answer for in its perpetuation of such a myth. However, perhaps the road these families follow is easier for them as they travel, the destination for that child is for him to handle when he gets there. After all, those who have little or no spoken language and limited reading and writing skills may never really appreciate what they have missed.

REFERENCES

Bloom, L., & Lahey, M. (1978). *Language development and language disorders*. New York: Wiley.

Bock, J. K., & Mazzella, J. R. (1983). Intonational marking of given and new information: Some consequences for comprehension. *Memory & Cognition, 11*(1), 64–76.

Boone, D. R., & Prescott, T. E. (1972). Content and sequence analysis of speech and hearing therapy. *ASHA; 14,* 58–62.

Brown, R. (1977). Introduction. In C. E. Snow & C. A. Ferguson (Eds.), *Talking to children*. Cambridge, England: Cambridge Univ. Press.

Bruner, J. (1976). Learning how to do things with words. In J. Bruner & A. Garton (Eds.), *Human growth and development*. Oxford, England: Oxford Univ. Press.

Cheskin, A. (1982). The use of language by hearing mothers of deaf children. *Journal of Communication Disorders, 15*(8), 145–153.

Clezy, G. M. (1979). *Modification of the mother child interchange*. Baltimore: University Park Press.

Clezy, G. M. (1984). Interactive analysis. In D. Muller (Ed.), *Remediating Childrens' language; behavioral and naturalistic approaches*. London: Croom Helm.

Clezy, G. M., Brown, I., & Moore, D. (1983). A longitudinal linguistic study of children with a conductuve hearing loss. *Proceedings 29 Congress IALP*, Edinburgh.

Cornett, R. O. (1967). Cued speech. *American Annals of the Deaf, 112*, 3–13.

Cross, T. G., Johnson-Morris, J. E., & Neinhuys, T. G. (1980). Linguistic feedback and maternal speech. Comparisons of mothers' addressing hearing and hearing impaired children. First Language, *1*, 163–187.

Crystal, D. (1981). *Clinical linguistics*. New York: Springer-Verlag.

Crystal, D., Fletcher, P., & Garman, M. (1976). *The grammatical analysis of language disability*. London: Arnold.

Dale, P. S. (1976). *Language development structure and function* (2nd ed.). New York: Holt, Rinehart & Winston.

Dore, J. (1974). A pragmatic description of early language development. *Journal of Psycholinguistic Research, 3*, 343–350.

Duncan, S., Jr. (1972). Some signals and rules for taking speaking turns in conversations. *Journal of Personality and Social Psychology, 23*(2), 283–292.

Garnica, O. K. (1977). Some prosodic and paralinguistic features of speech in young children. In C. Snow & C. Ferguson (Eds.), *Talking to children*. Cambridge University Press.

Ginsberg, H., & Opper, S. (1979). *Piaget's theory of intellectual development* (2nd ed.). Englewood Cliffs, NJ: Prentice–Hall.

Gregory, S., Mogford, K., & Bishop, J. (1979). Mothers speech in young hearing impaired children. *Journal of British Association of Teachers of the deaf, 3*, 2.

Halliday, M. (1975). *Learning how to mean*. London: Arnold.

Healey, J. H. (1982). The speech pathologist's role in the management of the hearing impaired. *Australian Journal of Human Communication Disorders, 10*, 59–62.

Kahan, V. L. (1971). *Mental illness in childhood*. London: Tavistock.

Ling, D. (1976). *Speech and the hearing-impaired child*. Washington, DC: Alexander Graham Bell Association for the Deaf.

Lund, N. J., & Duchan, J. F. (1983). *Assessing children's language in naturalistic contexts*. Englewood Cliffs, NJ: Prentice–Hall.

Muma, J. R. (1981). *Language primer for the clinical fields*. Lubbock, TX: Key Printing Aids.

Nelson, K. (1978). Early speech in its communicative context. In F. D. Minifie & L. L. Lloyd (Eds.), *Communicative and cognitive abilities*. Baltimore: University Park Press.

Phillips, J. (1973). Formal characteristics of speech which mothers address to their younger children: Age and sex comparisons. *Child Development, 44*, 182–185.

Ramey, C. T., Farran, D. C., & Finklestein, N. W. (1978). Observations of mother–infant interactions; Implications for development. In F. D. Minifie & L. L. Lloyd (Eds.), *Communicative and cognitive abilities*. Baltimore: University Park Press.

Snow, C., & Ferguson, C. (1977). *Talking to children*. Cambridge, England: Cambridge Univ. Press.

Stern, D. (1974). Mother and infant at play. The dyadic interaction involving facial, vocal and gaze behaviours. In M. Lewis & L. A. Rosenblum (Eds.), *The effect of the infant on its caregiver*. New York: Wiley.

Taplin, P. S., & Reid, J. B. (1973). Effects on the institutional set and experimenter influence on observer reliability. *Child Development, 44*, 547–554.

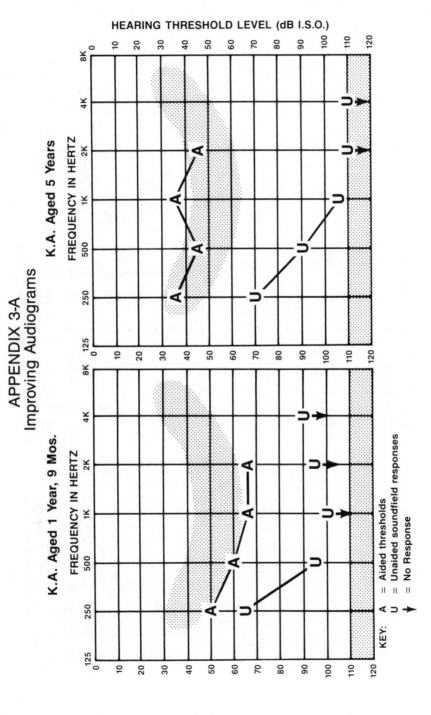

APPENDIX 3-A
Improving Audiograms

K.A. Aged 5 Years

K.A. Aged 1 Year, 9 Mos.

HEARING THRESHOLD LEVEL (dB I.S.O.)

FREQUENCY IN HERTZ

KEY: A = Aided thresholds
      U = Unaided soundfield responses
      → = No Response

APPENDIX 3-A (Continued)
Improving Audiograms

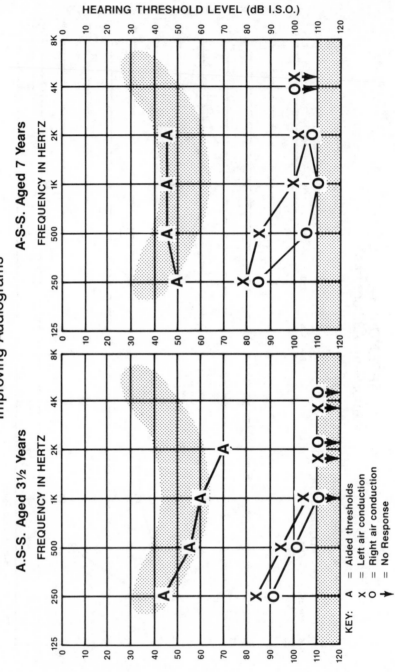

HEARING THRESHOLD LEVEL (dB I.S.O.)

A.S.S. Aged 7 Years

A.S.S. Aged 3½ Years

KEY: A = Aided thresholds
X = Left air conduction
O = Right air conduction
→ = No Response

APPENDIX 3-B
Flow Chart Showing Progress of Children Currently
Attending Programme

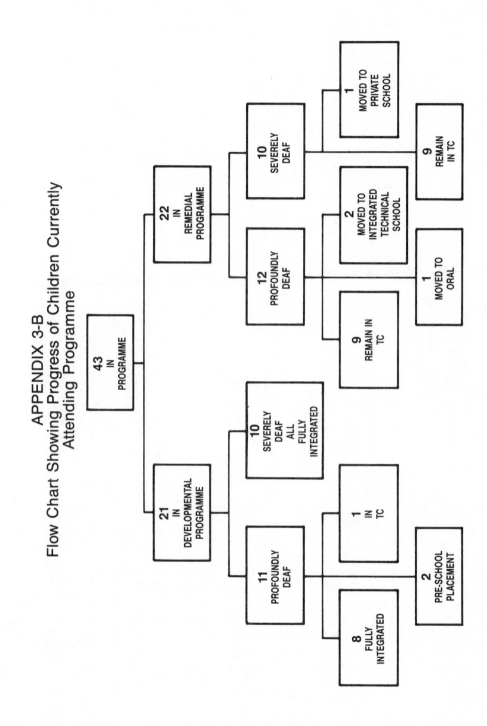

4
THE MCGILL UNIVERSITY PROJECT

Elizabeth B. Cole
Marietta M. Paterson

INTRODUCTION

The McGill Project for Hearing-Impaired Children was officially established in 1966, with financial support from a Canadian federal–provincial health grant, the Junior League of Montreal, and from private sources. Since that time, the Project has undergone several changes in locale, funding sources, staff, and numbers of children served. Basic philosophical tenets, however, have remained steadfastly the same, including a commitment to early detection and optimal amplification; a focus on the parent as the change agent; and an auditory–oral approach to facilitating spoken language development. The Project has the following major functions:

1. Community service providing:

   a. Audiological evaluation specializing in the assessment of young children (ages 0 to 5 years) and hearing aid users of any age.
   b. Parent guidance and habilitation of hearing-impaired infants, Ages 0 to 3 years. (The focus in this chapter is primarily on this aspect of the McGill project.)

2. Graduate training for MSc (applied) students in the McGill University programs in audiology, speech–language pathology, and in auditory–oral habilitation and education of hearing-impaired children.

3. Research investigating issues related to early detection and management of hearing-impaired children (e.g., newborn screening, phonologic development, frequency transposition, auditory and visual speech discrimination, vibrotactile cues in speech discrimination, earmold coupling systems, care giver–infant interactive behaviors).

Children in the Project

Most of the children in the project reside within the metropolitan area of Montreal, although it is not unusual for parents to drive as much as 2 hours each way for the weekly sessions, when services are lacking in their home districts. All services are offered in both French and English, with the present distribution about 50% English and 50% French. Since its inception, The McGill project has provided ongoing training to more than 90 children and their parents.

The age at detection of children enrolled in the project has ranged from a few months to over 3 years (mean 19.7 months). Usually a month or two elapses between detection, the completion of diagnosis, and the fitting of a hearing aid. The mean age when children first used amplification was 26.3 months and, since some children were referred after hearing aid selection, the mean age at the beginning of treatment was 28.2 months. The average age at detection of hearing loss is viewed as unsatisfactory by the McGill project staff, on the obvious rationale that the earlier the detection and amplification, the earlier the child can begin learning to listen. Consequently, early detection remains an ongoing, active concern of the staff members, who are constantly engaged in public education efforts and infant screening programs. Many more children have been seen only for diagnosis and assessment. The number of children enrolled in the project has fluctuated over the years from as few as 3 children to as many as 30.

The distribution of hearing levels averaged over the three frequencies (500, 1,000, and 2,000 Hz) for 19 of the 24 children enrolled in the project during the last 3 years (1980–1983) appears in Table 4-1. Data on the remaining five cases is still incomplete.

It can be seen that the majority (79%) have hearing levels conventionally described as severe-to-profound. The etiology of the hearing impairment was undetermined for 21 of the 24 children enrolled during the last 3 years. Two had hearing impairment believed to be of genetic origin, and in one case, the hearing loss was due to meningitis. Only 5 of the 24 children seen over the past 3 years have been viewed as free from problems other than hearing impairment. The remainder had one or more additional problems: Nine were severely delayed in general development; seven had chronic ear infections; a further seven had behavior disorders; two were from homes where neither English nor French was spoken; two had visual anomalies; but in five cases, parents were unable to follow the program.

TABLE 4-1. Distribution of hearing levels of 19 children in the McGill Project (1980–1983)

Hearing Levels	Conventional Label	Number of Children
20–55 dB	Mild	2
55–70 dB	Moderate	2
70–90 dB	Severe	3
90–110 dB	Profound	11
110 dB	Profound	1

Location of the Project

At the present time, individual sessions are normally held once a week for 1 to 1½ hours, in one of the McGill project clinic rooms within an off-campus house, part of McGill University's School of Human Communication Disorders. Each of the two therapy rooms is a child's playroom with a small round table and chairs and several closets full of toys for various activities. The rooms are equipped with one-way mirrors and external speaker systems. However, these observation arrangements are little used by the parents, since they, themselves, always participate in the sessions. Since audiological management is one of the major aspects of intervention with very young hearing-impaired children, the project is fortunate in having audiologic facilities across the hall from the therapy rooms. This means that services such as serial audiological testing, impedance testing, hearing aid evaluation, electroacoustic testing, and consultations are always easily accessible.

Each family is visited at home at least five times during the year. More frequent home visits occur at the initiation of therapy when the parents are just beginning to accept the fact of the child's hearing loss and its implications, and when the therapist wants to become quickly acquainted with the family. Home visits also become more frequent when the parents need additional support in utilizing everyday events for communication activities, or when there are special problems needing attention, such as behavior management.

There is no charge to the parents for the services they receive through the McGill project. Present financial support is accomplished through a combination of donations from charitable organizations and private individuals, with the staff funded primarily through McGill

University. Funds are additionally raised through a 5-day international summer colloquium given by staff members and other distinguished speakers on various themes of importance to habilitative intervention with hearing-impaired children.

Project Staff

Staff members who are routinely involved in the present habilitative program include the director, the assistant director, the supervising clinician, and the audiologist. Because the McGill project is closely associated with the university's teacher–clinician training program, staff members are expected not only to possess, but also to teach a variety of competencies to others. These include ability to

1. Demonstrate general teaching/clinical skills; to ascertain the child's level of cognitive, social, linguistic, psychomotor, and academic development; to plan and implement appropriate educational intervention for both the child and the parent; to stimulate vocal/verbal communication by the child, and to help the parents do the same; to be aware of child or parent understanding or lack of it, and to modify events or techniques according to the child's or parent's responses and needs; to manage the child's behavior, and to guide the parent.

2. Use strategies and information to maximize the child's use of residual hearing; to select hearing aids, and ensure their maintenance; to utilize the acoustic cues available to each child; and to focus on the child's use of audition in both scheduled and incidental speech and language-learning situations.

3. Employ knowledge and techniques for assessing the child's language-learning needs, select targets, and plan appropriate intervention events; to ensure that the child comprehends; to provide for varied practice of language targets in limited-to-wider contexts; to "seize the moment" for facilitating the child's language growth; and to make automatic and appropriate use of techniques such as modeling, expansion, and prompting.

4. Show sensitivity to and strategies for helping the parents facilitate the child's spoken language development.

5. Evaluate the child's speech-learning needs; to select speech targets and elicit new sounds; to provide for varied practice of the sounds in limited-to-wider contexts (syllable practice as well as meaningful usage in words and discourse).

6. Judge when to listen and when to talk with parents, as well as when to refer to other professionals.

7. Provide warmth, enthusiasm, and vitality in interactions with the child and the parents.

8. Self-evaluate, and continually improve one's own level of information and one's own competencies.

9. Have ability and interest in teaching university graduate students in auditory-oral (re)habilitation and education of hearing-impaired children. This includes lecturing in courses, as well as supervising practical training.

10. Assume other abilities and responsibilities including organization of parent group meetings; presenting information to clinic staff meetings and community organizations; participating in publicity efforts (radio, television, newspapers); and maintaining liaison with outside agencies and schools.

One additional requirement exists since the project is located in Quebec: staff members must be fluent in both English and French.

Parents

The parents are expected to become the primary facilitators of spoken language for their child. This involves a variety of areas which are easily enumerated, but which each represent long-term processes of growth and development. These areas include the parents' striving to cope in an emotionally healthy manner with fact of the child's hearing loss and its ramifications; interacting with the child in ways which will promote the child's acquisition of spoken language, as well as ensure his social, emotional, cognitive, and psychomotor development; becoming skilled at hearing aid maintenance; transferring the use of strategies modeled and practiced in the sessions to everyday routines at home (particularly for specific auditory, language, and speech targets which have been determined by the teacher/clinician).

Children

The fundamental goal for any child in the McGill project is that he/she develop to the fullest the potential for communicating through spoken language. The aim is for the child to be ready to be integrated into the regular educational stream at as young an age as possible. However, these goals must automatically be adjusted in accordance with a number of factors such as age of detection and subsequent full-time wearing of the hearing aid, degree of hearing loss, parents' willingness and ability to be involved in the child's habilitation, and the presence of additional handicaps or learning problems.

Initial Enrollment Procedures

Children typically come to the McGill project through referral from physicians, other audiological clinics, or through direct request by the parents. In order to make known the need for early detection and educational intervention, as well as the availability of audiological and habilitation services, project staff members periodically speak on television and radio, produce articles for local newspapers, and make personal contacts with community physicians and nursery school programs. All hearing-impaired children between the ages of 0 and 5 years are eligible for enrollment in the program, although all initial referrals in the last 3 years have been in the 0 to 3-year-old age range. Neither additional problems nor degree of hearing impairment are determining factors in enrollment.

At the present time, financial constraints require limiting the number of children in the program to approximate the number and language abilities (French or English) of the 2nd-year McGill University graduate students who receive supervised training with the children and their parents. Consequently, this enters into the initial decisions regarding possible enrollment or immediate referral to other programs. Once a child is enrolled, he/she remains a part of the project up to or even beyond 5 years of age, regardless of the university training program needs. Parents are made aware from the beginning that the intervention sessions are always considered to be diagnostic teaching sessions. This means that if it becomes apparent over time that the child's needs are not being met by the project program, he/she will be referred to another more appropriate program.

Evaluation Procedures
Staff

Evaluation of ongoing work by staff members occurs through a continual process of self-evaluation. As a prerequisite to employment, staff members are expected to possess a high level of competency in a broad variety of areas. Obviously, however, a given individual will have strengths and weaknesses in some of these areas which may be identified through reflection, use of the evaluation form (see Appendix 4-A), or experience in the habilitation sessions. On request, another staff member may aid in the self-evaluation process through providing requested feedback on specific issues. Instruction in techniques for self-evaluation has become an integral part of the teacher-training program, and although the complete process is not implemented in every situation, staff members and students alike have found it useful to have a set of guidelines for this kind of problem solving. The basic steps in the self-evaluation process are listed below.

1. Reflection in order to determine present strengths, or weaknesses in specific areas including both professional and interpersonal skills.

2. Planning a reasonable course of action in order to accomplish necessary change.

3. Examining specific relevant events and considering:

    a. What were the actual events which occurred (observable behaviors)?
    b. What inferences am I drawing about those events? (That is, what am I thinking about what happened?)
    c. What were the choices or alternatives for me in that situation?
    d. How (why) did I choose the alternative I did?
    e. How did I intend to proceed?
    f. Was there a discrepancy between my intentions and what actually happened?
    g. What impact did my response have on the child or parent?
    h. How effective was my response?
    i. How would I do it differently if I were to do it over again?

This process promotes both the exploring and the understanding of various interactions; for example, between teacher/clinician and the child or parent and teacher/clinician, as well as the generation of specific interpersonal and pedagogic techniques for change and development. The information is largely based on models for supervision (Anderson, 1981; Caracciolo, Rigrodsky, & Morrison, 1978; McCrea, 1979) whose goal is to produce professionals who self-supervise in a conscious effort toward continual improvement, and as a hedge against the infamous "burn-out" phenomenon.

Parent and Child

An extensive assessment of the child and parent(s) occurs at the beginning of the school year (September), or at the time that the child enters the program if that is after September. The primary purpose is to assess all areas which affect the child's development, with a particular focus on audition and communication, in order to select target areas and plan habilitation. A secondary purpose is to provide a base for evaluating progress. Information is collected over several weeks in settings which include home visits, therapy sessions, and audiological testing. Table 4-2 outlines the general areas assessed using the mentioned assessment tools. As can be seen in the table, data is gathered from formal standardized testing, developmental scales, videotape analysis, systematic observation, parent interviews, and parent records. Parts of this extensive assessment may be carried out by 2nd-year graduate students, each of whom is assigned to one child and family. As this is a training experience for them, all of the student work is closely guided and supervised.

After the relevant areas have been examined, a formal report is written following the format outlined in the Report Writing Guidelines (Appendix 4-B). Results of the assessment allow the teacher/clinician to set targets in areas of demonstrated need. While the most extensive assessment generally occurs at the beginning of therapy sessions in the fall, records are updated as intervention on particular aspects takes

TABLE 4-2. Comprehensive Assessment Battery

Areas Assessed	Measurement Tools
I. Child's medical, audiological, and educational histories.	Parent interview, reports from physicians, audiologists, previous educational programs.
II. Special concerns of the parents.	Parent interview.
III. Audition	
A. Audiological responses	Standard audiological testing for children and infants (as appropriate: conventional finger-raising, play conditioning, visual reinforcement audiometry, and/or behavior observation procedures). Results sought include (as possible) pure tone responses under earphones or soundfield warble tone responses; speech detection, reception, discrimination; 5-Sound detection and discrimination levels; soundfield unaided and aided responses, the latter preferable single ears and both ears; impedance test battery (tympanometry, static compliance, acoustic reflexes); hearing aids' electro-acoustic performance with and without the earmold coupling systems.
B. Auditory Behavior	Schedules of Development (Ling, 1977) for audition, hearing aids, vocalization; supplemented by parental questioning and teacher/clinician observation of the child's abilities to detect, discriminate, and identify environmental sounds and spoken language. Particular interest is in child's abilities to use audition for comprehending and producing spoken language (both with and without visual cues). As appropriate, Carrow's Test for Auditory Comprehension of Language (1973) is used.
IV. Developmental information. Areas assesed include gross motor, fine motor, self help, social-emotional, cognitive behaviors and abilities.	Developmental scales such as the Early Learning Accomplishment Profile: Birth to 36 Months, (Glover, Preminger, and Sanford, 1978); Learning Accomplishment Profile, Sanford and Zelman, 1981); Reynell Developmental Language Scales, 1969.

V. Communication

A. Interactional aspects. Includes the caregiver's communication facilitating behaviors and techniques; both interactant's observation of conversational devices for attention-getting, turn-taking, initiating, maintaining, and changing topic; ending conversations.

Parent Behavior Progression (Bromwich, 1981) and "Caregiver–Child Interactive Behaviors: A videotape Analysis Procedure" (Cole and St. Claire-Stokes, in press) which includes parent self-evaluation.

B. Function: use of language by both interactants to accomplish specific purposes.

"Caregiver-Child Interactive Behaviors: A Videotape Analysis Procedure" (Cole & St. Clair-Stokes, in press); also, particularly for children using 2-word phrases or more, communication act categories from Dore, Gearhart, and Newman, 1978.

C. Semantic/syntax: expression of meaning through structural relationships; ordering words in sentences; grammatical modulation.

Parent records and analysis of spontaneous language samples based on information in Kretschmer and Kretschmer, 1978; Streng, 1972.

D. Lexicon: word meanings.

Parent word tallies; in-house 500- and 2000-word vocabulary checklists (*Thesaurus*, Ling & Ling, 1977; *Peabody Picture Vocabulary Test* (Dunn, 1965); *Boehm Test of Basic Concepts* (Boehm, 1969).

E. Speech

1. Phonology: emergent use of speech sounds in unelicited jargon and/or spoken language.

Phonologic evaluation of spontaneous language samples based on Ling (1976) and Cole and Paterson (1984).

2. Motor speech production: sounds elicited and practiced on demand.

Phonetic Level Evaluation (Ling, 1976).

3. Vocalization development: sounds produced by child in spontaneous babbling.

Developmental sequence described by Oller (1977); also *Schedules of Development* (Ling, 1977) for speech ("Pre-speech and Babbling").

place and/or normally developing changes occur. At the end of therapy sessions in the summer, a summary report is prepared which details progress made in all areas, as well as recommendations for further intervention.

Referrals

Referrals for audiologic testing are an integral and ongoing part of the child's involvement for the duration of his/her enrollment in the McGill project, and all of the audiological testing is done on site. The close proximity of the audiological and intervention clinics has a number of advantages. First, since both persons are always present for testing, the audiologist and the habilitationist exchange information regarding both measured audiometric responses and observed auditory behaviors. Second, if there is any doubt that the child has comprehended the task, testing temporarily ceases until the habilitationist and the parents have trained the child to respond consistently to vibratory and/or auditory stimulation. It has also been useful occasionally to do "serial" testing; that is, repeated short testing sessions over several weeks in order to capture the child's maximal performance. Initial selection and fitting of the hearing aids can usually be accomplished rapidly even with relatively minimal information (sound field warble tone testing and the impedance battery). However, continued testing is usually necessary in order to obtain complete data for each ear, both unaided (under earphones) and aided (in free field). Other reasons for frequent audiologic involvement include the need to recheck responses following changes in the child's earmolds, and to identify middle ear problems, which frequently occur in this age group. Impedance testing is routinely carried out at 6-week intervals, but more frequently if problems are suspected. Hearing aids are also checked electroacoustically once every 6 weeks, but more often if the earmolds are changed or problems are noted by parents or teacher/clinician when they check the aids by listening to them.

Immediate referral to a physician is made when abnormal impedance results are found. Other medical referrals are made on an individual basis following the extensive initial assessment. These referrals for the child have included physical/occupational therapy, psychometric evaluation, neurologic evaluation, psychiatric evaluation, and brainstem-evoked response audiometry.

Progress is formally and informally evaluated on an individual basis, comparing performance at separate points in time. Differential factors in this population (such as the child's degree of hearing impairment, age at which it was detected, age when hearing aids were first worn regularly, and presence of other physical or learning problems, the child's personality, drive, and behavior, and the extent of parental involvement) preclude the use of totally objective or rigid decision-making procedures. The fundamental issues are: Is this child progressing optimally in our program? Could he/she be making more progress in another program? For children from the age of 3 or 4 years onward, there are programs in this locale which include all possible combinations of French or English language, auditory–oral or total communication educational options; and all degrees of self-containment or integration within the regular classes. Decisions to refer to another program are always made in consultation with parents and colleagues on a case-by-case basis. A child of 3 years of age who is progressing well with no complications might continue the weekly guidance sessions with the McGill project and be additionally enrolled in a preschool for normally hearing children. Another 3-year-old who also appears to have a great deal of potential for learning to communicate through spoken language, but whose parents are unable to cope with the child's education and/or behavior might be placed in a self-contained auditory–oral preschool program. Children who demonstrate very little potential to learn spoken language would be referred to a program which provides sign language instruction. Information about the children's abilities and needs, possible alternatives, and the staff's recommendations are all thoroughly discussed with the parents who, after investigating options for themselves, make the final decisions on continuation or follow-up provision for their children.

As appropriate, parents may be referred for genetic counseling and for more extensive psychological counseling than the teacher/clinician can provide. Counseling has been a problem area for several parents for more than one reason. Part of the difficulty lies in the local scarcity of French- and English-speaking professionals who specialize in working with parents of severely handicapped children. Another limiting factor is the expense to the parents of ongoing professional counseling. At one point, the project required all of the parents to have at least one session with a counseling psychiatrist, and provided funding for it. Some parents were predictably reluctant to recognize the need for such counseling. Many parents learn to cope with the various impacts of the child's hearing loss with only the teacher/clinician's help. However, for those who seem to "get stuck" and even for some who appear to be coping normally, extensive psychological counseling can be vitally helpful (Moses, 1979).

Content of Habilitation

The overall plan for the habilitation process for a hearing-impaired child and parents in the McGill project has the following diagnostic teaching components:

A. Assessment
B. Goal Selection
C. Intervention
D. Evaluation of Progress.

After assessment of the variety of areas related to the child's development (particularly of audition and communication), goals for parent, child, and teacher/clinician, which are intended to facilitate growth and change are selected. Unless there is evidence to the contrary, it is assumed that each hearing-impaired child is neurologically intact. Although rate of progress may be somewhat delayed due to lessened auditory exposure, the child's learning is expected to proceed following normal developmental lines (Bloom & Lahey, 1978; Kretschmer & Kretschmer, 1978; Streng, Kretschmer, & Kretschmer, 1978; West & Weber, 1974). Intervention stragegies for parents and therapist center around the use of play and care giving activities as the obvious and usual vehicle for the child's learning of communicative/interactional competencies in infancy (Bruner, 1975; Bullowa, 1979; Freedle & Lewis, 1977; Ling & Ling, 1978; Schaffer, 1977; Snow & Ferguson, 1977; McLean & Snyder-McLean, 1978). Thus, the specific topics for intervention activities are most often governed by the child's focus of attention within ordinary, everyday events. In later stages of treatment, this naturalistic intervention is supplemented by short sessions of adult-directed activities which provide intensive practice on selected linguistic aspects. Evaluation of progress is continual in order to closely monitor the child's growth. As progress is noted, new targets are selected in order to appropriately challenge the child and continue growth. Or, if a child is not responding as expected, intervention is adapted to better fit the child's individual learning style or rate.

Based on the changing needs and abilities of the parents and child, five stages in the habilitation process can be identified, as outlined in Table 4-3. The time frames indicated are estimates based on our clinical records and experience, and they refer to an exemplary situation where the child's hearing loss was detected by approximately 12 months of age, and where severe-to-profound hearing loss is the child's sole handicap. Under other conditions, the time frames can be expected to differ. It should be noted that the delineation of stages

TABLE 4-3. Stages in the Habilitation Process

Stage	Approximate Hearing Age[a]	Major Characteristics
I. Pre-Hearing Aid	—	Initial diagnostic period.
II. Post-Hearing Aid	0–2 mos.	
III. Moving On	3–6 mos.	(Re-)Establishment of a spoken language communicative base through everyday play and caregiving activities.
IV. Gathering Impetus	6–16 mos.	Naturally enriched activities, gradual introduction of brief adult-directed activities; child progresses toward syntactic utterances (2 or more words).
V. Snowballing	16–36 mos.	Exponential expansion of conversational competencies including pragmatic, semantic, syntactic, phonologic abilities; more adult-directed activities as appropriate for insuring that specific speech and language targets are achieved.

[a]"Hearing Age" refers to the length of time the child has been wearing hearing aids. The time frames indicated in this table are for a situation where the child's hearing loss is identified by approximately 12 months of age, and where severe-to-profound hearing loss is the child's sole handicap.

is merely a theoretical construct for the convenience of discussing a complex, synergistic process. With the exception of Stage I, movement from one stage to the next is a gradual blending, with the beginnings and endings difficult to perceive in an absolute sense. Needs, goals, and intervention strategies are often carried throughout the entire process, although in increasingly complex form. It is hoped that, perhaps in spite of the stages, the detailed description of the exemplary case which follows will clarify the *dynamic,* and *synergistic, process* of habilitation as seen by the authors.

MANAGEMENT

An illustrative case is described in this section in order to provide a clear and detailed explanation of the McGill project habilitation process. This case is an exemplary one in which the child's hearing loss was detected by approximately 12 months of age, and where severe-to-profound hearing loss was the child's sole handicap. Throughout the case description, the reader may find it helpful to refer to Table 4-3 in order to fit a particular stage into the overall schema. Similarly, Table 4-2 may be useful for pinpointing the areas assessed and the measurement tools used for each part of the assessment. For each stage (I through V), the parents and the child are both discussed with regard to the assessment, goal selection, intervention, and evaluation of progress components of the habilitation model espoused by the McGill project.

Stage I: Pre-Hearing Aid
Assessment

Assessment procedures involved both parents and child. Using selected measurement tools and procedures from Table 4-2, three kinds of information were collected from the parents and from available records during the initial days of habilitation. The first of these is general background information as shown below. (Fictional names are given in this example.)

Child's name: Frank Zed	Degree of hearing loss: severe to profound
Birthdate: 4 August 1981	Age detected: 11½ months

Age: 11½ months (at beginning of evaluation)	Age first aided: [During Stage I, the aids are not yet being worn. However, for the purpose of this case presentation, the child will begin wearing the aids at 12 months of age].
Parents' names: Kathy, Mike	
Phone: 987-6541	Aids: ECMP select (2 aids)
Address: 1354 rue Belle, Montreal	
Pediatrician: Dr. Enfant	
Otolaryngologist: Dr. Oreille	
Hearing aid dealer: Mr. Audio	

The etiology of the child's loss is unknown according to the physician's report, although anoxia occurred at birth. There is no family history of congenital sensorineural hearing loss. No major illnesses to date; two ear infections medically treated prior to 9 months of age. According to the parents, developmental milestones have been achieved within normal age limits, with the exception of hearing, speech, and language abilities.

The second type of information noted is that relating to the early sessions. Frank's parents asked the following questions, which are not unusual for parents at this stage: "How do you know these are the right results?" "How is it possible to learn to talk with such a degree of deafness" (severe-to-profound)? "What can we do now?" (while waiting for earmolds). "Frank mostly makes a raspy kind of sound from deep in his throat right now. Will he ever learn to make sounds normally?" Will he have to learn sign language?" "Is he ever likely to go to regular school classes?"

On several occasions during her first visits, the mother expressed a great deal of anger at previous professionals who had assured her that the child's hearing was fine, that she was simply an overanxious mother, and that in any event reliable measurements could not be obtained until the child was at least 3 years of age. The mother also brought up the topic of the parents' dreams for the child which now seem hopelessly out of reach. Both parents mentioned present and future changes brought into their lives by Frank's hearing loss. In addition, one of the parents' very real concerns centered around the extended family's bilingualism (French and English). The question was, "Will he ever be able to learn both languages so he can communicate with both sets of grandparents?"

The third kind of information recorded is gathered from observation. This data reflected early impressions of the parents' communication strategies as they were interacting with the infant. These impressions were noted by the teacher/clinician in order to begin immediately to provide the parents with strategies for improving communication with the infant. Another reason for noting the initial impressions was to provide a base for indepth analysis and exploration of interactive behaviors in later stages. For this exemplary case, the teacher/clinician's notes included the following.

The parents' primary means of attempting to capture Frank's attention has been using voice to call him. Since Frank has been without hearing aids, these verbal attention-getting attempts have been unsuccessful. When voice is supplemented with touch or visual strategies, the parents are more successful in attracting Frank's attention. However, Frank usually maintains eye contact only long enough to obtain social reinforcement (i.e., smile, nod of head, a hug, a kiss). The parents say they are discouraged by Frank's lack of responsiveness, and that they feel as if their contacts with him are mainly for care giving, with little communicating. Very subjectively, Frank seems to have almost trained his parents *not* to try to communicate with him. At least partially due to the lack of conventional feedback from the child, the parents' language is not appropriate in either length or complexity of utterance. They alternate between the use of single-word labels which they attempt to have the child imitate and the use of utterances which are too lengthy and complex.

In this, the pre-hearing aid stage, direct measures of Frank's behaviors, responses, and development were also made as follows.

a. Audiological responses. Using visual reinforcement audiometry, Frank made the following unaided responses to warble tones in sound field:

250	500	1000	2000	4000	Hz
70	90	100	> 110	> 90	dB

His speech awareness level was 85 dB. Previous brainstem-evoked response testing elicited no identifiable response to 90-dB stimulation in either ear. Tympanometric results were within normal limits, with acoustic reflexes bilaterally absent, which is not unexpected in view of the degree of hearing loss.

b. **Auditory behavior.** During these first 3 weeks (of Stage I), Frank was not yet wearing amplification. No repeatable responses to voice or environmental sounds were noted during the sessions.

c. **Overall development.** Developmental information was obtained using the procedures mentioned in Table 4-2. These indicated that gross motor, fine motor, social–emotional, and nonverbal cognitive abilities are approximately at age level. Information regarding self-help skills is incomplete at this time.

d. **Interactive aspects of communication.** Frank tended to stay within easy physical proximity of his parents, but did not often initiate interaction. When he did elicit their attention, it was by touching them or offering them a toy, and was generally without any vocalization. When picked up or faced directly, Frank responded by smiling or cuddling. However, as mentioned previously, eye contact tended to be very brief, and occasions for more extended communication rare because Frank's attention was immediately directed elsewhere.

e. **Vocalization development.** Frank's vocalizations have been infrequent in the sessions to date. The only sounds he has used are a neutral-sounding /a/ and a repeated guttural rasping sound. At this time, the production of these sounds does not appear to be clearly connected to particular communication situations.

Goal Selection

Parent goals. The following represented the teacher/clinician's goals for Frank's parents during Stage I.

1. Express questions, concerns, and feelings about the child's hearing impairment and the habilitation process so that the teacher/clinician can deal with problems or can refer the parents elsewhere when special expertise will better fit their needs.

2. Obtain hearing aids for the child.

3. Keep appointments for habilitation.

4. Attempt to carry out suggestions offered by the teacher/clinician.

Teacher/clinician goals. Over several meetings with parents and child during Stage I, the pre-hearing aid stage, the teacher/clinician's goals were as follows.

1. Deal with the delicate emotional/psychological issues.

2. Give the parents suggestions for immediate action directed toward building communication with their child.

3. Inform the parents about hearing impairment and habilitation. Since the parents often asked questions precisely about these areas, it was possible to impart the information in direct response to parent questions. Otherwise, the topics were simply introduced by the teacher/clinician. The following guidelines were followed to achieve the goals listed above: (a) Give first priority in the sessions to parent queries, concerns, and expressions of feelings. Follow the interests of the parents first in discussion, and *listen actively.* (b) Attempt to adroitly and skillfully tie new information to known information in such a way that growth is continuing, but not overwhelming to the parents. (c) Provide the parents with practical suggestions for beginning to facilitate communication even before fitting of the aids such as: "During this time before he has his hearing aids, talk to Frank at a very close distance (directly into his ear when you are holding him). Talk with a normal intensity: that is, do not shout." (d) "Reinforce and encourage all of Frank's vocalizations through looking at him when he vocalizes, by smiling, imitating the sounds, coming nearer, patting him." (e) "Engage in back and forth (imitative) face-making and sound-making. That is, you imitate him, and then wait expectantly for him to take his turn." (f) "Attract Frank's attention to your face when you are communicating. For example, use a large sweeping hand motion or pass a toy through his field of vision and up to your face. Use an interesting animated style of communicating and visual expression, although not overly exaggerated." (Note that this goal, in particular, may not be appropriate for all children. For Frank, it is important since he needs to learn that mouth movements can have communicative significance. The first step is to get him to focus his visual attention on the face long enough to communicate something to him. At a later time or with other children, it will be appropriate to direct attention away from the face in order to maximize reliance on residual hearing.)

4. Inform the parents about the necessary steps for obtaining the hearing aids, as well as the aid's function, maintenance, benefits, and limitations.

5. Provide the parents with information regarding local, national, and international support groups and organizations. If they have not already done so, encourage the parents to visit and observe other educational programs.

6. Provide the parents with written materials on deaf education on request or as appropriate. Encourage discussion of the materials.

7. Outline the philosophy, aims, and function of the McGill project including the type, quantity, and frequency of services, as well as parent and clinician roles. Obtain signatures on permission forms for release of information and videotape recording of sessions.

There are no specific goals for the child during Stage I, since this time prior to hearing aid fitting is primarily diagnostic.

Intervention

In Stage I, intervention is essentially focused on responding to parent-generated queries and remarks. While the teacher/clinician has goals, these are secondary in importance to responding to the parents' feelings and need for support rather than information. In many cases, as in this exemplary case, both support and information were sought and provided.

Evaluation of Progress

Most of the goals in Stage I were attained in the course of ongoing discussion of events with questioning, information-giving, and clarification by all participants. In addition, the goal of providing practical suggestions for beginning to facilitate communication was accomplished through discussion with modeling and coaching of new strategies by the teacher/clinician. There was evidence that the habilitation process had been proceeding satisfactorily in Stage I. Frank's parents had obtained the hearing aids, they kept appointments for habilitation, and they attempted to carry out suggestions which were offered by the teacher/clinician. They also asked questions and began to express feelings with increasing openness.

Stage II: Post-Hearing Aid
(Hearing Age = 0 to 2 Months)

Stage II may be considered as the period covering the first 2 months of hearing aid use. Normally hearing children have auditory experiences from birth onward. We find it convenient to describe a hearing-impaired child who has his first auditory experience when the hearing aids are first fitted as having a *hearing age* of 0 months. Thus, as normally hearing children develop listening skills during and beyond their first year, so most hearing-impaired children also learn to use their residual hearing not from birth but from a *hearing age* of 0 months onward.

Assessment

Assessment of parents' needs and abilities. The parents' needs are most aptly assessed at this stage by means of the questions they raise and the issues which arise as they work with the teacher/clinician. Stage II has two major characterizing events, both of which introduce unsolicited change and newness into their lives, from the parents' point of view. The first event is the new daily reality of putting hearing aids on the child; the second is participating in an extensive evaluation of their own parent–infant interaction. Similar to many other parents of children with a newly discovered hearing loss, Frank's parents have had no previous experience with anyone who has worn a hearing aid. Their questions about hearing aids can be grouped into three categories: (1) hearing-aid-wearing practicalities; (2) technical information; and (3) action. The questions asked included: "How long every day should Frank wear the hearing aids? What do I do if he keeps pulling them out? How long do the batteries last? What do we do if he won't wear them? If these aids are so powerful, how do you know they won't cause discomfort or further damage his hearing? How does a hearing aid sound? If the aids already make all sounds louder, what happens when a really loud sound occurs? Explain again how the aids can help if the hearing nerves are so profoundly damaged? Do I need to make my voice louder now? How close do I have to be? Should we test him at home to make sure he is hearing? How will I know if the aids are making as much difference as they are supposed to?"

Frank's parents were experiencing a great deal of emotional stress in connection with the new daily event of putting on hearing aids. Their questions occurred in sessions or telephone calls which were anxious, teary, or sometimes hostile. In essence, the parents were simultaneously dealing with their grief about the child's hearing loss, their fledgling hopes and uncertainties about what the hearing aids and education might be able to do, and their anxieties about their own abilities to cope with it all. Real support for the parents during this period came primarily from the clinic personnel. Even with the best of intentions, the extended family, friends, and neighbors seem to be contributing to the stress as they ask their own many questions ("What is that annoying little high-pitched noise?"), offer observations ("Those little radios make his ears stick out a little bit, don't they?"), and provide opinions ("I saw this show on television, and they said _____"). The reader is referred to Luterman (1979) and Moses (1979) for more discussion of the emotional impact of hearing loss on the family.

The second major characterizing event of Stage II is the extensive evaluation of parent–infant interactions, which is carried out by the teacher/clinician and the parent(s). At least one parent is videotaped as he or she is interacting with the child during the course of ordinary everyday care giving or play activities (Cole & St. Clair-Stokes, in press). If possible, the videotaping occurs in the child's home. Some parents are initially self-conscious about being videotaped, but the subsequent benefits (both emotional and educational) seem to quickly outweigh any discomfort. The parent role during the indepth analysis of the videotape is that of a consultant. As the teacher/clinician is transcribing the segments to be analyzed, the parent may be directly involved in activities such as listening for vocalizations and interpreting parent–child communicative behaviors and intentions. This dual analysis process may offer opportunities for the teacher/clinician to provide positive feedback to the parent regarding, for example, specific facilitative strategies he or she utilized in communicating with the child or their observational insight. The analysis also involves detailed observations of the child's communicative behaviors which can become an opportunity to emphasize the child's accomplishments and cleverness. In addition, the event can become a self-evaluation which culminates in the parent's spontaneously selecting aspects of his or her own (or the infant's) behaviors which need to be modified. (The reader may note that this is an adapted application of the self-evaluation process mentioned above under staff evaluation procedures.)

For the assessment of parent–infant communicative behaviors, Frank and his mother were videotaped playing together for about 20 minutes in the child's home.[1] This took place 2 weeks after Frank had been wearing his hearing aids (5 week's total contact with the McGill Project.) A 3-minute segment was selected, which the parent and teacher/clinician agreed was a fair representation of ordinary interaction. The following is a summary of observations gleaned from the indepth analysis (Cole & St. Clair-Stokes, in press).

1. Communication-facilitating behaviors. Frank's mother's style of interacting has the following facilitative aspects: she talks to him well within his hearing range; she speaks at an appropriate intensity; she speaks in a normal, unexaggerated fashion; she uses an appropriate amount of normal gesture; she usually accepts communication from the child by smiling and verbally responding. Aspects to be monitored and/or altered include her speaking in a high-pitched, repetitiously sing-songy manner; too-frequent elicitation of single words; ignoring a variety of nonverbal cues to Frank's focus of attention and interest; too-frequent imposing of adult-determined communication topics; infrequent or too brief pause intervals for Frank to take his turn or to initiate communication.

2. Use of conversational devices. In the 3-minute segment analyzed, Frank's mother used voice alone in the majority of her attempts to attract his attention (30 out of 33 attempts). Only one of the voice-alone attempts was successful. The other successful attempt to attract Frank's attention during the 3-minute segment occurred when the mother manipulated an object close to her face (a visual strategy).

---

[1]Frank's father was able to take off work to attend sessions approximately once per month. Consequently, for habilitative purposes, the mother was considered to be the primary caregiver, and she was videotaped with Frank at this time. Frank's father was very interested and involved in the process, however, and the mother said that information from the sessions he had to miss was always thoroughly discussed in the evening. Several mothers later, he requested that he and Frank be videotaped for the same purpose. Space does not permit a discussion of that videotape. To simplify references, the pronoun *she* will refer to the parent, and *he* to the child.

3. Use of language to accomplish specific purposes. In the segment analyzed, Frank's mother used her talking for a variety of
communicative functions. The total number of utterances by the
mother was 37. Of those the most frequent categories were imperative (13 utterances), closed questions (6 utterances), and continuants
(6 utterances). Lacking normative research data and with only a
3-minute segment of interaction being analyzed, one cannot make
sweeping generalizations regarding the adequacy of the mother's use
of language to accomplish specific purposes with Frank. However, these
observations could motivate the teacher/clinician to be alert in other
communicative situations for the occurrence of other functions, and
to encourage the mother to continue (or begin) using her talk to
expand Frank's utterances, ask open-ended questions, reply to Frank's
utterances or questions, and to imitate Frank's vocalizations or
utterances.

Assessment of the child. Assessment of Frank during Stage II
included further evaluation of his residual hearing, general development, and interactional communication.

Audiological responses were obtained using visual reinforcement
audiometry. Aided testing of Frank in the 2nd and 3rd weeks of hearing
aid use revealed the following results.

	250	500	1000	2000	3000	4000	Hz
Right ear aided	40	50	55	55		> 80	dB
Left ear aided	45	45	50	50		> 80	
Binaural aided	40	40	50	60	(?)55	> 80	

Frank cooperated in this testing situation and reliability of the results
was judged as good. We noted that it was possible for these results
to be minimal responses. When Frank was a bit more accustomed
to the task of responding to the very quietest sounds, he was retested
(see below). Frank would not tolerate headphones at this time.
(Unaided testing under earphones must be postponed for several
sessions until Frank will cooperate for it.)

With regard to Frank's auditory behavior, we found that he readily
accepted the idea of wearing hearing aids, and wore them full time
from the first day. Examples of early responses to sound which occurred
in the first 3 weeks of hearing aid wearing include the following.

Chronological age	Hearing age	Auditory/Vocal Behavior
12 months	1 week	Accepted hearing aids immediately.
		Banged toys with apparent delight at the sound.
		Turned to mother's voice at home.
		Stilled as if listening to adult conversation which began nearby.
	2 weeks	Increased amount and variety of vocalizations according to the mother.
		First usage of serially repeated consonant /bʌ, bʌ, bʌ/; also /m:/.
		Reduction of frequency of raspy sound.
	3 weeks	Alerted to sound when person knocked three times on the door.
		Looked back and forth as speakers changed in a nearby adult conversation (one male, one female speaker).

These behaviors were prognostically positive regarding Frank's likely ability to benefit from his residual hearing. Developmental testing begun in Stage I was completed during the early part of Stage II. For the one remaining area, self-help, Frank's skills were found to be appropriate for his age level.

Interactional/communication behaviors were assessed through analysis of the videotaped segment described above in the Stage II parent assessment. Analysis of Frank's conversational devices showed that he attempted to initiate an exchange with his mother only five times during the 3-minute segment, as compared with the 33 attempts made by his mother in the same time period. One reason for the small number of attention-getting attempts was that it simply was not necessary: his mother was already giving him her full attention. Frank's strategies for attracting attention need to be explored in other situations when the adult(s) are less vigilant. Of the instances which did occur in the videotaped sample, three were strategies for soliciting attention visually (e.g., gazing at the mother). The other two involved visual and tactile attention getting (e.g., glancing at mother while tapping her or offering a toy). One of these attempts was accompanied by vocalizing; all were successful.

Frank's use of language to accomplish specific purposes could not be assessed, since he had no verbal language at the time of this first videotaped session. However, he was communicating nonverbally. In the analyzed segment, there were 11 events which were interpreted by Frank's mother and the teacher/clinician as nonverbal communicative contributions. These contributions were used by Frank to accomplish 5 different communicative purposes. These included greeting, answering, requesting action, repeating action, repeating, and practicing. (See explanations of categories in Cole & St. Clair-Stokes, in press.) Half of his contributions were nonvocal, while the other half included voice. Eight out of eleven total contributions by Frank were successful in that the mother responded to them.

Vocalization development occurred within the first 4 weeks of hearing aid usage. Frank's interest in and ability to engage in vocal turn-taking play had increased greatly. The raspy, guttural sound which Frank's parents initially mentioned as his "favorite sound" was now seldom used. Frank now said /m:/ (as in "Mmmmm!") when fed grapes by his mother and produced it spontaneously on several occasions. He had also begun to use /b/ after 4 weeks of hearing aid use.

Goal Selection

Some of the goals in Stage II were carried over from Stage I, and/or were slightly more demanding modifications of Stage I goals. *Goals for the parents* included those relating to emotional/psychological support, hearing aids, and audition and communication.

The goal relating to emotional/psychological support was to encourage the parents to express questions, concerns, and feelings about the child's hearing impairment and the habilitation process so that the teacher/clinician could deal with the problems or refer the parents elsewhere for special expertise to better fit their needs.

The parents' goals relating to hearing aids were (1) to expect and establish full-time wearing of the hearing aid by Frank, and (2) to check the functioning of the hearing aids at home on a daily basis including use of the five sound test (Ling, 1978, 1981b, 1981c).

The parents had five goals in relation to audition and communication. These were

1. To keep two written records of Frank's behavior at home, one for instances of his responses to environmental noises and voice, and the other for vocalizations he produced;

2. To encourage Frank to listen and to vocalize consistently by using a variety of techniques suggested as follows: (a) Continue to show Frank that you notice and care when he alerts to a sound, searches for it, and/or points to his ear. (Frank's mother was doing this quite naturally: She smiled, hugged or patted him, and talked about the sound they just heard, "I heard that, too! Look—it's the garbage truck coming"); (b) Mention and talk about sounds as they occur and are meaningful, such as someone knocking on the front door, an appliance buzzer, someone calling from the next room; (c) Call Frank or ask him simple questions the first time from outside of his line of vision (but close by) when giving his attention can be very rewarding to him. For example, "Frank, do you want a cookie?" when he is in the kitchen; (d) Continue to encourage him to vocalize by looking at him when he vocalizes, smiling, moving closer, responding verbally, imitating him; and (e) expect Frank to vocalize when he wants something. In other words, when he is pointing at something he wants you to give him, simply do not respond until he vocalizes—and then respond immediately.

3. Continue responding appropriately to Frank's preverbal communicative behaviors (see teacher/clinician goals).

4. During everyday interaction, begin being conscious of aspects noted in the continuing videotape discussions as needing change (see teacher/clinician goals).

5. During everyday activities, begin associating routine events and toys with particular speech sounds (see teacher/clinician goals).

The teacher/clinician had three principal goals. These related to emotional/psychological support, audition and communication, and parent education. Emotional/psychological support goals were (a) to continue to give first priority to parent queries, concerns, and expressions of feelings. Follow the interests of the parents first in discussion, and *listen* actively; (b) to reinforce and encourage the parents for their contribution toward Frank's quick adjustment to hearing aid wearing and, as appropriate, for the way they are coping with all the changes and new information coming their way; (c) to continue to attempt to adroitly and skillfully tie new information to known information in a way that growth progresses, but is not overwhelming to the parents.

Goals for the teacher/clinician were (a) to give the mother positive feedback concerning the ways in which she is already encouraging Frank to listen and to vocalize in varied ways, stressing that she is helping him learn that sounds have meaning and value; (b) to use re-viewing and discussion of the videotape and any other instances which occur to give the mother positive feedback for ways in which she has shown insight into Frank's preverbal communicative behaviors, and has responded appropriately to them (e.g., sometimes no response is the appropriate one; other times an action may be called for, while talking about what is happening); (c) to use repeated re-viewings and discussion of the videotape to gradually focus the parent's attention on additional areas noted in the analysis as needing change, such as varying the parent's techniques for getting the child's attention; helping the mother better modulate voice pitch; avoiding eliciting single words from Frank; being more aware of Frank's nonverbal cues; following Frank's interest rather than always introducing something new; pausing for Frank to take his turn; coming near, but waiting for Frank to initiate communication before giving him visual attention or leaning in close to him. (At this time, the mother is not expected to immediately and simultaneously begin changing all these aspects. Rather, the goal is that she becomes aware that there are behaviors which are more and/or less facilitative of communication, and to try to notice what her own behaviors are in everyday situations, in order to see if the videotape was representative of her usual behavior; and (d) to demonstrate how ordinary routine activities with the infant are actually providing repeated, but fun and meaningful, exposure to particular aspects of speech by pointing out to Frank's mother that she is already doing this naturally when she always responds to Frank's moving near the stove with, "Look out! It's *hot*! The stove is hot! [putting hand toward the stove] Ow! It's hot! Let's move away—it's too hot." Or saying "All gone!" in a consistent way whenever appropriate or "Shhh!" when a toy or a person is sleeping. With a little forethought, the repertoire of these little routines can be expanded to provide nearly effortless opportunities for consistent exposure to any number of specific speech aspects, as they are incorporated into the course of everyday talking and playing with Frank. For example, the mother can made an immediate list of five or six favorite toys and the sounds that can be associated with them (e.g., "ah ^{ee} ee" when making an airplane fly, "Boom! Boom! Boom!" for his wind-up bear that beats a drum, "buh-buh-buh-buh" for a toy boat in a bowl of water).

The teacher/clinician's goals for parent education during Stage II relate to providing information on three aspects of intervention, as follows:

1. Discuss approaches to intervention in terms of nondirective (experiential) and directive (structured) learning and teaching; how the intervention will be one or the other, or a combination of the two at various points in the process; how the choice of approach relates to the child's social and cognitive maturity, the child's ability and willingness to imitate on demand, and the parents' style of behavior management.

2. Review or introduce information on (a) the wearing, care, and maintenance of hearing aids, earmolds, batteries; (2) low probability of noise damage from the aids and output limiting; (c) how Frank's responses relate to the "speech banana" (speech acoustics) (Ling, 1976, 1978, 1981b, 1981c; Ling & Ling, 1978; Pickett, 1980); and (d) the decrease in intensity as speaker's distance from the microphone increases; good listening distance (Ling, 1981c).

3. (a) Relate the early stages of auditory and linguistic (including early vocal behaviors) development in the normally hearing infant to that of the hearing-impaired child who has just begun wearing hearing aids; (b) explain the Hirsh model (1970, see also Ling, 1978) of auditory learning (detection, discrimination, identification, comprehension) as it is useful for emphasizing the necessity of proper amplification and the significance of subsequent vocal and linguistic developments as they occur; (c) discuss auditory-related expectations for Frank during Stage II: increasing responsiveness to environmental sounds and voice; increasing variety and quantity of vocalizing both in play by himself, and in attention getting (as he learns that vocalizing can often gain attention, smiling, vocal play games, delivery of desired objects, etc.); increasing interest in vocal play games (back-and-forth vocalizing with adults); increasing attentiveness to talk directed toward him, particularly talk occuring during often-repeated routines (e.g., all gone, bye bye).

4. Emphasize the importance of everyday care giving and play activities as the child's language-learning time for both normally hearing and hearing-impaired infants.

Goals for the child in Stage II included the following target behaviors, which were expected to begin occurring during the 2 months of initial hearing aid wearing. Similar to the goals for the parents, these were areas which were expected to continue expanding and becoming more complex throughout the habilitation process.

1. Increasing responsiveness to environmental sounds and voice.

2. Increasing tolerance for wearing headphones (even stereo headphones at home).

3. Increasing quantity and variety of vocalizing.

4. Increasing attention and interest in vocal play.

5. Increasing use of voice for communicative purposes (e.g., getting attention, requesting objects or actions) with or without accompanying gestures.

Intervention

Parent-related goals in Stage II, as in Stage I, were addressed through discussion and through modeling or coaching of new strategies or behaviors by the teacher/clinician. Parents' questions and problems were treated first within a session, and may have occupied the entire session. In addition, the reviewing of the videotape analysis by the parent and teacher/clinician together provided the vehicle for centering discussion and demonstration around changes which the parents could make in order to facilitate the child's auditory and communication development.

Intervention to meet the goals for Frank during Stage II was directed toward (a) full-time wearing of his hearing aids and (b) implementation by the parents of the activities and strategies selected for them as goals. In other words, the parents in carrying out their goals should thereby help Frank increase his responsiveness to environmental sounds and voice, increase the quantity and variety of vocalizing, increase his attention and interest in vocal play, and increase his use of voice for communicative purposes.

Individual intervention sessions are planned and evaluated using a form developed by the authors. This individual session plan (ISP) specifies the objectives for that session and the activities to be used to accomplish those objectives. Table 4-4 illustrates the ISP with a sample Stage II session for Frank and his mother. Space has been provided for the teacher/clinician to predict likely examples of conversation which may be generated in the course of the activities.

At this session (see Table 4-4), the column of "predicted language" for the session was shown to Frank's mother to demonstrate a level of talking which was age appropriate for Frank. It consisted mostly

TABLE 4-4. Example of Individual Session Plan

Child: Frank Zed	Date: January 23	Teacher/Clinician: M. Paterson (Mother present, grandmother observing)	
Objectives/Purpose	Activities/Materials	Predicted Language	Comments
1. Audiological: continue aided binaural testing.	Visual Reinforcement Audiometry (VRA) or Puppet in the Window		Frank much more consistent and cooperative in responding than in previous sessions.
2. Attention-getting: Use auditory, visual tactile means (in that order as necessary). Model for mother; have her do it.	Model for mother; have her do it. Activity: blow lightweight plastic balls from person to person on the table.	Let's blow the balls! Get ready, Frank! (Mom, Marietta) Puff! That was a good try, Frank. Blow it again. I caught the ball. It's my (your) turn. Blow it to me! I'm ready!	Mother and Frank both seemed to enjoy the game. Breath control for impulsion of ball improving. Good "get ready" posture already; also nice attack.
3. Turn-taking: Once attention is established, pause deliberately for Frank to take his turn. Wait him out! Expect a response. Model for mother; have her do it.	Imitation of hand-clapping, bouncing nodding, waving.	I'm clapping my hands. What are you doing, Mommy? Clap your hands! Clap, clap. That's it, clap your hands.	Did not do.

TABLE 4-4. Example of Individual Session Plan—Cont'd

Child: Frank Zed *Date:* January 23 *Teacher/Clinician:* M. Paterson (Mother present, grandmother observing)

Objectives/Purpose	Activities/Materials	Predicted Language	Comments
4. Vocalizing in communicating (requesting): Frank's request for help must include vocalization. If he does not vocalize, ask the mother (who then models for Frank).	Hopping animals hidden in barrels that Frank cannot open by himself.	I hear something in the barrel (shaking it). Do you hear that, Mom? (Frank) That's right, open it. Oh, that's hard to open. Try again. Oh—you want me to help you. That's hard. Mom, can you help me? Wind it up, Mommy! (Frank) Let it go! Look at the frog! The frog goes hop, hop, hop. Catch the frog! You caught the frog.	Frank enjoyed this, and he knew immediately to search for the object. Mother has trouble keeping the conversation going. Watch her turn-taking; not enough pause Other instances: Frank pointed babbled, and looked at Marietta— and then went to get the ball; Frank waved and said /ba-ba/ for "Bye-bye" on departure without prompting.

Parent Discussion Topics		Observations	Parent Questions/Comments
1. Attention-getting, turn taking, here-and-now talking. Explore this again with mother; model in play with Frank. Coach her with dialogue if necessary to help her when she is stuck. Ask mother at end of session whether this was a useful exercise.			Is he doing well? Will he have normal speech language by age 5? Grandma expects him to be bilingual by age 3 because his progress is so encouraging now. She said it was helpful.

2. Ask what Frank's favorite toy or games are at home. Offer suggestions for maximal exploitation of these activities. If mother would like, generate some typical appropriate talk for one or several of these toys or games.

She is going to write out some possible conversations (her idea).

Good to clear up this misunderstanding, as mother was really anxious; stress interactive nature of real conversation.

3. Arrange for a home visit in the next two weeks. Discuss the videotape of mother-child interactive behaviors which will be done during that visit.

Reinforced mother for maintaining lower voice pitch and losing repetitive sing-song pattern—much improvement!

I never gave a thought to how children learn language before. I was the youngest child, and I never was around small children much before. I can't "talk, talk, talk" at Frank the way it says to do in that book I read last week.

of phrases and sentences, and employed several of the sound and toy or activity associations. She then decided it might be helpful to rehearse some possible conversation for a number of other everyday activities. This kind of planning and rehearsal might not be helpful for every parent, but Frank's mother said that it gave her a concrete idea of appropriate talking, and that it made it easier to have confidence and fluency in real situations. Space in the ISP is also provided for the teacher/clinician to jot down notes regarding each event during the sessions, or to make observations afterward. The parent discussion form includes preplanned topics and suggestions to be discussed, as well as space for recording questions and comments from the parents during that session. The latter column is usually filled out after the session. Systematically noting parent questions and comments allows the clinician to reconsider the response provided in the session and to determine whether or not to bring up that topic in the subsequent session. It may also enable the teacher/clinician to discover patterns in parent thinking and reactions to intervention strategies and information.

One final note regarding this individual session plan: The items do not need to follow in the order indicated on the form. For this session, since the audiological testing had to be scheduled, it occurred for about 20 minutes at the beginning of the session. This was followed by allowing Frank to play by himself for 10 or 15 minutes while the teacher/clinician and parent discussed the first topic. Frank then appeared to be ready for some attention, so the activity with the animals hidden in barrels was next. When it had run its course, the plastic ball blowing was introduced. At that point, Frank seemed to be at the limits of his attention span, so he was allowed to play by himself while the teacher/clinician talked about the remaining items.

Evaluation of Progress

Assessment of parents' progress in the three areas described above show gains in each: *Emotional/psychological adjustment* to Frank's hearing impairment has been marked. The parents have continued to ask questions and express feelings, but now, at the end of 2½ months, the majority of their questions have become habilitation oriented, and the period of acute emotional distress seems to be abating as changes are occurring in Frank. Not unexpectedly, however, the parental feelings of sadness, anger, guilt, and anxiety about the future continue to surface in every session. The parents have grown accustomed to the *hearing aids* and Frank now wears them as if they were a normal part of his clothing. The mother seems comfortable with the procedures for maintaining and checking the aid, and has heard some aids which are not functioning well so that she has a better idea of what to listen for. In the areas of *audition and communication* Frank's mother has begun to keep careful observational records of his responses to environmental sounds and his vocalizations. She is including information about the context, which is very helpful. For example, she includes the distance at which Frank has heard sounds and a note about the circumstances: "Frank was playing quietly with his trucks in the living room when my brother knocked on the front door (14 feet away). He looked up, but didn't seem to connect the sound to someone being at the door." Both parents seem to be making every effort to reinforce Frank consistently for responding to sounds and for vocalizing.

The mother has been observed to wait for Frank's vocalization before granting his gestural requests on several occasions (once he wanted her to come look at something, once a drink of water, once a toy he could not reach). His mother has become a keener observer of her own and Frank's communicative behaviors. For example, she has begun self-monitoring her voice pitch. She is also aware that she often uses and tries to elicit single words from Frank, and that she tends to be so attentive to him that he does not often have to make much of an effort to initiate communication. Frank's mother was delighted to be "given" words to associate with toys and everyday activities. She mentioned that she has been using "shhh," "flash-flash-flash" (for a digital clock), "hop hop," (for blowing out a candle), /a long high ee (for the airplane) and "all gone." However, she still tends to use only single words, rather than accompanying phrases and sentences.

All of the target topics for the teacher/clinician mentioned above were touched upon in discussions during the 2 months, but it is expected that all of them will require further discussion.

Evaluation of Frank's progress was undertaken through a combination of parent records and teacher/clinician observations. They yielded the following chronology of Frank's auditory and vocal behaviors in the first 2 months of hearing aid use.

Hearing age	Auditory behaviors	Vocal behaviors
1 week	Accepted hearing aids immediately	Vocalized to light box in clinic: /m-m-m/
	Turned to calling voice 3 times during session	Increase in quantity of sounds
	Seems to be listening to himself	

Hearing age	Auditory behaviors	Vocal behaviors
2 weeks	Intonational contours beginning to vary	Imitated in play: /baba/, /u-u/
	Normal sounding voice	Imitates /m:/ for grapes
		Quantity of vocalizations increasing
		Noticeable reduction of "raspy" guttural sound
3 weeks		Imitating blowing with feathers, mobiles, plastic balls
4 weeks	Turned to door knocking after 3 knocks	
5 weeks	Vocal play with /a,m,b/	More control over breath stream in blowing
		Vocalizations becoming more connected and babble-like
8 weeks	Developing control of vocalizations and one-word utterances which suggests auditory discrimination and comprehension abilities	Imitated /u,a,wa,m:,ba/ several times in the clinic
		/ba/ and waved bye-bye twice
	(See Hirsh, 1970; Ling, 1971; Ling, 1976)	/bʌbʌ/ used constantly in babble
9 weeks	Constant variegated babble including /ba,ma,wa/ which suggests auditory discrimination by manner of these three sounds	Babbles constantly: /bʌ, bi, ba, wa, m: ma/
		Spontaneous utterances in context include /bʌp bʌp bʌp/ for hop hop hop; /bʌ/ for bird

Stage III: Moving On (Hearing age = 3 to 6 months)

Stages I and II comprise the initial diagnostic period during which time the teacher/clinician is gathering and analyzing data pertinent to the child's development of spoken language competence. By the end of the diagnostic period, goals have been selected for both the parent and the child, which guide the thrust of habilitation for at least the next several months. Typically, the child has learned to wear the hearing aids, and has taken initial steps toward using his residual hearing and his voice. The parent has regained some degree of emotional/psychological equilibrium. The child has become familiar and comfortable with the clinic room and staff, and the parents and teacher/clinician have established a congenial working relationship. Thus, the stage is set so that everyone involved in ready for the tasks of "Moving On": firmly (re-)establishing a spoken language communicative base through everyday play and care giving activities (Stage III).

Assessment

The assessment of the strengths and needs of Frank's parents in Stage III is addressed first in terms of questions they asked and second in terms of interactive behaviors they demonstrated during Stage II.

Parents' questions focused on vocalizing and speech. They asked, "Which sounds will come out first? Which ones do we have to teach him? What about sounds he can't hear, like the "s"? How will Frank ever learn to say all the sounds? When? Does he have to babble all the sounds before he will start using words? If it will take a few years to learn all the sounds, shouldn't we be trying to teach all of them right now?" They also focused on spoken language comprehension and production: "How can I tell when Frank understands something if he doesn't use the word? I've already been trying to get him to say the word "dog." I think he has a hard time with the "d" sound because it comes out like "gaw." Why does he make this kind of mistake if he can hear both the "d" and the "g"? How can we correct his mistakes and teach him the "d"? How can we ever teach him all the words he needs to know? Recently, Frank has started kind of screaming around the house. It's really annoying. I've tried to stop him and explain to him, but he just keeps on. Why is he doing this? Is it because he's frustrated about talking? I know I should be making him say more, but I'm not sure of what to say to him to make that happen? I'm trying to pause and give him his turn, but what should I say if he doesn't talk?"

These questions seem to center more around what to do to get the spoken language learning process underway, which may be viewed as prognostically positive. It would be ridiculous to suggest that there is a fixed timetable for parents "handling" the complex of emotions evoked by the new knowledge of their child's hearing impairment. However, the sooner they are able to focus attention on the child's habilitation and growth, the sooner it will begin.

Assessment of Frank's parents were made through the Stage II videotape, which was collected and analyzed in order to determine goals and begin intervention by working toward attaining those goals. This information was also utilized in working with Frank as Stage III began. (The reader is referred to the Stage II assessment.) However, after another 2 months (hearing age = 5 months), a further videotape was collected because the teacher/clinician believed that both parent and child behaviors had altered enough to warrant a new indepth assessment. A 25-minute session of free play and a tea party in the clinic playroom were videotaped. Both parents were present that day, and each interacted alone with Frank for part of the videotape. Three-minute samples of each were subjected to indepth analysis by the parents and the teacher/clinician. Space permits discussion of interactions between only the mother and Frank.

As in the first videotape, Frank's mother generally spoke in an unexaggerated fashion; she used an appropriate amount of gesture; she spoke within Frank's hearing range at an appropriate intensity. Furthermore, she had modified her overall pitch to a lower level, and almost never used repetitious sing-song prosody.

In looking at the videotape, Frank's mother said that she could see that often she was talking to Frank when he really was not paying attention at all. She also mentioned that even when she was able to get his attention, she then had trouble keeping him involved, so that all of the exchanges seemed very brief. She wanted to know if she could be saying things which would keep him involved longer.

Although not stated in precisely this manner to the parent, the teacher/clinician's analysis concurred with the mother's impression that she needed assistance with attracting Frank's attention and keeping it. One of the problems seemed to be that the mother assumed that because he was capable of hearing her, he was probably also listening to her. Consequently, she was generally continuing to use voice alone when she was attempting to get his attention, and she often talked when his focus of interest was not the same as hers. In the videotape, it was clear that this resulted in the mother carrying on a monologue, or a narration of events, which was far from communicative. That is, she was using the "talk, talk, talk" approach that she read about, but what was going in was minimal. It seemed most likely that the listening habits (auditory attentiveness) were new enough that Frank needed more practice with having his attention clearly drawn to the fact that the mother wanted to engage in a communicative exchange. Additionally, the analysis revealed that the mother tended to begin interactions with Frank by introducing a completely new topic of her own, or making some kind of demand on him (e.g., "Look over there, Frank!" "Tell Mom ____." "What's that?") The following section presents additional evidence of this.

The mother's use of language to accomplish specific purposes was also assessed. In the 3-minute segment, nearly all categories of communicative function could be identified in her talk. However, 63 of her 67 utterances were in the following categories:

Continuants	18 utterances
Informatives	14 utterances
Closed questions	17 utterances
Imperatives	14 utterances

These are all perfectly normal functions for communication, but may be less facilitative of real exchange and child-initiation of communication than some other categories. That is, continuants and informatives do not necessarily include a "hook" for drawing a response from the child. Closed questions and imperatives, while intended to elicit a response from the listener, can often evoke only a single word or a nonverbal response. Furthermore, all four categories tend to emphasize speaker domination. Again, this is a perfectly normal phenomenon in parent–child exchanges. But if the goal is to encourage the child to initiate communication, then some of the control may need to be relinquished to child some of the time. This problem is likely to be contributing to the mother's frustration at not being able to maintain Frank's attention for longer exchanges. Function categories which may be more facilitative of communication (and which were infrequently used by Frank's mother) include expansion of child utterances, imitation of child utterances, replies to child utterances and questions, and open-ended questions.

In making an assessment of the child's needs, items from both the Stage II "Evaluation of Progress" and the Stage III "Assessment" are used, since they actually overlap in both time and content. After 4 months of hearing aid usage (that is, during Stage III, which includes hearing ages 3 to 6 months), Frank's mother and the clinician reviewed the mother's record of the words and phrases Frank produced and comprehended. For a word to be recorded, it had to meet several requirements which were discussed and clarified several times with Frank's mother. The productions were words which Frank either said or imitated spontaneously (i.e., without direct elicitation). The words and phrases comprehended occurred within appropriate contexts without gestural cues. The summary list for Frank at a hearing age of 4 months follows, without the contextual notes also recorded by the mother:

Words Produced[a]	Words Comprehended
/o/	nose
/aɪ/	eye
/eɚ/	hair
/maʊ/	mouth
/iɚ/	ear
/ba-baɪ/	bye bye
/o–o/	no no
/wɔl/	doll
/bɚ/	bird
/b/pʊ/	poo
	yes
	Do pick up
	come
	Find Dad
/ɔp̄–ɔp̄/	hop–hop
	Mom
/mo/	milk
	downstairs
/ʌp̄/	up
/bø/	bread
/ba/	ball
/au/	ow, ouch
	close the door
/opɛ̃/	open the door
	Give it to me.
	light
Total = 16	Total = 27

[a]The mother's notations have been translated into International Phonetic Alphabet (IPA) symbols.

Perusal of the mother's list with the contextual notes indicates that the first 16 words are being used to indicate the relationships of existence, recurrence (requests), cessation, rejection, and action as described by Bloom (1973). Other categories of the one-word functional utterances Bloom observed in her longitudinal study (of a normally hearing child) include disappearance, non-existence, and location. The words were also categorized according to Nelson's (1973) system of word classes for the first 50 utterances. Frank's words were primarily object nominals (both specific and general), with some demand-descriptive action words and personal–social assertions and expressions. No attributes or function words (as defined by Nelson) have yet appeared. Obviously, Frank's early utterances are similar to those described in the literature for normally hearing infants. The preponderant use of nominals was mentioned by both Bloom and Nelson as characteristic of their subjects. However, in Frank's case, it will be important to monitor this aspect carefully as it may also be a reflection of the mother's strong tendency to elicit one-word labels for objects.

The words comprehended also fit into categories identified in the literature for normally hearing children by Huttenlocher (1974). These include the following:

Name of family member or pet:	Mom
Label for game or social ritual:	light, Go pick up, come, Find Dad, ouch, bye bye, no no, yes, downstairs
Manipulable object/toy:	doll, bird, hop–hop, ball
Body parts:	nose, hair, eye, mouth, ear
Food-related:	milk, bread
Other:	poo, close the door, open the door, give it to me

It should be noted that the larger number of words comprehended versus those produced is not surprising for this early period of verbal development (McLean & Snyder-McLean, 1978).

By Stage III, Frank's vocalization development was moving rapidly toward normality. The guttural, raspy noise Frank was producing prior to hearing aid fitting was no longer heard. His repertoire of speech-like sounds produced in vocalized combinations or in words now included the following:

Emerging vowels: a, aɪ, au, u, o, ɝ, e, ɔ, ɪ, ɔ, ʌ, ẽ

Emerging consonants: b, m, w, l, v, d, p, p̄

The range of vowels and diphthongs produced indicates that Frank is exhibiting differential tongue movement for the vowels. In addition, the consonants include contrasts of manner, place, and voicing. Frank has also amply demonstrated well-controlled blowing abilities in play activities. He is thus, after 4 months of hearing aid usage, producing and manipulating a number of the parameters fundamental to fluent speech.

Goal Selection

A number of goals from the two previous stages continue to be goals in Stage III, some in identical form, some modified in accordance with recent developments.

Emotional/psychological goals for parents continue to include the expression of questions, concerns, and feelings about the child's hearing impairment and the habilitation process so that the teacher/clinician could deal with the problems or refer the parents elsewhere when special expertise will better fit their needs. The goal relating to hearing aids was that the parents should continue to consistently monitor the functioning of the child's hearing aids on a daily basis. In the area of audition and communication, parents' goals werre to continue keeping written records of Frank's auditory and vocal or verbal behaviors, including vocalizations and words or phrases produced, as well as words, phrases, and sentences he understood. (After the mother has noted approximately 100 words as "understood," word/phrase checklists can be begun as described in Stage IV "Intervention.")

Further goals for the parents in Stage III were (a) to continue encouraging Frank to listen and to vocalize (see specific suggestions in Stage II "Goals"), (b) to give Frank every opportunity to initiate communication (for example, by simply moving within fairly close physical proximity to him, thus making yourself available without talking or looking directly at him; reading a book or playing with a toy, and waiting for him to contact you and to try to communicate with you); (c) to initiate communication with Frank by *following his focus of attention* rather than introducing a totally new topic; (d) by *securing his attention before you communicate with him.* (This can be attempted first with voice alone, but if that fails, use visual or tactile cues. It will be appropriate to drop the visual and tactile cues at a point in the near future (see Stage III intervention), but for the time being, it is important to be sure Frank knows that he is being addressed); (e) by *continuing to talk with Frank* as you have been: asking questions, telling him things, talking about what is happening, and asking or telling him to do things, but in addition trying occasionally just to imitate what he has just said in an affirming manner; and/or to expand on what he has just said, also trying to ask some more questions that are not just answered with yes or no or with one-word labels and by continuing to expect Frank to vocalize when he wants something.

The goals for Frank from Stage II were modified in accordance with his progress. The five most important were (a) increasing responsiveness to environmental sounds and voice, now with some immediate awareness of the sounds' significance, (b) increasing accuracy in responding to routine phrases and words without looking at the speaker's face, (c) continually increasing variety in vocalizing aiming at vocalized productions nearly always occurring as reduplicated syllable strings or as variegated babbling (see Oller, 1979; Stark, 1978), (d) consistent use of voice for communicative purposes, with or without accompanying gestures, and (e) increasing the use of words for people, objects, animals, actions, social assertions and expressions, questions, attributes, states, locatives, possessives. These may be expected to occur in the midst of babbled utterances as well as in isolation.

Intervention

The teacher/clinician's approach and strategies for intervention in Stage III were similar to those described in Stages I and II. One change, however, was that speech imitation games were increasingly consciously employed by the teacher/clinician in the course of play and care giving activities. Frank's mother was a part of the games, and was encouraged to do them at home with Frank.

After Frank was clearly reinforced by verbal communicating, and usually turned immediately when an adult solicited his attention, then it was appropriate to introduce more reliance on audition alone in communicating with him. The teacher/clinician modeled and encouraged the mother to provide increasing opportunities for Frank to respond to spoken language in familiar, routine context without seeing the speaker's face. This was best accomplished in the most natural manner possible, and well within Frank's listening distance. For example, the speaker could simply talk to Frank when he was beside or slightly in front of the speaker, as opposed to directly facing him or her, and/or by talking to Frank when his visual attention was elsewhere. Covering the mouth with a hand or paper was another option, but was the least preferred by the authors since it can introduce an unnecessary element of artificiality into the communication event. Covering the mouth as part of a specific, planned teacher-directed activity seems to be a more acceptable usage of the technique. If Frank did not understand an auditory-only message, then he was allowed to see the speaker's face; if this was ineffective then the spoken message was accompanied by gesture. The idea was to give Frank an opportunity to use his auditory capabilities to the greatest extent possible, and to do this initially within well-known routines so that he experienced success.

Evaluation of Progress

There had been a continuing trend toward increasing parental coping with the emotional demands of Frank's hearing impairment, as well as the new information and skills. The most demonstrable changes in the parents occurred with regard to the issues which have become important to them, and their behavior as they were interacting with Frank. In the course of Stage III, the majority of the parents' questions came to be centered on habilitative concerns as can be seen from an examination of the questions listed in the assessment. This suggested that Frank's parents may have shifted from focusing on the child's disability and its implications to promoting the child's communicative growth. Naturally this was not a total shift, but it made it possible to move forward with habilitation. As will be evident in Stage IV, Frank's mother did begin to consistently put into practice the habilitative suggestions for getting and maintaining Frank's attention.

Stage IV: Gathering Impetus (Hearing Age = 6 to 16 months)

The diagnostic teaching process is one of continual assessment of abilities and needs with goals and intervention directly related to observed and measured changes. This means that particularly in Stage II and beyond, assessment and evaluation and intervention overlap and blend into each other. All aspects are an integral part of the intervention process. Consequently, in order to avoid repetition and to conserve space, the descriptions of the remaining two Stages (IV and V) will consist primarily of a combined asessment/evaluation section. Modifications in the goals and intervention will be noted as appropriate.

In previous stages, the status of the child's auditory and communication abilities and needs were assessed, and habilitative procedures put into practice for beginning the process of facilitating the child's development of spoken language. In Stage IV, the process continues. The teacher/clinician's role continues to be one of active listening, astute diagnostic observation, and educational guidance and modeling for the parents as they continue to learn how to facilitate the growth of communicative competencies in their child. Stave IV is considered to be starting as the child establishes consistent use of some single word utterances, with or without accompanying babble and gestures. Its ending, approximately 6 to 16 months later, coincides with the child's developing ability to put two words together in early spoken syntactic utterances. In addition, at this point, the child is also likely to continue to be using babbled jargon and single-word utterances.

Assessment/Evaluation of Progress

After Frank had been wearing the hearing aids about 9 or 10 months, the parents seemed to be in a period of emotional stability. They commented that they were impressed by the amount of work involved in this process; that they still became discouraged from time to time, but that they now believed that it was possible for the child to use his residual hearing, and to learn to talk; that they could and would cope with the major commitment of time and energy. At the same time, Frank's emerging ability to communicate verbally was a source of excitement and sustenance for the parents. They expressed amazement and delight as Frank strung words together (e.g., "dad, go." "No, shoes." "Lion, roar."), thus producing more than one single word within a given context. The parents were encouraged by comparisons made at friends' homes where they encountered some normally hearing 2-year-olds whose verbal development did not seem to be so very far ahead of Frank's.

The mother continued to keep careful records of the words and phrases Frank comprehended and produced. She made an observable effort to make herself available to Frank more frequently, but then to allow him to initiate communication with her. When she did communicate with him, she generally followed his focus of attention. She said she felt comfortable with the (initially uncomfortable) strategies of imitating Frank and/or expanding on his utterances. She still asked quite a lot of questions that elicited single-word labels, although some progress was noted as she asked him more questions such as "What happened?" "What did ____ do?" "Do you want to ____ or ____?"

During Stage IV, Frank passed through the audiometrically difficult period of being too old for visual reinforcement audiometry (i.e., quickly satiated by the reinforcers), and too young for conditioned play audiometry (i.e., he could/would not perform the task in response to the stimulus). However, by the end of Stage IV, he was cooperating for conditioned play, and it was possible to obtain reliable single-ear responses under earphones, as well as reliable single-ear aided responses. These are shown below.

	250	500	1000	1500	2000	3000	4000	Hz
Sound field aided								
Right ear	35	35	30	35	45	80	80	dB
Left ear	35	35	30	35	50	80	80	
Earphones								
Right ear	75	95	100	105	110		90	
Left ear	75	90	100	100	110		90	

The unaided responses are not markedly different from those obtained in previous testing. The apparent improvement in aided responses is primarily due to changes made in the gain function of his hearing aids. However, it may also reflect Frank's greater understanding of the testing task, as well as a possible element of greater (learned) listening ability. His unaided responses suggest that his physiologic capabilities have not changed over the last 16 months, but it is possible that the acuity of his auditory awareness has been sharpened through hearing aid usage, listening experience, and habilitation.

Frank now removes his aids by himself, switches them off, and attaches them to the stethoscope for real ear checking in the clinic. He is also beginning to try to help insert the molds. With regard to auditory behavior, Frank responds to /a, i, u/ and /ʃ/ of the Five-sounds test (Ling, 1981b, 1981c) at a distance of about 3 feet. He responds to /s/ inconsistently at about 6 in. from the hearing aid. In auditory comprehension games performed in the clinic, he is able to select items with the same initial consonant, the same number of syllables, but with varying vowels. He can also auditorily discriminate some words which vary according to manner differences in the initial consonant (e.g., monkey vs. donkey).

Words and phrases comprehended using audition alone are described below. Frank uses his voice to communicate extensively both at home and in the clinic. He attends to communication from others in a natural manner. He uses his voice and verbal communications to perform a variety of the early functions described by Dore (1975). These include calling, repeating, requesting action, greeting, answering, reporting, protesting, and labeling. According to ongoing parent and clinic records, Frank now has a receptive vocabulary (words understood without gestures) of approximately 240 words. This compares favorably with the 27 words he understood 6 months ago. All of the categories described by Bloom (1973) and by Nelson (1973) are represented in Frank's receptive repertoire. Frank's expressive vocabulary presently consists of 184 spontaneously produced words in comparison with the 16 recorded for him 6 months ago. In addition to the parents' continuing tally of sounds, words, and phrases responded to and used by the child, the teacher/clinician and parent are by Stage IV recording the receptive and expressive vocabulary on 500- and 2000-count word/phrase lists. The 500-word list is begun after the child has approximately 100 words listed in the parents' continuing tally. Each word is checked according to whether it was used "with cue," "without cue," "through imitation," or "spontaneously." These classifications have been useful for discussion of different levels of comprehension and production, as well as in tracking the acquisition of individual words over time.

In addtion to the one-word utterances, Frank is beginning to use some multiple-word utterances. The following have been observed:

no squirrel	big dog	all wet
more juice	small dog	Daddy go work
Tammy, wake up	no hat	bye bye in the car
want milk	Daddy beard	brush your teeth
riding bike	Tammy cup	up the sky

The semantic/syntactic relationships of agent–action, action–object, possessor–possession, entity–attribute (recurrence, nonexistence, attribute), and agent–object are all represented in Frank's present two-word capabilities. Demonstrative–entity, entity–locative, action–locative, and conjunctive relationships have not yet appeared. These capabilities appear to conform with observations of two-word utterances in normally hearing children (MacDonald & Nickols, 1974).

Frank is beginning to imitate short phrases as well as speech sounds now. In both spontaneous productions and in imitation, Frank has good voice quality and produces the following sounds:

Vowels and diphthongs: /a, i, u, o, e, ɛ, ʌ, ʊ, ɝ, æ, au/

Consonants: /m, b, p, w, f, j, d, l, n, g, k/.

Stage V: Snowballing (Hearing Age = 16 to 36 months)

Stage V is considered to occur as the child begins to demonstrate an exponential expansion of pragmatic, semantic/syntactic, and phonologic abilities. Semantic/syntactic abilities, for example, are more and more frequently of greater length (three- and four-word utterances).

Utterances are also beginning to be marked by inflectional morphemes and function words. In Stage V it becomes possible to implement more adult-directed activities to accomplish specific targets. (The adult-directed activities are described in the Stage V intervention section).

Assessment/Evaluation of Progress

Frank's parents seemed to be very encouraged by his growing communicative abilities. In nearly every session, the mother mentions some event or observation that has occurred such as his making a comment in a new context, expressing a simple abstract notion, his enjoyment of a particular story book or nursery rhyme, or his ability to abstract ideas from one situation in order to generalize to another. For example, during a teacher/clinician-directed hiding game in the clinic, Frank suddenly told everyone to close their eyes and say the magic word "Abracadabra"—whereupon he produced a toy from under the table with a magician-like flourish. (He had seen a children's magic show on television the previous day.)

After Frank had been wearing his aids for 23 months, his mother mentioned that it was difficult now to remember how it had been just after the detection of the loss; the despair they had felt at the loss and at the magnitude of the task facing them. She said she knew there was still a great deal to be done, but with his obvious progress she felt it was all much more possible. She said she was really able to enjoy Frank for himself now, and not think of him in terms of his hearing impairment or his language deficits. Also, both parents revealed that they had been giving a lot of thought to how difficult all this "intervention" must be for Frank himself.

Parent questions in Stage V included the following: "When should we begin to teach Frank to read? Won't that help Frank learn to say some of the sounds he doesn't have or doesn't say well? Wouldn't reading early give him a head start at school? What about preschool placement? I like the idea but it worries me. The children make so much noise—how will he ever hear people talking? Also, the children will not be patient with him, and I'm afraid he'll be left out. Or else, like the 8-year-old girl next door, they'll treat him like a little baby, and just say single words at him. How can he still learn from that environment?"

Frank's mother says that he enjoys wearing his aids and protests when they are removed. He is able to remove his aids by himself, to help insert the molds, and to switch the aids on and off.

Frank turns consistently and differentially to his name being called, including situations where three or four other names might just as easily be called.

He is now repeating back (auditorily identifying) four of the five sounds in the Five-sounds test. In conversational situations in the clinic with contextual but not gestural cues, Frank was observed to comprehend a number of the mother's utterances, such as "Do you want a drink of water? Go get another book! Let's go put our jackets on," through audition alone.

A videotape was made of Frank and the mother in order to assess interactional aspects, semantic/syntactic abilities, and speech development in Stage V. A 3-minute sample of Frank and his mother playing with toy cars and a ramp was selected for indepth analysis. The mother assisted in compiling the transcript and in the analysis. It showed that the mother consistently encouraged Frank's awareness and use of the auditory–oral channel for communication. She talked within the child's hearing range with appropriate intensity and pitch; she spoke in a normal, unexaggerated fashion; she used an appropriate amount of gesture; her language appeared to be appropriate to Frank's level of comprehension; and she paused long enough to encourage Frank to take his turn. Furthermore, Frank's mother was skillful in attending to and following Frank's interests, and she reinforced Frank's contributions to the conversation. The videotape demonstrated that Frank had become an active communicative partner and was motivated and interested in communicating with his mother. As in Stage I, Frank used talking to accomplish a variety of communicative functions. In the segment, the majority of his comments could be categorized as requesting or reporting (included comments and/or descriptions of an object or event; also expressions of emotion or intent. These verbal utterances were often accompanied by a natural indicative gesture of some kind. For example, while looking at his mother, Frank pointed to the bottom of the ramp and said, "You catch the cars." Or, as Frank was asking for all of the cars, he said "Give me the whole thing" while making a quick sweep with one outstretched hand. (The gestures are mentioned since, in each case, they are an element of additional information to the message which is being communicated.)

During the 3-minute section of the videotape, Frank produced approximately 90 separate verbal contributions. Of these, the average length of verbal productions was 3 words (range = 1 to 5 words). The average length of babbled production was two syllables. Examination of the transcription indicates that his utterances nearly always included approximations for all the major meaning elements of the sentence patterns he was producing. For example, he said the following:

/ai keʌ go gɛ ı/
(I can't go get it).

Analysis of sentence patterns, semantic cases, and inflectional morphemes (grammatical modulations) show that Frank's knowledge of how to encode semantic relationships in conventional syntactic forms had become sophisticated. Examples of syntactic sentence patterns (SP) observed in the 3-minute segment included the following:

SP I:	NP (± Aux) + V (± Adv) The car is sliding down.
SP II:	NP (± Aux) + V + NP (± Adv) Mommy catch them. I have more.
SP IV:	NP + Be-verb + Adj I'm ready.
SP V:	Wh-question Where is the box?
SP II Elaboration:	NP + V + NP (± Inf clause) (± Adv of place) I want the car to go downhill.

With the various sentence patterns he used, Frank demonstrated appropriate use of the following major semantic cases:

Nouns:	agent, patient, mover, experiencer, possessor, patient, locative, recipient, entity;
Verbs:	action–causative, action–affective, process–causative, process–affective;
Modifiers:	recurrence (another, more); nonexistence (not any); disappearance (all gone); color; amount; shape;
Adverbials:	locatives, time (already);
Question form:	where.

The grammatical modulations observed in his videotaped sample included:

Beginning form of present progressive: (e.g., I playing, I going);

Prepositions: down, over, under, in, on, with;

Negative modals: don't, can't;

Pronouns: I, them, me;

Interrogative: where.

The parent tally and the word lists indicate that Frank presently (hearing age = 23 months) had a receptive vocabulary of 635 words. His receptive vocabulary increased rapidly from the 240 words reported when Frank's hearing age was 10 months. Although the growth was probably not linear, these figures suggest that since a hearing age of 4 months (chronological age of 16 months), Frank has been learning to understand 30 to 35 new words per month. During Stage V the Peabody Picture Vocabulary Test (PPVT) (Dunn, 1965) was also administered. This test showed that at chronologic age 2 years 11 months and hearing age 1 year 11 months, his PPVT receptive vocabulary age was 2 years 7 months.

Before he was 3 years old, Frank's voice quality was natural and pleasant sounding. He usually used appropriately varied intonation patterns to mark his questions and expressions and cooperated consistently for imitative speech babble activities in the clinic sessions and frequently repeated short phrases modeled by his mother in free play. According to Sanders' (1972) age estimates of consonant production for normally hearing children, Frank's phonetic abilities were within the range which would be expected for his hearing age.

In summary, in Stage V, Frank demonstrated progress in a number of ways. He responded well to voice and environmental sounds, and he auditorily comprehended increasingly longer phrases. Frank's main mode of communication was voice (with eye contact and gesture supplemented as needed) which he used to communicate effectively. Analysis of his language revealed that Frank was expressing numerous semantic relationships using a variety of sentence patterns, with some inflectional morphemes. Both his receptive and expressive vocabularies were expanding at a tremendous rate. Frank's phonetic repertoire consisted of a wide variety of vowel and consonant sounds, many of which were appropriately used in his expressive communication.

This concludes the detailed description of the management of an exemplary hearing-impaired child. The characteristics which made this child "exemplary" were (1) early detection of hearing loss; (2) early wearing of amplification; (3) presence of some usable residual hearing; and (4) no handicap other than profound hearing impairment. Other factors which may have been deduced from the case presentation were that the parents were able and willing to make a major time commitment to the child's development, and that the child did not display anything other than normal behavior management problems.

Given all these factors, the child and parents were able to become a highly successful family. From this detailed case description it is possible to gain an estimate of the kinds of abilities which were acquired, as well as the approximate rate of development for one particular child. Frank has every likelihood of being able to attend regular classes for normally hearing children, with supportive help, starting in his early elementary years.

But life and people seldom jibe precisely with exemplary models such as this one. Experience in the McGill project has shown that the absence of any one of the factors listed above can substantially alter the developmental process of spoken language acquisition. The requirements constituting satisfactory progress can become extremely fuzzy as attempts are made to weigh the present realities against the alternatives and the future possibilities. It is certainly not our view that a child must be "integratable" by first grade in order to stay in an auditory–oral educational program. However, it would be futile indeed to attempt to detail here all of the factors involved in making placement decisions for each possible type of situation. Suffice it to say that when substantial progress is not being made, the project team will have consulted and discussed the case with each other and the parents multiple times. If the situation remains static for approximately a 6-month period, and all of the project's resources have been exhausted, then an alternative placement is recommended to the parents, with whom alternative educational placements will already have been discussed.

The project specializes in helping hearing-impaired children develop spoken language, since we view that as a distinct advantage for communicating and coexisting with a large part of the world as it is today. However, a child's growth and development as a "successful" human being are certainly not totally dependent upon acquisition of spoken language. The team strives to keep parents' expectations realistically high with a focus on their individual child's overall well being. If a child's learning and development will be enhanced by place-ment in a setting that includes (or uses exclusively) sign language, then an attempt is made to facilitate transition as early and as smoothly as possible.

Placement of Graduates

Clinical records are available regarding 90 children who have been enrolled in the McGill project since its official establishment in 1966. (Records are missing for 1973–1975.) Research is presently underway to locate all of those former project children, and to obtain a measure

TABLE 4-5. Number of children referred to various educational placements by the McGill Project (1966–1972, 1976–1983).

Educational Placement	Number of Children	Percent of Total
Full integration in normally hearing nursery or kindergarten (supportive services assumed)	27	30%
Public or private oral school self-contained classes with partial integration, as appropriate	37	41%
Program for children with retardation or learning problems	3	3%
Total communication programs	9	10%
Referral information not available	14	16%
Total	90	100%

of their present language abilities, academic achievement, and social/emotional adjustment. At the present time, the clinical data generally indicate only the program to which the child was referred (and in which he/she was then presumably enrolled) upon leaving the project. This information is presented in Table 4-5. Of the children whose placement is known, 36% of the recommendations were for full integration and 49% were for self-contained classrooms with partial integration, which means that 85% were known to be referred for continuing education in spoken language environments.

One published research study needs to be mentioned, which was carried out on seven profoundly hearing impaired graduates of the McGill project (Ling, 1981a; Ling & Milne, 1981). Upon leaving the project, these children were fully integrated in regular classrooms, with supportive services provided by itinerant teachers from the Montreal Oral School for the Deaf. All of the children had attended the project for 3 years or more from the age of 18 months or less. Since the study began when the children were 6 to 12 years of age, the results obviously cannot be solely attributable to the children's enrollment in the project. But the data do provide support for the contention that an early intervention program providing an oral option (which for these children was initially the McGill project) can provide the type of help which will result in academically successful hearing-impaired children whose speech in many cases is just as intelligible (even for unfamiliar listeners) as that of their normally hearing peers.

DISCUSSION/SUMMARY

In spite of libraries full of publications classified as educational research, the surface has barely been scratched regarding issues surrounding learning and the educational process. And, in fact, generalizability of the results from much of that research is limited to carefully controlled situations or to selected abilities which have been isolated from the overall learning process (Mishler, 1979). Research on the spoken language, learning, and education of children with sensory handicaps such as hearing impairment, is proportionately less abundant. Furthermore, since prelingual and sensorineural hearing impairment is a relatively low-incidence handicap with widely varying resulting effects (presumably depending upon factors such as degree of hearing impairment, age of onset, early amplification and education, and the family situation), it becomes extremely difficult to draw together an adequate number of hearing-impaired subjects who are sufficiently similar to each other that standard, traditional research procedures are viable. In addition, when considering the quickly traversed and unrepeatable preschool years, the pressure of not wanting to lose precious time can make it difficult to assign children randomly to particular treatment groups for longitudinal studies. Probably one of the more useful solutions to this problem will come from application of ethnographic research procedures which are intended to derive an understanding of the learning process keeping social, physical, and linguistic contextual features intact (Pike, 1971).

In the meantime, educators are forced to make decisions based on incomplete research evidence, and on their own sense of what seems cogent for both general and particular situations. Obviously, there is no "one way" even to facilitate spoken language development in hearing-impaired infants and children. The McGill project's approach to intervention has evolved to the one detailed in this chapter through consideration of the cited research evidence from others and ourselves, and ultimately through what seems rational, workable, and humanistic. For example, the overall plan for intervention (assessment, goal selection, intervention, and progress evaluation) is one which the team agrees is logically sound and workable, particularly in the university training situation. In another situation where clarifying each step of the procedures in order to train someone else is not a factor, it may be less vital for the experienced and skillful teacher/clinician to operate in such an open-to-detailed-examination manner.

In summary, then, decisions regarding what seems cogent to the McGill project team are undoubtedly governed by our view of habilitation: that it has dynamic, synergistic, and process aspects which are all crucial. Habilitation is dynamic in that it is active, continuous, and energetic. It is synergistic in that it involves cooperative interactions such that the total effect is greater than the sum of the independent actions of the teacher/clinician, the parent, or the child. As a process, it is a whole course of gradual, mostly natural, changes and growth on the parts of everyone involved.

REFERENCES

Anderson, J. L. (1981). Training of supervisors in speech-language pathology and audiology. *American Speech-Language-Hearing Association, 23*(1), 77–82.

Bloom, L. (1973). *One word at a time: The use of single word utterances before speech.* The Hague: Mouton.

Bloom, L., & Lahey, M. (1978). *Language development and language disorders.* New York: Wiley.

Boehm, A. (1969). *Boehm Test of Basic Concepts.* New York: Psychological Corporation.

Bromwich, R. (1981). *Working with parents and infants.* Baltimore: University Park Press.

Bruner, J. (1975). The ontogenesis of speech acts. *Journal of Child Language, 2,* 1–19.

Bullowa, M. (Ed.). (1979). *Before speech: The beginnings of interpersonal communication.* Cambridge: Cambridge University Press.

Caracciolo, G. L., Rigrodsky, S. R., & Morrison, E. G. (1978). Rogerian orientation to the speech–language pathology supervisory relationship. *ASHA, 20,*(4), 286–289.

Carrow, E. (1973). *Test for auditory comprehension of language.* Austin, TX: Learning Concepts.

Cole, E. B., & Paterson, M. M. (1984). Assessment and treatment of phonologic disorders in the hearing impaired. In J. Costello (Ed.), *Speech disorders in children.* San Diego, CA: College-Hill Press.

Cole, E. B., & St. Clair-Stokes, J. (in press). Caregiver–child interactive behaviors: A videotape analysis procedure. *Volta Review.*

Dore, J. (1975). Holophrases, speech acts, and language universals. *Journal of Child Language, 2,* 21–40.

Dore, J., Gearhart, M., & Newman, D. (1978). The structure of nursery school conversation. In K. Nelson (Ed.), *Childrens language* (Vol. I). New York: Gardner Press.

Dunn, L. (1965). *Expanded manual: Peabody Picture Vocabulary Test.* Circle Pines, MN: American Guidance Service.

Freedle, R., & Lewis, M. (1977). Prelinguistic conversations. In M. Lewis & L. A. Rosenblum (Eds.), *Interaction, conversation and the development of language.* New York: Wiley.

Glover, M. E., Preminger, J. L., & Sanford, A. R. (1978). *Early learning accomplishment profile for developmentally young children: Birth to 36 months.* Winston-Salem, NC: Kaplan Press.

Hirsh, I. J. (1970). Auditory training. In H. Davis & S. Silverman (Eds.), *Hearing and deafness.* New York: Holt, Rinehart & Winston.

Huttenlocher, J. (1974). The origins of language comprehension. In R. Solso (Ed.), *Theories in cognitive psychology.* New York: Halsted Press.

Kretschmer, R. R., & Kretschmer, L. K. (1978). *Language development and intervention with the hearing-impaired.* Baltimore: University Park Press.

Ling, A. H. (1971). Changes in the abilities of deaf infants with training. *Journal of Communication Disorders, 3,* 267–279.

Ling, A. H. (1977). *Schedules of development in audition, speech, language and communication for hearing-impaired infants and their parents.* Washington, DC: The Alexander Graham Bell Association for the Deaf.

Ling, D. (1976). *Speech and the hearing-impaired child: Theory and practice.* Washington, DC: The Alexander Graham Bell Association for the Deaf.

Ling, D. (1978). Auditory coding and recoding. In M. Ross & T. Giolas (Eds.), *Auditory management of hearing-impaired children.* Baltimore: University Park Press.

Ling, D. (1981a). Early speech development. In G. T. Mencher & S. E. Gerber (Eds.), *Early management of hearing loss.* New York: Grune & Stratton.

Ling, D. (1981b). *The detection factor* [Videotape]. Instructional Communication Center, McGill University, Montreal, Canada.

Ling, D. (1981c). Keep your child within earshot. *Newsounds, 6,* 506.

Ling, D., & Ling, A. H. (1977). *Basic vocabulary and language thesaurus for hearing-impaired children.* Washington, DC: The Alexander Graham Bell Association for the Deaf.

Ling, D., & Ling, A. H. (1978). *Aural habilitation: The foundations of verbal learning in hearing-impaired children.* Washington, DC: The Alexander Graham Bell Association for the Deaf.

Ling, D., & Milne, M. (1981). The development of speech in hearing-impaired children. In F. Bess, B. A. Freeman, & J. S. Sinclair (Eds.), *Amplification in education.* Washington, DC: The Alexander Graham Bell Association for the Deaf.

Luterman, D. (1979). *Counseling parents of hearing-impaired children.* Boston: Little, Brown.

MacDonald, J. B., & Nickols, M. (1974). *Environmental Language Inventory manual.* Columbus: Ohio State University.

McCrea, E. S. (1979, November). *Supervisee self-exploration and four facilitative dimensions of supervisor behavior: Preliminary findings.* Presentation at ASHA, Atlanta, GA.

McLean, J. E., & Snyder-McLean, L. K. (1978). *A transactional approach to early language training.* Columbus, OH: Merrill.

Mishler, E. G. (1979). Meaning in context: Is there any other kind? *Harvard Educational Review, 49,* 1–19.

Moses, K. (1979). Parenting a hearing-impaired child. *Volta Review, 81,* 73–80.

Nelson, K. (1973). Structure and strategy in learning to talk. *Monographs of the Society for Research in Child Development, 38,* No. 149.

Oller, D. K. (1979). Infant vocalizations and the development of speech. *Allied Health and Behavioral Sciences, 1,* 523–549.

Pickett, J. M. (1980). *The sounds of speech communication.* Baltimore, MD: University Park Press.

Pike, K. L. (1971). *Language in relation to a unified theory of the structure of human behavior.* The Hague: Mouton.

Reynell, J. (1969). *Reynell Developmental Language Scales.* Windsor, England: N.F.E.R. Publishing Co.

Sanders, E. (1972). When are speech sounds learned? *Journal of Speech and Hearing Disorders, 37,* 55–63.

Sanford, A. R., & Zelman, J. G. (1981). *Learning accomplishment profile: A guide for individualizing educational programming (Age Range 36–72 Months).* Winston-Salem, NC: Kaplan Press.

Schaffer, H. R. (Ed.). (1977). *Studies in mother–infant interaction.* New York: Academic Press.

Snow, C. E., & Ferguson, C. A. (Eds.). (1977). *Talking to children.* Cambridge: Cambridge University Press.

Stark, R. E. (1978). Infant speech production and communication skills. *Allied Health and Behavioral Sciences, 1,* 131–151.

Streng, A. H. (1972). *Syntax, speech and hearing.* New York: Grune & Stratton.

Streng, A. H., Kretschmer, R. R., & Kretschmer, L. K. (1978). *Language learning and deafness.* New York: Grune & Stratton.

West, J., & Weber, J. (1974). A linguistic analysis of the morphemic and syntactic structures of a hard-of-hearing child. *Language and Speech, 17,* 68–79.

APPENDIX 4-A
Teacher/Clinician Evaluation Form

McGill University   School of Human Communication Disorders

Teacher/Clinician Evaluation Form

Check one:

☐ Self-Evaluation
☐ Cooperating teacher's/supervisor's evaluation

Student's Name: _____
Dates of practicum: _____
School; clinic; agency: _____
Cooperating teacher;
  supervisor: _____
Ages of children: _____
No. of children: _____
                  Observation: _____

Approximate
number of   Participation: _____
hours or
days of   Full-time
                       teaching: _____

EVALUATOR'S FRAME OF REFERENCE

In order for us to be aware of the frame of reference being used, we would appreciate your responding to the following question:

I am filling out this evaluation and describing this student (or myself) on the following basis: (Check one)

☐   the change which has occurred during the course of this practicum; or

☐   a comparison with other students at the same stage in the training program; or

☐   a comparison to performance by a skilled and experienced teacher (i.e., the goal)

☐   other:

EVALUATION PROCEDURE

The following is an outline of desirable skills and characteristics of a teacher of hearing-impaired children. You may use the outline in either of the following ways:

EITHER: (1) Rate performance (as applicable to this practicum experience) using the following scale:

1	2	3	4	5	6	7
	Very poor			Average		Outstanding

Explanatory comments are welcome

OR: (2) Use the outline as a reference list, and simply write a descriptive evaluation with regard to the items.

I.   **GENERAL PERFORMANCE**

_____   awareness of children's present level of cognitive/social/psychomotor/academic development;

_____   ability to plan appropriate education programs (including individual lessons within the overall curriculum, i.e., short- and long-term planning);

_____   selection of appropriate materials in accordance with present levels of functioning;

_____   well-organized, clear presentation of ideas, events or lessons;

_____   ability to adjust own language to the needs of the children;

_____   ability to stimulate talking by the children;

_____   awareness of children's understanding or lack of it;

_____   ability to modify lessons or techniques according to the children's responses and needs;

_____   ability to help children use information learned in structured practice sessions, in their spontaneous conversation, as appropriate;

_____   ability to maintain and interpret adequate records; report writing;

_____   ability to select, design, produce and/or utilize media, materials, and resources appropriate to lesson objectives.

II.   **EMPHASIS ON AUDITION**

_____   facility at hearing aid checking and troubleshooting;

_____   attention and reference to audiological information in determining appropriate sense modalities to use in speech and language instruction (including, especially, knowledge of auditory cues available to each child for speech and language targets);

_____   attention and reference to audiological information in considering appropriateness of child's amplification system;

_____   Ability to assess child's present listening ability through detection; discrimination, identification, and/or production of phonemes;

_____   knowledge of the sequence of auditory development;

_____   consistent focus on maximizing audition in scheduled speech and language teaching;

_____   consistent focus on maximizing audition in incidental learning situations;

_____   facility in use of techniques for encouraging listening by the child, as opposed to watching (e.g., sitting behind or beside the child, focusing on toys or activities, use of attentioning, phrasing, intonational contour, concealing lips, as appropriate).

III. **SPEECH TEACHING SKILLS**

_____   ability to evaluate speech learning needs of children from formal assessment, as well as from ongoing diagnostic learning/teaching events;

_____   ability to select speech targets;

_____   ability to plan speech lessons;

_____   range of techniques for eliciting new sounds;

_____   ability to adjust speech teaching activities/strategies in accordance with child's errors and sensory capabilities;

_____   provision for transfer of sounds from phonetic to phonologic levels of automaticity in both scheduled and incidental learning situations.

IV. **LANGUAGE TEACHING SKILLS**

_____   ability to assess language learning needs of children;

_____   ability to select language targets;

_____   ability to plan language lessons;

_____   flexibility of techniques for ensuring that children have comprehended;

_____   ability to "seize the moment" (as appropriate) for facilitating the child's language growth;

_____   provision for varied repetition of target language items in teacher-directed activities;

_____   appropriateness of correction/acceptance of child's productions in spontaneous conversation;

_____   ability to appropriately use modeling, expanding, prompting (etc.), techniques;

_____   provision for incorporation of learned language items into conversation.

V. **MANAGEMENT SKILLS**

_____   management of routines;

_____   flexibility to teach in both group and individual situations;

_____   behavior management.

VI. **RELATIONSHIP WITH PUPILS**

_____   warmth, enthusiasm, vitality;

_____   response of children to teacher.

VII. **RELATIONSHIP WITH PARENTS**

_____   sensitivity to their needs and capabilities;

_____   provision of information in a meaningful way;

_____   ability to elicit and encourage active participation by parents (as appropriate).

VIII. **PROFESSIONAL QUALITIES**

_____ self-evaluation;

_____ response to feedback;

_____ relationships with colleagues and other professionals.

IX. **OTHER COMMENTS**

Student and cooperating teacher or supervisor have discussed this evaluation.

Date:_____ Signed: _____

                                                    Student

                                       _____

                                       Cooperating teacher/supervisor

APPENDIX 4-B
Report Writing Guidelines

REPORT WRITING GUIDELINES
(1982–1983 E. Cole)

Child's Name: Degree of hearing loss:
Birthdate: Age detected:
Age: Age first wearing aid(s):
Parent's Name: Hearing Age:
Phone: Date of evaluation:
Address: Evaluator(s):

I. **BACKGROUND INFORMATION**

    A. A very brief paragraph including

        Etiology of loss (if known)

        Medical history (including other developmental delays or problems)

        Audiological history—age detected, by whom, age first wearing amplification; most recent test results; aids presently wearing

        Educational history—what programs has child been in; dates and names

    B. Reasons for present assessment

        Initial, periodic, end of year, etc.

        Special concerns of parents, teacher (as appropriate)

II.   **ASSESSMENT**

    A.   Audition

        1. Audiological test results
        2. Auditory behavior

    B.   Developmental: gross motor, fine motor, cognitive (as possible and useful), self-help, social–emotional, etc.

    C.   Communication

        1. Interactional aspects

            a. Caregiver's facilitating techniques
            b. Conversational constraints (as appropriate)
            c. Strategies for establishing joint attention—caregiver and infant
            d. Nature and function of comments—caregiver and infant

      2. Semantics

          a. Precursory cognitive/semantic/relational knowledge
          b. Semantic relationships and lexicon

             (1) One-word utterance (apparent) meanings

                semantic class
                word class

             (2) Multiple-word utterances
                conventional case grammar labels
                word counts or vocabulary tests (as useful)

      3. Syntax

          a. Mean length of utterance (MLU); Word/morpheme count; type–token ratio

          b. Sentence frame description

             (1) Modalities
             (2) Basic sentence patterns; expansions
             (3) Elaborated sentences—kinds; frequency

          c. Grammatical modulations

      4. Speech

          a. Vocalization development
          b. Phonologic; phonetic

III.   **SUMMARY**

As briefly as possible, outline findings in each area. The question to be dealt with in this section is: Is the aspect or skill within your expectations for this point in the child's development?

    1.
    2.
    3.
      (etc.)

IV.   **RECOMMENDATIONS**

1. Audiologic
2.
3.
  (etc.)

5
AN ACOUPEDIC PROGRAM

Doreen Pollack

AN ACOUPEDIC PROGRAM
The Development of an Acoupedic Program

The acoupedic program was developed as a program of educational audiology to meet the needs of those acoustically handicapped children whose hearing losses are detected in infancy.

As a result of technologic progress in the 1940s it became possible to test infants and fit them with appropriate, wearable hearing aids, thus creating the opportunity to try a different remedial approach to the problem of childhood deafness.

The author began a program in 1948 at Columbia Presbyterian Medical Center in New York City, under the direction of the late Dr. E. P. Fowler, Jr., and Mrs. Lorraine Amos Roblee. We had several goals: We wanted to develop a screening program for neonates, determine how soon hearing aids could be fitted, how hearing aids could be selected, and how infants could be educated to use their residual hearing. From the inception of this program it was recognized that parents would be partners in the process, and that our expectations for the children would change as a result of utilizing residual hearing, to the extent that our aim might be integrated rather than segregated education.

Audiologic evaluations using the psychogalvanometer (Hardy, 1965), which we soon discarded in favor of play conditioning and visible or edible reinforcements, showed that at least 95% of the children labeled "deaf" possessed residual hearing of varying degrees.

At this time, we assumed that it was possible to hang hearing aids upon the young child and continue to teach lip reading, but with a dependency on visual clues selection of hearing aids posed a problem. We began to structure the formal teaching so that the child was taught to depend on listening, processing, and responding to sound, and lip reading was deemphasized. The results were surprising to us, even though hearing aids did not supply adequate gain to the profoundly deaf at that time.

The program aroused the interest of the late Dr. Henk Huizing of Holland, who was engaged in research at Columbia Presbyterian in 1949–1950, and he suggested using a new term, *Acoupedics,* to differentiate this approach from traditional oral and auditory training. Dr. Huizing defined the new philosophy as "a process of integrating hearing in the deaf child's personality, with the ultimate goal of successful biosocial integration of the deaf in a normal environment" (Huizing, 1959).

The author moved to Denver, Colorado, in 1951, and developed programs in a number of different settings. The first one was initiated in 1952 in association with the University of Denver and the Denver Hearing Society, but this was transferred in 1957 to the Audiology Section of the University Speech and Hearing Department. The second program was begun in 1965 as part of the new Speech and Hearing Services of Porter Memorial Hospital in Denver. In addition, the author saw some patients in their homes, and was a part-time paedo-audiologist at the University of Colorado Medical Center (Pollack, 1974).

THE BASIC PRINCIPLES OF THE PROGRAM

During this period, eight basic principles for an acoupedic program* were formulated:

1. Early detection of hearing impairment: An ongoing audiologic assessment is begun at the earliest possible age, ideally in the newborn nursery.

2. Early fitting of hearing aids: Hearing aids are used as soon as the diagnosis of permanent hearing loss has been made, and they are selected after a period of diagnostic training. Binaural fitting is usually advocated.

3. A unisensory approach: Unisensory training is designed to develop hearing perceptions and integrate hearing into the child's personality. There is no formal teaching of lip reading to the infant.

4. A normal learning environment: A normal learning environment is created in which the child is bathed in sound and all his training is done in the meaningful context of his daily experiences.

*Copyrighted 1969

5. The use of an auditory feedback mechanism: Speech is learned through the child's auditory feedback mechanism and his innate reaction to echo all we say.

6. Development of language following normal patterns.

7. The parent as the first model of communication: This is accomplished by visits to a home, by observation and participation in the clinic, and by group meetings. Experienced parents are encouraged to volunteer their help to new parents in the program.

8. Individualized training: There is no grouping with other deaf children until it may become necessary for formal education. There are two reasons for this: (a) Speech is normally learned as a process of unconscious identification with the mother in a one-to-one relationship, and (b) normal behavior patterns develop from communication with normal-hearing people.

The Geographic Area Served

The program has served a wide geographic area because of lack of services outside the urban centers in Colorado. In the 1950s, families traveled to Denver, usually on a once-a-week basis, from four or five neighboring states. As late as 1975–1976, the Colorado State Department of Education reported very few preschool programs in Colorado, particularly in the rural or mountain communities. There were no statistics given for the 0–2 population, but among the 42 preschoolers served by public schools, 31 were in self-contained units, with 12 in residential facilities, 3 in resource rooms, and 8 served by itinerant personnel. It was estimated that 562 hearing-impaired children Ages 3–5 were not receiving an education.

Until the advent and local implementation of Public Law 94-142, hospitals and private agencies or universities provided most of the early intervention programs in Colorado.

The Numbers Served Since Inception

Approximately 100 children were served in the original program sponsored by the University of Denver, but most of them were seen for a short period of time, and went into special education school programs.

At Porter Hospital, 179 children were seen on a regular basis. In addition, a large number of families came for evaluation and intensive training from all over the United States and from other countries to stay in the LISTEN House for periods of time ranging from 1 week to 1 month. These families are not included in the statistics given under Results.

Age Range of the Children

The first Acoupedic cases seen in Denver were often not detected until their preschool years and their attendance ended with entrance into the local schools, sometimes within 1 year. A few of the families, however, chose to continue either privately or in the university clinic, and the results for this group were markedly better (see section on Results). Therefore, the Porter program was organized as an open-ended program and families received help from the child's early infancy until they chose, or were counseled, to terminate. The emphasis changed from parent guidance to child therapy and back again to parental support as the needs of the family changed. For example, crises often arose as the child entered new phases: entering school, changing schools, the teen years, and so on.

In general, children continued to attend the clinic through the junior high years, some for tutoring, others for speech refinement, but they were expected to work independently by the time they reached high school. Some reached this stage of independence in elementary school, at least in communication skill, and returned to the clinic only for annual reevaluations.

Age of Entry into Programs

The National Demographic Survey of 1975–1976 (published by Gallaudet College) showed that 93% of the hearing-impaired children in classes for the deaf were reported to have had their losses by the first birthday, and only 10% after the first birthday.

During that same period, an inspection of the children in the acoupedic program showed the following ages upon entry into the program:

TABLE 5-1

Before 1 year of age	4
Between 1 and 2	13
2 years	23
Between 2 and 3	11
By 4 years	4
Over four	11
Total	**66**

Nationally there is still a lag between suspicion of deafness and initiation of treatment, or confirmation of the loss. The national statistics of age of enrollment in special schools showed only 1.3% enrolled in programs by Age 3, with the numbers increasing to 60%

in the teen years. In acoupedics, the majority of children were enrolled in infancy with the numbers decreasing to 1.9% at Age 14.

The Degree of Hearing Loss of Children in Special Programs

Charts showing the percentages of children (from classes for the deaf) in each group of hearing loss—from normal to profound—do not vary significantly from one year to the next. 1975–1976 was a typical year.

TABLE 5-2. Degree of Hearing Loss of Children in the Acoupedic Program

	Acoupedic Program Percent	National Percent
Total known information	100.0	100.0
Normal (under 27 dB)	0.0	2.4
Mild (from 27 to 40 dB)	3.8	4.0
Moderate (from 41 to 55 dB)	5.7	8.2
Moderately severe (56 to 70 dB)	17.0	13.3
Severe (from 71 to 90 dB)	24.5	26.3
Profound (91 dB and above)	49.1	45.8

Etiology of Hearing Impairments

A majority of children are said to have deafness of genetic or viral etiology. Other causes are meningitis, prematurity, Rh incompatibility, birth trauma, and childhood illnesses. Following the 1964–1965 rubella epidemic, a large number of the hearing losses in the Acoupedic program were of rubella etiology. Recently, there has been a higher incidence of meningitis and cytomegalovirus deafness.

PROGRAM FUNDING

In the early years, private delivery of service involved the problem of financial support. Insurance coverage was very limited. Some families relied on donations from groups such as Lions, Kiwanis, and Red Feather agency (later called Mile High United Way). The Colorado State Department of Public Health provided partial payment for families who met their criteria for support under the Handicapped Children's program. The majority of parents paid their own fees.

The author found herself traveling along country roads at night trying to find the group which had requested a presentation about the program. She talked to anyone who would listen, from sororities to Girl Scouts. Donations were often "in kind" rather than in cash. We gladly accepted volunteers who cut out pictures, made decorations for the holidays, and so on. Eventually, the LISTEN Foundation assumed most of the responsibility for community presentations and fund raising, while the clinical staff presented papers at professional meetings.

While it is true that such a program in a private hospital can be expensive, it usually compares favorably with the costs of special education in the public schools. Residential education is, of course, even more expensive. A public school teacher may be responsible for a group of only five to eight children during the school year, may also have an aide, and work with other school personnel such as the speech pathologist, physical education teacher, school nurse, psychologist, and so on. In the clinic, each staff member worked with approximately seven families per day on an individual basis. Some of the children were seen two or more times a week for time periods ranging from 30 minutes to 2 hours. While this may not be the answer for all families, the results show that individual therapy and strong parent participation and commitment result in higher communication, educational, and social achievement levels, thus reducing cost to the community later on.

The LISTEN Foundation

In 1969, a group of parents (whose children had been seen in the Acoupedic program) and their friends formed an association which they named the LISTEN Foundation, to raise funds, to help young parents and to perpetuate the Acoupedic approach. At first their fund-raising efforts were modest: They sold fruit cakes and memberships in the organization. After the formation of an Auxiliary, there were radiothons, letter campaigns, ski days, art auctions, thrift sales, golf tournaments, and other major social events. Over the years the board of LISTEN included more representatives from the business community, and even the president of LISTEN was no longer chosen from the parent group. This increased the fund raising effort and brought in significant contributions from local foundations, but it had some disadvantages in that the lay community did not always fully appreciate, as did the parents who were board members, the effects of hearing loss and the ramifications of a program in a medical setting.

Without the tremendous efforts of LISTEN members, the program would have remained a small clinical service. Over the years they increased their budget and activities to include the following:

1. provision of fees for school visits and parent meetings for all families in the program;
2. payment of fees for speech and language services and for occupational therapy evaluations and remedial therapy to families who met the criteria for financial support;
3. payment of the salary of a family counselor whose services were free of charge to families in the program;
4. provision of traineeships in the clinic for teachers or audiologists. These varied in length from a few weeks to 9 months;
5. provision of annual introductory and advanced workshops for professional personnel, with graduate credit from the University of Northern Colorado;
6. payment of an annual donation to Porter Hospital in exchange for more room space. This area was named the LISTEN Acoupedic Center;
7. provision of a library of toys and books for parents.
8. distribution of pamphlet: *Does Your Baby Hear?* to hospitals and physicians around the state;
9. publication of a book for schools entitled, *They Do Belong* about mainstreaming;
10. purchase of a house close to the hospital which was used in two ways: (a) as a demonstration home, and (b) as a residence for families who came from out-of-town or out-of-state for evaluation and short term consultation;
11. purchase of equipment to be used in the clinic. (For example, an audiometer, a hearing aid analyzer, neonatal screener, loaner hearing aids, loaner FM units);
12. public education and awareness: LISTEN members gave presentations around the state and at national conventions, appeared on local television stations, and arranged interviews with local newspaper reporters;
13. financial assistance to staff members and parents so they could attend national conventions;
14. pay for a LISTEN Foundation executive director and office staff.

A number of other ideas were tried. Some were discarded, as for example, transportation assistance, and the "Auntie Mame" program in which volunteers spent time with a child to relieve the mother. Another was ECHO.

ECHO

During one period LISTEN sponsored an unusual group of our former graduates (all young adults or late teens) who felt that they could serve as models for the younger children, and especially those in their early teens, which is a difficult time socially for all children. They called the group ECHO, an acronym for "Enthusiasm and Concern for Helping Others."

ECHO was led primarily by Mark Fletcher (who later worked at the AGBAD headquarters in Washington and obtained a master's degree in Guidance and Counseling), and by Sherry Nieman (a graduate of the University of Northern Colorado and now the mother of four children). They organized many social activities with the idea of helping young teens become more independent out in the community. They also organized picnics and Christmas parties for clinic families. Later, they wanted to expand and serve as models for other young oral people who did not have the same communication skills.

The ECHO group served as a support group which gave an opportunity to young teenagers to "open up" and discuss their feelings about being a hearing-impaired person in a normal-hearing world, something they did not want to do with their parents or other normal-hearing adults at that time in their lives.

The group ended as the older graduates moved away, married, or became involved in careers. No other mature leaders came forward to take their places.

Other Professional Activities

Students from local universities served practicums at the clinic, and many visiting professionals observed for several days at a time.

The author, and sometimes other staff members, were invited to act as consultants or lecturers across the country. The author herself accepted 57 such assignments, in addition to a great deal of public speaking at local and national conferences, and she also served as an adjunct professor.

PHYSICAL PLANT IN THE HOSPITAL

In 1965, the author started a speech and hearing program at Porter Hospital in one room and on a part-time basis. As the program expanded, staff and space were added until the clinic offered a full range of services in a new wing on the ground floor of the hospital adjacent to the department of physical medicine, that is, to Occupational and Physical Therapy. (The clinic program continues, but in a new location on the hospital campus.)

A comprehensive array of services to both inpatients and outpatients was offered, including audiology, ENG, speech and language pathology, Acoupedics, and learning disabilities. Thus, the Acoupedic Program was part of a multidisciplinary service (see Figure 5-1).

The LISTEN Acoupedic Center

Space is at a premium in a medical setting, but the Acoupedic program continued to grow. The hospital board, therefore, agreed to allot additional space in return for an annual donation from the LISTEN Foundation.

The LISTEN Acoupedic Center for infants and preschoolers contained one large room used for meetings, videotaping, and other activities; a kitchen unit; a bathroom; two therapy rooms with observation windows; a storage room for equipment; and a small office which was sometimes used for therapy and sometimes as an office for students

FIGURE 5-1. Early Intervention for Hearing-Impaired Children

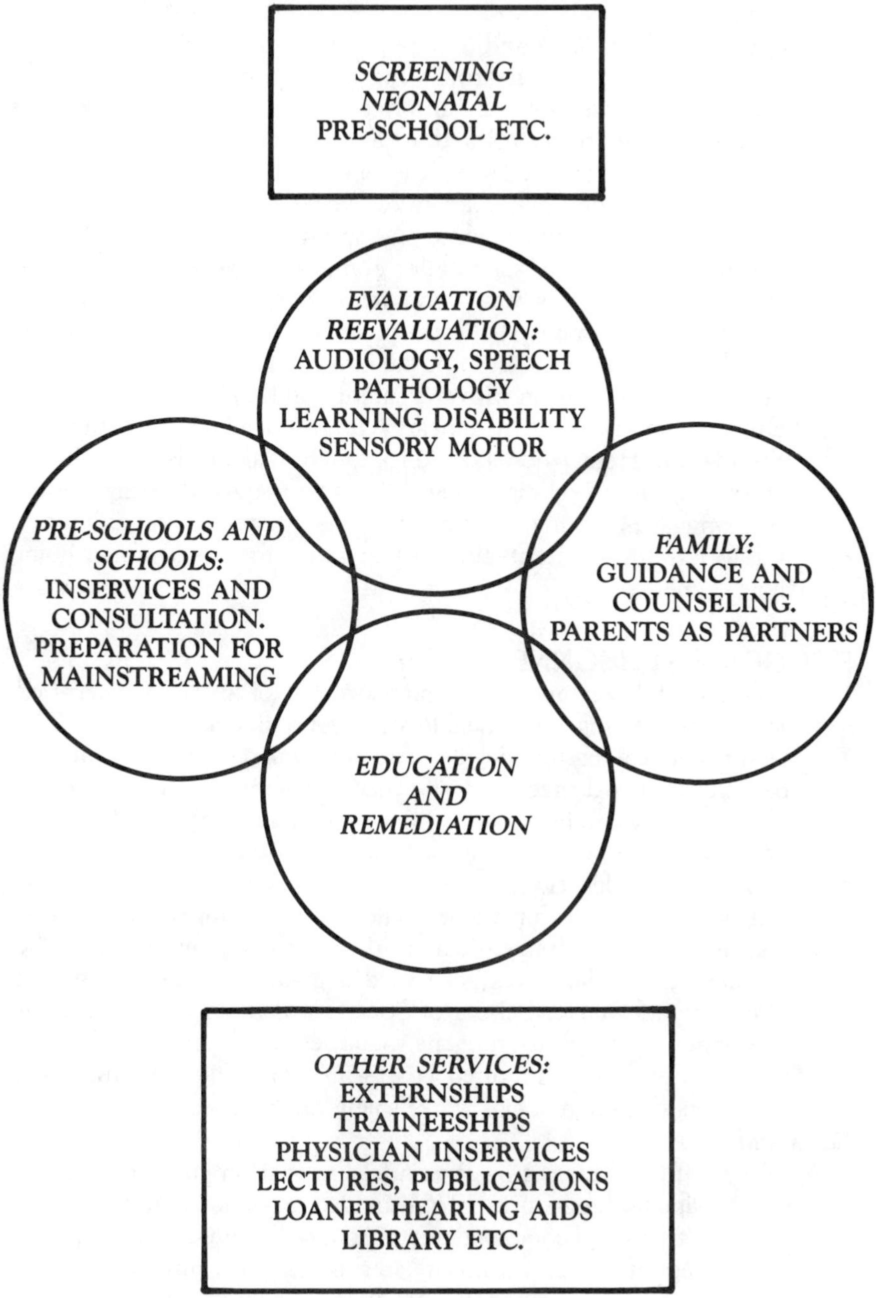

**SCREENING
NEONATAL
PRE-SCHOOL ETC.**

**EVALUATION
REEVALUATION:
AUDIOLOGY, SPEECH
PATHOLOGY
LEARNING DISABILITY
SENSORY MOTOR**

**PRE-SCHOOLS AND
SCHOOLS:
INSERVICES AND
CONSULTATION.
PREPARATION FOR
MAINSTREAMING**

**FAMILY:
GUIDANCE AND
COUNSELING.
PARENTS AS PARTNERS**

**EDUCATION
AND
REMEDIATION**

**OTHER SERVICES:
EXTERNSHIPS
TRAINEESHIPS
PHYSICIAN INSERVICES
LECTURES, PUBLICATIONS
LOANER HEARING AIDS
LIBRARY ETC.**

or trainees. In the large room was a piano and a library cupboard containing books and toys which the parents could take home.

The audiology suite and therapy rooms for older children were in the main speech and hearing wing across the hall. The LISTEN Foundation offices were in another part of the hospital as were additional meeting rooms and an auditorium.

The hospital is situated in a pleasant suburban campus, and we used the grounds for some of our activities: We took listening walks outside, we gathered rocks and flowers, and so on.

When the program was smaller home visits were also made, but as the city grew this was found to be very time-consuming and expensive. We learned to guide the parents in two ways: (1) by working together in a therapy session in the clinic, with part of each session devoted to conversation with the parents, and (2) by guiding parent–child communication in a nearby house owned by the LISTEN Foundation. Here, parents could fix lunch, make beds, wash dishes, and so on, with the clinician suggesting ways to use these daily routines as a language-learning experience. It was interesting and enlightening to watch the parent–child interaction in a more normal home environment.

PROGRAM PERSONNEL

Because the Acoupedic program was part of an *ASHA* certified speech and hearing clinic, qualifications for staff members met *ASHA* requirements: a master's degree in audiology and/or speech–language pathology, or a degree in deaf education with a CED certificate. Because of the emphasis placed on audiology, the majority of the staff had certification in audiology, with undergraduate degrees in speech pathology or education.

It was recognized that there would be a need for social services, and at first the hospital social worker donated some time to the Acoupedics families. Next, we used a graduate student from the University of Denver School of Social Work on a practicum basis and under the supervision of the social service department. Finally, the LISTEN Foundation hired a part-time family counselor (who had a master's degree in social work) solely for acoupedics.

Roles and Tasks

The Office of Education Personnel Preparation grant awarded to the Acoupedic Program in 1976 provided an opportunity to define the roles, tasks, and competencies of Acoupedic clinicians. Although the concept of acoupedics may seem theoretically simple, its success involved a broad and complex knowledge of human communication and interpersonal relationships. The roles which trainees were expected to fill were as follows:

1. Program developer: The tasks for this role include organization of early intervention programs adapted to a variety of settings, and the development of individualized prescriptive educational programs for children with a variety of problems.

2. Evaluator: This involves tasks of a wide range: conducting differential diagnostic evaluations and educational planning, both individually and as a member of an evaluation team; compiling data from audiologic, communication, perceptual, cognitive, and psychologic evaluations and writing reports which can be read to make recommendations for treatment.

3. Master teacher: The primary task of a master teacher is to provide high quality individual prescriptive programs designed around the principles of Acoupedics for children with communication and learning problems associated with a hearing impairment. However, teachers need to be cognizant of other teaching methods and philosophies, and of other programs in the area to which some children may be referred.

4. Parent Counselor: There are a number of tasks associated with parent guidance. First and foremost is to relate to parents in groups or individual sessions and so deal with parental feelings and the need for information. Through this positive and supportive relationship, the clinician helps parents live with a hearing-impaired child and create a learning environment within the home. The clinician demonstrates how to use and reinforce the skills developed in the therapy session. Parent guidance usually involves working with other community agencies, with social service personnel, family counselor, consultant psychologist, and with other organizations which offer support to families, such as the parent organization of Alexander Graham Bell Association, the LISTEN Foundation, and others.

5. Service Coordinator: The tasks for coordinating clinic services with other services and programs include learning how to structure an interdisciplinary service unit and how to communicate with medical personnel and school personnel. In the case of the Porter Hospital program, clinicians also worked with families who came from out of town or out of state to stay in the LISTEN House for consultations, and this service had to be coordinated with services available in families' home town or state.

6. Dissemination: Clinicians were expected to participate in, or conduct, inservice training, workshops, and so on; to share information

with professional colleagues and lay groups; to foster public awareness and work toward changing traditional attitudes. This involved
preparing materials, especially videotapes or publications.

Competencies

a. Academic competencies (primarily related to knowledge and skills):

1. Audiology

   Has basic knowledge of anatomy and physiology of hearing mechanism.

   Can organize an early detection project by using neonatal, infant, or preschool
   screening.

   Can follow up screening by completing case history and basic testing appropriate to
   child's age.

   If not an audiologist, knows when and where to make appropriate referrals.

   Understands audiology reports and can discuss them with family members.

   Understands the performance characteristics and maintenance of amplification devices,
   both individual and group, and how to "trouble shoot."

2. Parent–Family

   Can interview and orient family members to the program. Is a good listener and gains
   confidence of parents.

   Able to establish a good working relationship with family members to provide positive
   support and guidance for home program.

   Has the flexibility and creativity to adapt a program to meet family's individual needs
   and capabilities.

   Communicates evaluation results and recommendations in lay language.

   Is capable of supporting parents' work with their handicapped children by helping
   them to build the personal competencies necessary to stimulate and reinforce their
   children's normalized development.

   Can work with parent organizations and hold parent meetings.

   Is knowledgeable of community resources and knows when and where to refer families
   for appropriate services.

3. Child Development

   Has knowledge of normal child development: affective, social, sensorimotor, visual,
   auditory, cognitive, speech, language, and educational readiness.

   Uses a variety of child management and reinforcing techniques.

   Understands child motivation at different ages and stages of development.

4. Habilitation and Remediation

   Has knowledge of normal sequential development of auditory functioning, cognition,
   speech (or expressive language), receptive language, reading, and writing skills.

Can conduct an in-depth evaluation to determine levels of functioning in the areas listed above, and can produce a well-written report defining the problems and recommendations.

Can plan individualized prescriptive programs based on evaluation results and individual needs and abilities, to develop maximal use of an auditory function, to stimulate speech and language following the sequential stages of normal development, and to prepare the child for mainstreaming.

Has knowledge of other handicaps which frequently accompany hearing impairment (such as perceptuomotor problems, developmental lags, childhood aphasia, apraxia, dysarthria, learning disabilities, retardation, cerebral palsy, and other central nervous system dysfunctions).

Has differential diagnostic skills to evaluate the communication skills of the multi-handicapped, but knows when and where to make appropriate referrals for additional evaluations.

Is able to adapt and plan remediation programs for the multihandicapped hearing-impaired child.

Understands a team approach and coordinates program with that of associated disciplines, for example, social workers, classroom teacher, occupational therapist, psychologist, physical therapist, learning disability teacher.

Has knowledge of available materials, and can create own materials.

Capable of using media such as Language Masters, videotape, and so on.

5. Education

Has knowledge of different options and programs.

Keeps up with current literature and research.

Has knowledge of normal educational curriculum so that hearing-impaired child can be prepared for mainstreaming.

Can coordinate special programs with other programs: preschool, Head Start, normal kindergarten, and so on.

6. Administration

Can develop a program in different settings for children aged 0–6 with hearing impairment, and their parents.

Can devise a system of record keeping and reporting, so that progress can be measured and interpreted clearly to parents and to other personnel serving the child and family. Can use a problem-oriented record.

Has a system for data collection and retrieval.

Knows community resources and can work with community organizations for public awareness, fund raising, and so on.

b. Personal Competencies:

The complex responsibilities of a clinician in a parent–child program seem to appeal to those who have an openness to new ideas and the self-confidence to work with relative independence, together with the willingness to self-monitor.

The clinician has to be a person who has a genuine love of young children and can establish rapport with them and create excitement and eagerness for learning. The most successful person seems to be able to "look at the world" through a child's eyes, but is also able to relate easily to parents and professional colleagues.

One of the more important qualities is a positive attitude toward life and the ability to build a good self-concept in another person. Whatever the potential a child has, that child must feel good about himself *as he is*. This is also true of the parents so that they can grow into the role of helping their child and later assume the responsibility for working with the school system.

Patience, perseverance, a sense of humor, and good voice and speech are other personal competencies which are important. The best results stem from *continuity* for the family, which calls for maturity and commitment in the professional staff.

ENROLLMENT PROCEDURES
Referral Bases

There were never any selection criteria for entry into the Acoupedic Program. Because it was part of a hospital clinic, the majority of patients were referred by their physicians who expected that services would be provided. (In recent years, many families were referred by other agencies or by other families, but in every case the family physician was consulted.) Although Acoupedics was intended for infants or preschoolers, a number of older children were accepted for a modified program. (See Results and Case Histories.)

If there was a selection factor, it was that the decision to enroll in the program was made by the parents. During their first visit to the clinic the program was described in some detail, with emphasis upon the goals they wanted for their child and their responsibilities in habilitation. They were able to observe parent–infant sessions, and sometimes met with and discussed the program with parents already enrolled. They were then encouraged to visit other clinics in the city before making a second appointment. It was felt to be very important for parents to choose a program which met their needs and shared their goals.

Assessment Procedures

Assessment procedures were changed and expanded over the years. The children fell into three groups: (1) those whose audiologic and medical workups, and even hearing aid fittings, had been conducted in another center (sometimes in another state); (2) those children who were referred directly for an initial workup because of suspected loss; and (3) babies who were being followed as a result of our neonatal screening project.

Children in the first group were enrolled in the teaching program and were later reevaluated audiologically. In many cases, the hearing aid fitting had to be changed. Problems of audiologic management and errors of judgment have been described by Hanners (in Nix, 1977). She also had to change hearing aids prescribed by clinical audiologists who did not have a concomitant remedial program.

The second and third groups were enrolled for diagnostic teaching until the audiologic assessment and hearing aid fittings were completed.

The assessment period also included completing a case history and gathering information about the parent–child relationship, the child's cooperation in a structured situation, and other observations. Parent orientation was begun during this period including individual counseling and parent meetings. (See under Parents: Guidance and Counseling.)

Assessment procedures included a case history and some baseline communication testing, using the *Communicative Evaluation Chart* or the *Koontz Child Development Program* and the *Receptive-Emergent Language Scale* (REEL). These tests for young children did not usually yield much information about speech and language upon entry into the program because of the age and severity of the hearing loss, but they included a number of performance tests which indicated whether the patient was developing normally for his age in areas other than communication.

Ideally, if physical or sensorimotor deficits were found, the child was referred to the occupational therapist, but financial constraints sometimes delayed this evaluation.

Audiologic Evaluations

Since Acoupedics is a program of educational audiology and its success depends upon optimal use of residual hearing, early detection and audiologic management play a crucial role.

Neonatal Screening and Follow-up

The earliest possible detection is the first principle of Acoupedics. For some children, this meant a neonatal or infant screening.

The author has used a number of different instruments to accomplish screening beginning in New York in 1949, but at Porter's the nursery nurses were trained to use an instrument which produced a test tone involving a narrow band signal around 3000 Hz at 90 dB SPL, and also a white noise. The intensity level could be changed. Response categories were numbered 1–5, that is, ranging from no response to Moro's reflex, as described by Downs (in Northern & Downs, 1974). The audiologist retested those babies who did not show a 4 or 5 response. The best time to test neonates was found to be at least an hour before feeding when they were in a light sleep.

After the nursery at Porter's was closed, the neonatal project was continued at Swedish Medical Center, a sister hospital in the same area, where the High Risk Register was used in conjunction with screening with a 3000-cps tone. The "failures" were referred, together with those babies deemed at risk for hearing loss, to Porter's for continued follow-up.

Follow-up tests included a case history and repeated testing with the 3000-cps tone. The majority of babies passed this retest, but if not, warbled pure tones and the human voice (preferably the mother's voice) were used. In recent years, difficult-to-test babies were referred for brainstem testing (Mencher, 1981).

Babies who did not respond to tests in the soundproof suite were referred back to their physicians for further medical evaluation and approval of entry into the parent–infant program.

At risk babies who passed the preliminary test were followed and rechecked at regular intervals (usually 3–6 month intervals). Recheck visits included a standard audiologic battery.

For many years some mothers have reported that they observed better responses to sound in the early months of their babies' lives, and did not become concerned until close to, or after, the first birthday, or even until 18 months. Pollack has described a rubella baby who gave repeated Moro's reflex responses at birth, but developed a severe bilateral loss by 2 years of age. Some of the babies who were deemed at risk, because of an older sibling with a hearing loss, responded normally at birth and were found to have a permanent sensorineural loss by the first birthday or later. Thus, the mother's reporting is correct in many cases: infants do suffer from a progressive loss. On the other hand, when parents report concern to their physicians, they are often reassured or even called an "anxious mother."

Neonatal or infant screening was accompanied by an educational program which included: (1) talks to the medical staff to obtain their cooperation in setting up a program; (2) talks and demonstrations to the nursing staff and to the volunteers who assisted with the paper work; (3) talks to the general public, with use of film strips and movies; and (4) programs involving the local media.

In addition, pamphlets describing auditory and speech milestones were distributed to hospital patients and in doctor's offices. The educational program frequently brought in older infants who had never been tested before.

Audiologic Evaluations
a. Behavioral:

A routine battery used for young children included the following:

1. observation of responses in the sound-proof room to warbled pure tones and the human voice,
2. repetition of these tests monaurally through headphones,
3. the use of COR (Suzuki & Ogiba, 1961) or other visual conditioning strategies after 6 months of age, and
4. play conditioning (Pollack, 1970) around 2 years of age.

When speech and language developed, formal speech tests were added to the test battery. These included:

1. *A speech reception test:* At first, vocal sounds were used, as for example, "meow" for a cat; later words and toys representing spondees such as baby, doggie, mama; and finally, a standardized list (airplane, baseball, etc.).

2. *A discrimination test:* At first, one-syllable words known to the child and depicted on picture cards such as shoe, blue, mouth, house, cat, hat were spoken at levels at least 25–40 dB louder than the SRT level. As the child's vocabulary increased, the WIPI (Ross & Lerman, 1970) was the test of choice.

All tests were administered both binaurally and monaurally in the aided and unaided condition. Testing was not always completed in one session, but we found that the attention span was extended with the use of small, edible rewards placed beside the toys or pictures.

b. Nonbehavioral Tests

1. Acoustic Impedance

   The most frequently used nonbehavioral test was the *Acoustic Impedance test* (Fria, 1983) used to check the integrity of the conductive system and the locus of the hearing loss. It is known that perhaps 60% of all children have incidents of otitis media by 2 years of age (Howie, et al., 1975) and unfortunately the majority of hearing-impaired infants are not spared this additional problem. Because a conductive loss added to the sensorineural loss frequently took our patients "off the air" prompt referral for medical treatment and constant monitoring was critical.

2.   Electrophysiologic tests

Some of the difficult-to-test children were referred to another center for electrophysiologic tests. These included: brainstem audiometry (Finitzo-Hieber, 1982); electric response audiometry (Brackmann, 1977).

THE PARENT-INFANT PROGRAM
Diagnostic Therapy

Once a child was enrolled in diagnostic therapy sessions, earmolds were made and a loaner aid was taken home. It was found to be important to allot a certain amount of time for experience with amplification before hearing aids were selected. Many babies with a profound loss, who had never before responded to sound, began to show awareness and response. After a short time the original behavioral tests were repeated and the hearing aids selected. The optimum time period was a month, but in cases for which financial assistance had to be processed, it was sometimes as long as 3 months.

After purchase, the aids were checked on an analyzer for volume, frequency response curve, and distortion. Not all new aids were found to perform according to manufacturer's specifications.

Body aids were usually fitted for the severe to profound losses, because they provided a higher SSPL (maximum power), fewer feedback problems, were less prone to damage and loss, and gave better results for distance hearing and noisy environments. As the children grew older, ear level aids were selected. The atresic children (those with abnormal outer ears and canals) wore bone conduction aids.

Earmolds

Impressions for earmolds were also made in the clinic. Different materials and manufacturers were tried. The simplest earmold was made of Adcomold, which could be coated, drilled, and then used as the actual mold.

The Audiologic Reassessment Program

Each child's audiologic assessment was repeated at regular intervals: from 3–6 months during the first year, and then at annual intervals. However, retesting usually took place at more frequent intervals, that is, at any time the parent or clinician reported concern because of a change in the child's responses, as, for example, after a bout of otitis (ear infection). Rechecking of the hearing aid performance was also conducted at regular intervals and especially when a child's responses changed, or after the hearing aid had been repaired.

Progressive Loss

When children are followed for a number of years, it is apparent that at least 50% of them show no significant change regardless of the power output of their hearing aids. Varying numbers do show evidence of progressive loss, depending upon the length of time they are followed. For example, many of the rubella children retained the same configuration in one ear, but suffered a progressive loss in the other ear until it became a typical "left corner" audiogram. Some of the postmeningitic children and those with genetic losses also had progressive deafness. Recently, more sophisticated polytomograms revealed deformities of cochlear structure associated with a form of hydrops, as in the Mondini syndrome. These children were fitted with a shunt in the hope of stabilizing the loss and preventing further deterioration (Arenberg, 1979).

Some audiologists have stated that high power hearing aids cause progressive loss. This may be true in certain cases, but does not explain why so many children we have followed for 20 years have shown no change in spite of wearing power aids. It does, however, underscore the need for ongoing audiologic management and rigorous reassessment. In the survey conducted on 80 of the children who had attended the Porter Hospital Acoupedic Program, 59 parents reported that their children had suffered no additional significant loss of hearing.

TREATMENT PROCEDURES

The treatment program following audiologic assessment, hearing aid fitting and diagnostic therapy, included three main components: (1) a parent guidance and counseling program; (2) a program for auditory, speech, and language development following a normal sequence, which was often accompanied by an occupational therapy program for sensorimotor integration; and (3) an evaluation component.

Parent Guidance and Counseling: Informal and Formal

Since 90% of all children with a hearing loss have two normal-hearing parents, a diagnosis of deafness is always a traumatic experience, and parents cannot participate effectively in the habilitative process until their feelings have been facilitated. Parents, however, react differently to the diagnosis: some weep bitter tears, some go to different doctors seeking a "cure," and others are relieved that the problem is not mental retardation or whatever they thought it might be. For many of them, the early testing and medical diagnosis is an experience which causes unnecessarily severe and bitter feelings. One parent wrote the following:

> We started taking V- to doctors and hearing tests at the age of 3 weeks. After many doctors and many tests down the road for 2 years, we finally came to the Acoupedic Program. You took so much time to make her feel comfortable, no one else took the time you did, in fact they instilled a lot of fear in her. Consistently, all the other people thought and some actually told me, that I was a fanatically neurotic first-time mother who insisted on having something wrong with her child."

From the very first audiology visit, when they are helped to accept the diagnosis of hearing loss and to leave with hope that much can be done in remediation, parents play the most important role as partners in the acoupedic program. This requires ongoing support which may be given informally or formally, individually or in a group, or as part of the child's session.

Counseling

a. **Informal Counseling.** Each time the child attended for treatment, the parent was asked, "How did it go this week?" Sometimes it was necessary to say: "You are looking a little down—do you want to talk about it?" A clinician has to be ready to facilitate feelings, and to be sensitive to the need for more formal counseling.

We tried to send the parent away on an "up" note. Even after a stormy or otherwise difficult session, it was possible to point out something positive about the child's responses or behaviors. Many parents who had been to other programs told us that special education personnel or medical personnel emphasized what the child could *not* do because of the disability, and they always had negative feelings afterwards.

One of the program's graduates, now a wife and mother herself, wrote the following:

"When SF, MF, SH, SR, and I enrolled in the Acoupedic Program, Mrs. Pollack was just starting it. Our parents had to put a lot of faith in her because they didn't have any idea how it would turn out. She was able to build up their confidence and patience so that they could work with us on a day-by-day basis. I can still remember the scrapbook with the cut-out pictures. I think I will remember it when I am 80 years old!"

Teaching patience and giving encouragement are an integral part of an Acoupedic approach. But it is not always an easy relationship. Some parents transfer their anger and frustration onto the clinician, and sometimes a parent is so overwhelmed by the responsibility that she is not ready to assume her partnership role. Most parents *grow* into the role.

    b. Formal counseling. In every Acoupedic program the team has included a social worker or psychologist. At the University of Denver, Dr. Esther Shapiro, a psychologist, saw the parents for an individual session approximately 1 hour every 2 weeks. The sessions served many purposes, but in particular, a chance for the mother to talk about how difficult it was to have a hearing-impaired child. Topics ranged from toilet training, grievances about relatives, to concern about discipline and so on. The counselor was, in fact, helping parents work through the grieving process which accompanies the loss of their dream of having a perfect child (Moses & Van Hecke Wulatin, 1981). By the third quarter, not one mother requested appointments, but there were impromptu meetings.

    When the program was started at Porter Hospital, the social service staff was helpful but did not have time to undertake individual counseling. A graduate student from the University of Denver School of Social Work was therefore assigned for his practicum to speech and hearing. He offered his services to all families in the Acoupedic Program, sometimes visiting them at home and sometimes seeing them when they came to the clinic. For one family, he became a "Big Brother" to the normal-hearing son who was developing behavior problems as he competed for attention with two younger, hearing-impaired brothers.

    Eventually, the LISTEN Foundation funded a part-time family counselor solely for Acoupedic families, who were either referred by the clinician, or who could refer themselves, for problems which had to be related to having a hearing-impaired child. For longstanding problems, such as alcoholism, the family was referred to other centers or other private practitioners. In recent years many more families were found to have serious problems, including drug addiction, divorce, financial mismanagement, and so on. Some attempts were made to set up regular group counseling for parents with similar needs, as, for example, single parents, but scheduling proved to be very difficult, especially for families who traveled long distances. The most successful groups were those for siblings who related their mixed feelings about having a hearing-impaired child in the family, and who seemed to be able to give each other much needed support.

    Hearing-impaired children were also seen for individual counseling and play therapy as indicated. One mother wrote the following:

> One part of S's program that we feel contributed greatly to his accomplishments, in addition to the support and therapy in his earlier years, was the program added during his preteen

years. Working with Barbara MacDonald (the family counselor) in building his self-image and setting his standards and ideals for himself as a person. This part of his education was perhaps more valuable in those years than the academic therapy he received: a *must* for his being a total person.

Parent Education Meetings

There is no question that a group can be highly supportive, and all parents were encouraged to attend parent meetings which were usually held once a month in the evenings, or sometimes in the daytime while children were in therapy. But not all parents like groups, and in general it was the successful and committed ones who attended evening meetings to which they even brought their friends and relatives.

Parent meetings were sometimes conducted by the program director or another clinician, and sometimes by guest speakers, as for example, an otologist, local school personnel, visiting speakers sponsored by the Alexander Graham Bell Association, or by some of our older graduates and their parents. Videotapes and films were also used.

The content of the meetings varied according to the needs of the group, but usually included the following topics:

a.   orientation to the program,

b.   normal hearing, causation of hearing loss and the measurement of hearing loss (parents tested their own hearing and charted an audiogram),

c.   how hearing aids are selected and maintained. What an aid can and cannot do,

d.   how a listening function develops,

e.   how speech and language develop,

f.   how a hearing loss affects social and emotional health,

g.   how a hearing loss affects family life,

h.   the local educational options and the attitude of the community,

i.   legal rights of families and children.

A variety of approaches were used, from "lectures" to round-table discussions. Parents always enjoyed the strategies described by Luterman (1979), such as hypothetical families, role playing, and so on.

Over the years, after completion of the formal meetings, some parents attempted to continue groups in their homes or other meeting places. These parent-run groups did not seem to exist for any length of time, perhaps because of the emotional level generated which caused problems when it was not channeled into positive directions by a professional (who not only contributed information but did not generalize from one example as families were inclined to do). On the other hand, a parent-organized group in Canada, *Voice for the Hearing-Impaired*, has been extremely successful. The LISTEN Foundation, which began as a parent-organized group, has not assumed responsibility for informal parent group meetings. We were always pleased when parents moved on to help other parents, either by visiting new parents, or by becoming members of the auxiliary or board of the LISTEN Foundation.

Parents as Partners in Therapy

Unless we encountered an "out-of-control" child who needed to be removed temporarily from a parent in the clinic until the behavior was modified, parents (and sometimes siblings) were present in the therapy room during the early years. Usually, it took only one or two sessions for the child to realize that the adult was "the boss" and could not be manipulated or controlled. These were extremely stormy sessions but resulted in a complete change in the child's cooperation.

As the clinician demonstrated how to develop audition, speech, and language in a play situation that was highly motivating to a young child, family members present were encouraged to participate and gradually to take over an activity. There was constant interaction and conversation between parent and clinician, with the clinician explaining at times, or developing a parent's observational skills at other times. At the end of the session, ideas were presented for introducing and practicing new skills in their daily lives.

Many parents also kept daily diaries, noting the progress, or lack of it, or writing down questions and concerns as they came to mind. Their observations were very helpful in planning sessions. The partnership also included directives from the parents as Harris & Pollack (1979) said, "I was allowed to be heard, I was allowed to argue, I was allowed to question. I loved the idea of having a teacher accessible to my feelings and doubts and to hear me."

Parents' interaction with their children was also guided in the LISTEN demonstration home and occasionally in their own homes. Some parents are natural speech and language teachers, but the majority had to grow into the role of modeling, expanding, and verbalizing. They all had to learn how to gain better eye contact, and how to reestablish vocal and other playful interaction, or how to talk in short sentences and in well-inflected voices close to the hearing aids. But above all, we helped them to see their child as a child first and foremost, and not as a "deaf child." This is a lesson which reoccurs in the teen years when parents tend to blame many normal teen problems on the hearing loss.

Problems in Partnership with Parents

Can all parents act as partners? I do not think so. We had our share of parents who are still hoping for a cure and who did not follow through; who came to the clinic with broken aids or dead batteries; who were always late for appointments, or who never dealt with their child's behavior problems effectively, that is, never set consistent limits. We had parents who had so many other problems in their lives that they could not cope with the hearing impairment, and others who simply did not give enough conversational input. We dealt with all kinds of problems with the help of the family counselor. If all else failed, we had to encourage those families to seek a program where parent participation was not considered essential and where the child was seen daily in a formal group situation, as in the public schools.

Another type of parent who naturally had difficulty in an Acoupedic Program was the parent with an unaided, profound hearing loss, or the manual deaf parent. In these cases, which were infrequent because the adult deaf more typically sought help from the State School for the Deaf, we were able to arrange for the child to spend a great deal of time with a normal-hearing relative or in a Head Start program.

Factors for Success with Parents as Partners

The excellent response to the survey questionnaire (see section on Results) illustrates the responsibility felt by parents in an Acoupedic Program. One might wonder how this came about.

First might be the fact that parents chose to bring their children to the Acoupedic Program, knowing from the orientation that it would involve a great deal of responsibility on their part, although the *full* impact on their family life probably dawned quite slowly. The parents who could not, or would not, accept that responsibility and who wished for the problem to be solved by someone else, either left the program early or never enrolled.

Second, perhaps, was the fact that the program was individualized. The clinicians were giving 100% to that parent, listening to problems and helping find solutions. This was a parent-centered as well as child-centered program.

Third, during most of the years that the Acoupedic Program was at the University of Denver and at Porter Hospital, parents were not pressured by public and professional opinion to place their children in a sign language program, nor were they confused by different philosophies, even though there has always been controversy.

Fourth, the majority of our families stayed together as family units, a situation which changed dramatically in the last 5 years when few of the children lived with two parents.

Last, the graduates of our program and their parents served as models of what could be accomplished, giving the younger parents a long-term view.

It must be emphasized that good parenting was *not* a factor of income or education level. Because of the financial help available, the Acoupedic Program included a cross-section of the community.

THE CHILD-CENTERED CURRICULUM:
A DEVELOPMENTAL APPROACH

Since audition is central to learning spoken language, the curriculum for every child is based on sequential stages for normal development of hearing, speech, and language. Although these are interdependent, there are definable "milestones" which occur for a normal-hearing infant and which form the foundation for future learning. These skills, once gained, become more and more sophisticated as the child grows, sometimes in a circular (expanding) fashion, and sometimes in a spiral (leading to more difficult tasks).

At the same time, a child is also developing in other areas: motorically, cognitively, and socially, areas to which audition contribute important information.

Young children with hearing impairments differ in their rate of development to the extent that an individualized plan is essential. The "curriculum," then, is rather a flexible description of goals with strategies, and evaluation tools used to attain these goals.

The first goal is *awareness of the presence or absence of sound.* A normal-hearing infant becomes aware of sound even before birth, but from the moment of birth when his first cries bring his caretaker to him, he realizes that sound is used for communication. A severe to profoundly deaf infant usually shows little or no awareness of sound because it is meaningless and unimportant to him. Infants with lesser degrees of loss may also inhibit sound because it is not a *consistent* avenue of information. Allied with this is the fact that once parents realize that their child has a defect, they do not treat him in the same manner: They do not draw his attention to sound, nor expect him to respond. They may even stop talking to him.

The first remedial procedure is to create a learning environment in which we can teach awareness of sound. There are three important steps in this strategy: (1) to focus the child's attention upon a sound stimulus by showing him that other people hear something and respond to it; (2) to reward this attention by showing him the source or meaning of the sound; and (3) to encourage imitation of the activity which produced the sound, or to encourage imitation of the sound heard.

This is accomplished by an adult making a low-pitched, loud sound several times *out of the child's line of vision* but close to the hearing aids (as, for example, under the high chair); holding his hand over his ears and saying with a very pleased, alert expression: "I hear that. What's that?" The noisemaker is then shown to the child who is encouraged to make the sound himself to elicit a reaction from the family members present. The adult should alternate "I hear that" with "I don't hear that," shaking his head.

Although it is best to begin with loud sounds, different sounds should be used as soon as possible, such as high-pitched sounds, quieter sounds, noisy versus musical sounds, and so on.

The parent's assignment is to develop a listening environment at home, by demonstrating to the child that she hears the water running, the dog barking, and by showing him the source of the sounds. If these sounds are not made meaningful for the child he will ignore them.

At the same time, family members are reminded to talk naturally about everything that the baby is experiencing; in other words, to behave as if he is hearing, which he is—through his aids. This is not easy for most families because a severely impaired child gives little or no feedback at first.

Localization

As soon as it is apparent that the infant is aware of sounds, the next goal is *Localization*. An intact baby will develop an orienting reflex which forms the basis for a conditioned reflex (Luria, 1973). In other words, after thinking "I hear that," he wonders, "Where is it coming from?"

In the case of a severely impaired infant it is usually necessary for an adult to make a sound at one side, and out of the line of vision, and to gently turn the child's head in the right direction to locate the source of the sound. Then the location of the sound is changed to different parts of the room and even outside the room. Noisemakers and the human voice are used. The parent's home assignment is to expect the child to turn and look for a sound, and to repeat the stimulus until he does turn, rather than trying to attract his attention visually or by touching him. At the same time, the infant is taught to respond appropriately to many sounds as, for example, turning when his name is called, opening the door when someone knocks, dancing to music, and so on. An older infant delights in crawling around to find a hidden music box or a family member who has hidden and is calling his name.

Development of Distance Hearing

As soon as a child responds at close range, he is moved further from the source of the sound, or the sound is moved further from the child. Although some children have only a limited range, they should be given every opportunity to develop that range. Parents have often reported how surprised they were when a "deaf" child responded to the baby's cry upstairs, or turned at being called from a distance of 50 feet. As in every other phase of the program it is important not to place limits upon a child's learning.

Development of Discrimination

A normal-hearing child experiences hundreds of hours of listening before he begins to develop language. As he listens, he begins to discriminate between many different sounds. For example, he recognizes the voice of his caretaker by 6 weeks and is usually quieted by it. Eilers and colleagues (1975) found that babies between 3 and 6 months of age could be conditioned to respond differently to consonants, and Eisenberg (1976) demonstrated that infants respond differently to sounds on the basis of frequency, intensity, and stimulus dimensionality from an early age.

One of the games played to encourage discrimination is to place two of the noisemakers on a table. The child sits with his back to the table and has to decide which sound he has heard. In everyday life, he will indicate his discriminatory ability by opening the back door when he hears the dog scratching or barking, or by appearing excited when his father's car or the train whistle is heard. Eventually all children lose interest in, or habituate to, familiar sounds unless they are especially motivating, and thus they begin to inhibit background noise to focus on conversation. However, it is always wise to check a hearing-impaired child's awareness of environmental sounds. In this way, the infant is learning not only that he lives in a world that is full of sound and that sounds are meaningful and fun, but he is laying the foundation for communicating with sounds.

Vocal Play

The next milestone is vocal play. Even during the early weeks of life, adults and babies play at reciprocal vocalization, that is, a mother may echo back the sounds her baby makes and the baby responds by vocalizing to her. Normal babies also do a great deal of shouting, grunting, blowing raspberries, and so on, followed by months of babbling and lalling, usually with an object in their mouths. The voice of a young deaf child retains a more natural quality if aids are fitted at an early age, but strategies are needed to encourage vocalization and to develop prelinguistic skills.

Hearing-impaired infants also need a long period of vocal play. During this time, adults use a high-pitched, sing-song type of voice with rising inflections. Each family invents its own vocal games in addition to those widely known, such as pattycake or peekaboo. Some infants love to ride on a parent's back while the parent sings "Yankee Doodle," others love to be bounced on a knee to rhymes, or pretend to be scared when brother becomes a growling bear. If, however, they do not enter a program until close to school age, the activities have to be relevant to their age and interests. Humming on a kazoo is an excellent way to vocalize and develop breath control, puppets can be used for pitch change, and so on.

Strategies for vocal play include lots of play with toys for which the adult makes a consistent sound: For example, a car is accompanied by lip trilling (brbrbr) or beep-beep, an airplane by humming, and a bird by whistling. A toy flute is imitated by a high voice, a duck by a low quack-quack. The voice can be varied in pitch, intensity, and rhythm during vocal games. Older infants enjoy looking at picture books for which the same sounds can be made, "Look, there's a kitty cat. Meow, meow, I hear that kitty cat."

Auditory Schema

The next goal is to develop auditory schema for phonemes, leading to babbling and lalling. We begin with long vowels and diphthongs, AH, OO, OH, and OW, because they involve lower frequencies and are louder. We say them through plastic circles before we drop them onto a pole, or through rings of play dough we have made, or through cardboard tubes. Parents can introduce them into play at home: AH—— while stroking, OH—— while bubbles are floating to the floor, or OOOOO when the family marches through the house pretending to be a train.

To encourage vocalized imitation on the part of the child, we use the "hand strategy." The clinician makes a sound behind her hand. She places her hand in front of the parent's mouth for the parent to imitate the sound. Then the parent places a hand in front of the child's mouth to indicate that he should make the same sound. Once a child realizes that he is expected to imitate and will be praised, hugged, or otherwise rewarded for imitation, the hand strategy can be used occasionally to encourage more correct imitation, but it should not be overused. Young children are naturally imitative if they are enjoying an activity and feel comfortable with the person who is playing with them.

Other vowels will be learned spontaneously as part of an activity, as for example, "u" in *up* when building blocks, or "oo" when saying *pull* and *push* when playing with a toy wagon or popbeads.

The first consonants normally acquired during the first 2 years are the voiced phonemes: w, m, b, n, d, and g, and the voiceless h, p, t, and k. We stimulate them by associating them with a specific toy with which we are playing as for example:

b b b b b, as we push a toy motorbike across the table,
w w w w, as we wind up a musical clock or mechanical rabbit,
h h h h h, for a panting dog, and
p p p p p, for a toy sail boat.

We usually direct the parent to play with one sound for approximately 2 weeks. If it is not imitated by this time, another phoneme is selected for the next 2 weeks. Parents can incorporate babbling whenever they are playing with their baby, as, for example, playing with his toes and saying bbbbb for each toe. The parent has to be reminded that although a child with a hearing loss is programmed like a normal-hearing child (unless proved otherwise) to store what he hears until he is ready to use it, the deaf child may be slower to feed back what he has heard, and one should not become discouraged. He has to "make up" for lost time—the time before his aids were fitted, that is, his *hearing age* is not the same as his *chronological age*.

At the same time, depending on the age and motor skill development, we incorporate other activities to encourage prelinguistic skills such as suckling, blowing, moving the tongue around, and so on. As soon as a baby can blow, the high-frequency voiceless phonemes are introduced: we whisper kkkkk as we cut, ttttt for a toy clock or a galloping horse. When introducing words containing these sounds, such as *hot* or *cup*, it is well to whisper the whole word first so that the strong voiced components do not mask out the voiceless ones. Amplified whisper is quite loud and has excellent clarity.

Auditory Feedback and Feedforward

As a result of these activities, the infant begins to develop an auditory feedback loop whereby he monitors his own vocal and speech production to match those which are entering his ears through his aids. He appears to form a strong association between the auditory impressions and the movements which produce them.

It has long been assumed that a deaf baby cannot do this but has to depend upon visual or tactile cues. Again, this is a case in which the young deaf child does not know he is deaf and is not supposed to be able to do it, but will try to do everything he is given the opportunity to learn. He can accomplish this because modern hearing aids improve his threshold to the level of a conversational or even a quiet voice. Thus, he reaches the stage of *echolalia* just as a normal-hearing baby does, and in this way the foundation for imitating words and sentences is laid and the child is free to learn from everyone, wherever he goes.

Functional Words

As soon as a baby begins to babble a specific sound, the adult introduces a word beginning with that phoneme. For example, if he can hum *mmmmm* for the airplane, he is encouraged to say *more* at meal times, or to call *mama*; and if he can babble bbbbb, he can be expected to say *bye-bye*. These we call functional words and they are usually the first words attempted because they are often associated with gestures.

At this point, an evaluation of progress is important. If an infant is beginning to imitate, does he seem to hear the rhythm, that is, the number of syllables in bye-bye and mama? If he makes no attempt to imitate or does not seem to understand natural gestures, further testing in other areas of his development may be advisable.

The time frame for each child will vary from 6 months to a year for these early listening skills. Most teachers, however, seem to give up too quickly, whereas an experienced clinician knows that a great deal of input is necessary before a rather small amount of feedback is forthcoming. Progress also occurs in spurts: after a step forward, new information must be taken in before a new step forward is observed. Therefore, there will be many plateaus. Sometimes the child seems to regress before progressing because the new information causes disorganization before it is integrated with information already acquired and internalized. Eventually progress accelerates as a broader base of information is built up. In short, as much time as possible should be given to a preschooler to learn auditorily, but progress should be measurable or the program will have to be modified.

Symbolic Language: Auditory Processing

It is determined that a hearing-impaired child is ready to learn symbolic language when he can do the following: (1) indicate that he associates a sound with an object, that he is picking up the toy dog when an adult "barks," or the bird when she whistles, (2) recall and produce the correct sound for an object spontaneously, (3) use a few functional words, such as *bye-bye* or *no*, and (4) use vocalization (a sort of jargon) for communication.

After approximately 1 year of listening, a normal hearing child begins to understand that a "pattern of sounds" in a particular sequence indicates what he sees, touches, feels, and wants. Usually understanding occurs as a result of a great deal of repetition in a routine situation, such as, "pick up your toys," although the word *toys* may not be understood in any other context.

Although children with moderate to severe loses sometimes reach this stage naturally, we usually have to help severe to profoundly impaired infants by pointing deliberately to an object or person and asking, "What's that?" or "Who's that?" Then we supply the noun, "That's ____ ." Parents follow through by stressing that noun as often as possible during the next week, by playing with toys, by cutting out and hanging up pictures, and so on. The following week, a new noun is chosen. After several weeks, most children realize that people and things have names, and they begin to acquire symbolic language in a natural manner. For example, verbs are acquired during activities: we *push* the chair around; we *wash* the car; we *stir* the soup: it is hot, so we *blow* it.

New words are learned in units, with a core of words which can be used in the daily routine and around which vocabulary is gradually expanded. For example, in playing with dolls, a youngster may learn *eye, wash, all wet, sh! go nightnight;* in playing with cars, the words *car, drive, go,* and *stop.*

When Children Do Not Learn Symbolic Language

Unfortunately, a number of hearing-impaired children have a language learning problem, just as do the normal-hearing. The inability to learn nouns is especially important and may indicate a childhood aphasia. Usually these children respond quite well to environmental sounds and later appear to learn a word, but it is quickly lost and has to be relearned many times. It can take endless repetitions before a new word becomes a stable part of the child's vocabulary. Sometimes, words cannot be learned auditorily at first, and in this case the program must be modified to include visual learning and a highly structured, operant-conditioning approach, using pictures, not toys. We always continue to present a word auditorily, and encourage auditory learning.

Usually these children have other problems, such as attention deficits, hyperactivity, tactile defensiveness, left–right confusions, disordered sensorimotor integration, dysarthria, apraxia, or dyspraxia, and slow maturation (Ayres, 1979).

An outstanding problem associated with language learning disorders is the difficulty in handling stimuli that move in time, or sequentially.

The *printed word* remains stationary for as long as the child wishes to study it and process it, and therefore we have used the McGinnis method (DuBard, 1974) successfully with these cases. Other programs have used Cued Speech (Cornett, 1967) or sign language which, however, move in time.

The apraxic child may be unable to monitor his own speech, or recall how to form the motor speech patterns. Van Uden (1977) has described 95 children between 2½ and 6 years of age in his school, and found that 55% had no learning problem other than those associated with hearing loss, but 45% had varying degrees of other problems, ranging from the moderate dysphasics to the severe dysphasics who learned primarily through "graphic conversation," finger spelling, and an iconic form of sign. (For example, they can recognize that a rocking movement represents a baby.)

Development of Auditory Memory Span and Sequencing

Although auditory memory probably begins at birth, it becomes apparent as words and sentences emerge that the ability to remember larger and larger "chunks" in the correct sequence becomes very important.

By encouraging the hearing-impaired child to repeat back what he hears we can develop a lengthening span. As soon as he knows a few words, we move into the two-word stage as quickly as possible. From two-word units, such as *more juice* and *I'm tired*, we move on to three word units, such as: *in the kitchen, where's may hat, I want two* (cookies), and so on. (Bloom, 1973, 1975; Brown & Bellugi, 1964; Moskowitz, 1978).

One of the activities young children enjoy is "acting out" a simple story with toys. A favorite story is that of a cat and all the things that happen to him. We may say: "Where's kitty? Up in the tree. Come down, kitty. Don't fall!" Or we pretend to pour milk and say: "Come here, kitty. Pour, pour, pour! Here's your milk, Drink your milk."

All these activities can be adapted to the child's auditory memory span and need for specific syntactic structures. Later, we work on memorization of nursery rhymes, nursery stories, finger plays, and songs.

However, it must be stressed that although spoken language is learned by imitation, the most important input for receptive language development is the conversational interaction which occurs spontaneously all day long. It is in providing enough conversational input that parents sometimes need continued guidance.

Auditory Disorders on the Syntactic Level

Unfortunately, there is a group of children who function well on a vocabulary level, but demonstrate language learning disorders on the syntactic level, that is, when they have to formulate rather than imitate sentences. Some of these children have a short auditory memory span also, but the problem is basically one in which the child does not infer basic sentence patterns from a normal amount of input.

All hearing-impaired children need structured help with syntax, but the "intact" child moves into sentences just as does the normal-hearing child. The brain is normally preprogrammed to accomplish this from conversational input. For these children with problems in learning "how words go together," it is necessary to drill on the basic patterns of English. A variety of commercial materials are available.

Putting it Together

With the basic auditory skills of attention, discrimination, processing, and memory span now integrated into the child's total learning behavior, a long period of language stimulation occurs.

Throughout the program, anything and everything that is motivating to a young child is used: toys of all kinds, inlay puzzles, paints, dolls, dressing up, music, flannelboards, Montessori materials, as well as planting seeds, decorating the Christmas tree, flying a kite, and so on. At home, every daily routine is a learning experience, from making cookies to washing the dishes or making the beds.

All new vocabulary is checked for auditory recognition, that is, the child has to be able to recognize words and sentences without visual cues. If he can recognize or repeat or answer at close range, the teacher moves further away and especially speaks when she is behind the child's back. The child must feel he can depend on his hearing.

By this age, parents are not routinely part of the clinical sessions, although they continue to observe through the observation window and discuss the session with the clinician afterwards. This is because the child has to become an independent communicator without the tendency to rely upon his parent, and because he has to learn from different adults. (Sometimes, at this point, he was seen by two different clinicians, one of whom was responsible for academic preparation while the other emphasized speech correction.)

Preparation for Mainstreaming

As the child approaches the age for formal education, the Acoupedic Program prepares him for the auditory skills he will need at school. We teach reading through phonics, we use the tape recorder and the telephone; we learn the language for math; the formulation and answering of questions, especially the wh-questions; how to follow directions in a workbook; how to participate and listen in groups, and so on.

From this point the clinical program has to use materials which are relevant to the child's educational needs and which supplement the short periods he spends with an itinerant teacher, as for example, learning the science words; syllabification; rhyming; memorization of the alphabet and numbers to 100; tracking as other children read aloud, and so on.

A child who functions well auditorily not only remembers well because he can "self-talk" and hear himself, as in adding a long column of numbers or repeating a long direction, but he can monitor his written work, that is, he can hear himself as he reads back what he has written and thus correct himself.

At 4 to 5 years of age, when the child has some control over his speech muscles, we also begin speech correction or refinement. For example, some deaf children develop the "s" sound naturally, usually in a medial position as in *horsey*, but if they do not, a tactile clue or a visual cue can be used; the little finger can feel the breadth if it is placed against the incisors, or a circle of mist on a mirror can be seen if the sound is made through a straw placed against the incisors. Many of these techniques are described by Ling (1976).

Although the clinical staff were involved with the school in staffings to formulate individualized educational programs (IEPs), in school visits to observe the child's performance in the classroom and the classroom acoustics, and sometimes to demonstrate the use of FM units, the parents were always encouraged to be the primary link between school and clinic, and to keep in close contact with the classroom teacher as to new concepts and vocabulary to be learned or to discuss behavior problems.

Patental responsibility has been easier to implement since it was included in PL 94-142 (Nix, 1977). However, a professional facilitator, as described by Leckie, (1973), is an important member of the team.

Many of the strategies described in this section can be seen as demonstrated by Pollack on a series of videotapes available from the Alexander Graham Bell Association (Master clinician tapes, 1981), and are described fully in Pollack (1970, 1983).

Frequency of Sessions

When an Acoupedic Program is organized in a hospital which charges fees for each service and each visit, it is necessary to be able to accomplish a great deal in the shortest time possible. For some children only one visit per week was possible, for others, four or five visits. There were additional visits for parent meetings or parent counseling, for occupational therapy, and for audiologic reassessments.

Having all these services under one roof made it possible to coordinate services so that the family was not expected to undertake many journeys nor were they running all over town for different services, nor were they exposed to professionals with widely differing philosophies.

Because of an infant's relatively short attention span, we learned to demonstrate and teach at least one major skill or unit in about 30 minutes, but it was more comfortable to schedule another 15 minutes to give parents time to ask questions, share observations, and so on. It is this constant dialogue with parents that distinguishes a clinic program from a school program. Thus, in the first year or so, we preferred two short visits per week, the second visit being used to review and reinforce the development accomplished during the first visit.

As families began to travel longer distances, and with the increase in gasoline prices, one visit per week was requested by many. It was always necessary to be flexible for reasons of cost, patient's age, and the family schedules. In recent years the high incidence of divorce and the large number of mothers who worked outside the home brought new challenges of scheduling. Sometimes the babysitter or other caretaker was the "partner" instead of the parent.

That the goals of the program were accomplished in so many of the cases (see the section on Results) indicates, I believe, that an individualized program based on normal development within a normal family environment can produce results which have not been achieved within special education environments. (Reichenstein, 1978; Kretschmer, 1982; Quigley & Kretschmer, 1982).

Group versus Individual Learning

For teachers who are accustomed to seeing their hearing-impaired preschoolers in groups 5 days a week, the length of Acoupedic sessions may seem surprising. The efficiency of such a procedure has been researched by Dale (1979) who confirmed that short individual sessions on a one-to-one basis give the child many opportunities to respond directly, in contrast to a group situation in which he may only respond once or twice, that is, one-to-one therapy deals with the child's own special needs. It does not waste time in group games or constant repetition of activities until every child in the group moves forward. Furthermore, the language which is being constantly "fed" into the child always occurs simultaneously with his activities and at close range—input which cannot be reproduced in a group situation. Although the skills are learned in play activities that are highly motivating to a young child, socialized play, juice time, nap time, and other parts of a school day take place in the home or in a preschool setting with normal-hearing children. The professional personnel devote their time to their special area of expertise. This is not to say that the clinic session cannot be conducted in a public school situation. Gantenbein, (1979) in the Berrien Springs Schools of Michigan, organized a similar autitory–verbal parent–infant program, as did Northcott in the Minnesota Schools (Northcott, 1978).

This time frame is effective only when parents are expected to participate and have the responsibility of incorporating the new skills into their daily routines, in addition to providing a "global" stimulation by talking about everything their children are experiencing and feeling. School districts may need to provide a number of different options, with longer school periods and their own integrated nursery program for children whose parents are unable or unwilling to participate, or whose learning problems require more professional time. This type of programming is offered in Nassau County school district in Merrick, New York.

Group Activities in a Preschool or Nursery School Setting

When the acoupedic program was held at the University of Denver, the major priority was training college students. This was accomplished by having a nursery group of normal-hearing children into which the hearing-impaired children were integrated. They were taken out of the nursery for individual therapy by students supervised by the master clinician. The parents were able to observe their children and participate in the therapy. The nursery school teachers were trained in normal child development. In a similar program at Nashville, Tennessee, described by Horton (1976) a teacher of the deaf simply did not have the right orientation.

The Porter Hospital parents placed their children in a variety of normal-hearing preschools. Some of the mothers volunteered to visit a number of local nursery or preschools and devised a questionnaire so that they could combine all their information in a large notebook for other parents. Although some schools were deemed inappropriate because of teacher attitudes, large child-to-teacher ratios, or just very noisy environments, we had good relationships with many preschools providing that we, the clinic staff, provided some inservice and promised continuing support and advice. An article was written and distributed to the teachers (Pollack & Ernst, 1973). The LISTEN Foundation, through contributions from local clubs, donated some scholarships for preschool attendance.

EVALUATION PROCEDURES
Communication Tests

1. Initial testing. As described under enrollment procedures, a baseline test was administered. This was sometimes delayed because of the child's behavior. The choice of materials varied, depending upon the child's age and presence or absence of speech and language. Since few of the young children had developed any spoken language at enrollment age, we used tests which gave a profile of motor and perceptual development in addition to items for vocalization, babbling, and gestures and other prelinguistic skills (see Enrollment Assessment).

2. Routine evaluations. Test materials which had been standardized on normal-hearing children were used at regular intervals, but usually once a year because the early progress made by young children is not easily measured on a short-term basis and we did not want to "over test." Although a clinician had to be flexible in her administration of tests to hearing-impaired children, she adhered to the standardized procedures as closely as possible. Tests appropriate for a child's chronologic age were chosen from the armamentarium listed in the appendix.

Limitations of Standardized Tests as Prediction Factors

Testing sometimes occurred just as a child had progressed beyond one level but had not reached the next level, and the scores were felt to be depressed, whereas a few weeks later, he *could* pass on that level. This illustrates the sudden spurt of progress observed in all areas of development so that in the earliest years it is sometimes more helpful to use test results qualitatively rather than quantitatively as a guide to performance trends. The Peabody Picture Vocabulary Test (PPVT) is an excellent example of the limitations of standard test materials. In the preschool years, there are very few items on one level, so that one error may indicate a loss of several months. During the early school years only a few children with exceptional language facility scored at or above their chronologic age. One such case, a "rubella" child with a P/T average of 87 dB (ISO-1964) in the better ear, progressed from a Peabody Vocabulary score of 2.1 years at a chronologic age of 3.6 years, to a score of 7.6 years at the chronologic age of 5.7, which gives a mental age 2 years above her chronological age, an advantage which she maintained in all subsequent tests. However, she loved to read and came from a very articulate family. She was later accepted by Stanford University.

More typical was S.R. (etiology unknown, P/T average in the left ear was 87 dB and 92 dB in the right ear) whose PPVT score at age

11.2 was appropriate for a mental age of 6.10 years. However, by seventh grade he was on the Honor Roll in a normal junior high school, and eventually graduated from a well-known Texas university with a degree in business administration. He now runs his own insurance agency.

Progress Criteria and Determination of Future Placement

On the other hand, performance on our annual testing was used as a basis for realistic recommendations to the parents for future placement. Progress in communication skills must be measurable and consistent with expectations. A child who entered the program at Age 2 with no language must have reached at least Age 3–3½ years communicatively by school age if mainstreaming was to be considered. If not, placement was recommended in a variety of programs, from full day special education to part-time resource room.

One can expect a spurt between 6 and 8 years of age which seems to occur as a result of neurologic maturation, verbal stimulation through reading, or just because the child has finally acquired a foundation from which many other doors seem to open. Horton, (1976) also felt that if there is a question in the minds of the many people who make the decision for regular first grade placement (such as the parents, the audiologist, the clinician, the principal) the option should be made to jump in the direction of the regular, normal educational environment and provide special services.

The philosophy that a child should be integrated at the point at which he is "ready" to be integrated, that is, at the point at which his skills linguistically are comparable to his hearing peers, is a concept that is probably achieved or achievable in few instances. Horton believes that the hearing-impaired child moving into the mainstream at any point is not comparable to his hearing peers and he will be less so the longer he is kept out of the environment of his hearing peers. What we see the children learn as they move into the mainstream are things that are not measured in achievement tests. They are things like picking up the vernacular of their hearing peers, or understanding the subtleties of verbal humor, in other words, those things that make children "normal."

Of course, there are children who are not ready to move into the normal educational environment, but for too many years clinics which were working with children from an early age in a highly enriched environment had to send them into a traditional system where they "marked time." We are still, I think, trying to change that system, but it is improving.

Tests which helped us make recommendations for school placement and future program planning are listed in the appendix. Another factor which influenced placement decisions was the presence of a progressive loss.

In addition to standardized test materials, observation of responses to therapy sessions were charted after every session. Forms were devised to chart both problems and progress, patterned after the hospital "problem oriented record" (see appendix).

At first audiotapes were made as part of the ongoing evaluations, but later, at least one videotape of each child was made. Unfortunately, in a clinical program in which 60 or 70 children were seen every week, it was not possible because of financial reasons or time constraints to videotape each child consistently. Ideally, one would like a longitudinal tape record of every child's development. We accomplished this with only a few children, that is, those who were typical examples of the results of Acoupedics, and also those who had additional problems. These videotapes were also used to evaluate the performance of parents and clinicians in the therapy sessions.

Communication tests were very helpful in comparing the development of our hearing-impaired cases with their normal hearing peers, and in providing indications for future program planning. However, they were not infallible. Some children, who never scored well on tests, were nevertheless able to learn in the classroom and cope with the demands of their everyday lives. Some of them "caught up" in the teen years and graduated from college.

The author's experience has been that one must take a long-term view. If we are preparing children for the rest of their lives, it is not important if they take longer to reach an average level. It is often difficult, however, to convince school personnel to give this extra time to "catch up" without recommending referral to sign language, even though there is a wide range of achievement in a normal-hearing classroom.

PSYCHOLOGIC EVALUATIONS

For several years the LISTEN Foundation donated the services of a psychologist so that every child in the program received a psychologic evaluation. The psychologist was chosen because of her experience with children who had speech disorders or hearing impairment as well as with normal children, and because she was working in another state and was known to be an objective evaluator. Upon meeting each child, she was given only a name and a birthdate.

For the youngest children, the following tests were used:

Weschler Preschool and Primary Scale of Intelligence (performance only)
Developmental Test of Visual–Motor Integration
Draw a Person (Goodenough)
Cat Story Telling
Oseretsky Test
Leiter International Test

For the school age group, the following battery of tests were chosen:

Weschler Intelligence Scale for Children (Revised)
Wide Range Achievement Test
Bender–Gestalt

The psychologist also used a speech intelligibility rating scale, and gave a questionnaire to the parent accompanying the child, which proved to be very helpful in disclosing some of their underlying attitudes and concerns. The pscyhologist was impressed by the fact that profoundly impaired youngsters, Aged 8–13, were able to perform well on the verbal portion of the Weschler Intelligence Scale for Children (revised version) rather than with special nonverbal (or manual) testing standardly used with hearing-impaired populations. She also noted their success in mainstreaming into regular education, and their good acceptance of their hearing aids, possibly due to proper functioning and good parent education.

The psychologist further stressed that their ability to respond to normal conversational speech, that is, to relate in a testing situation to a stranger who used a normal tone of voice, was one of the largest differences between the children in the auditory program and other hearing-impaired children. There was a noticeable lack of internalization that they were "deaf"—that is, most self-concepts were free of seeing themselves as primarily hearing-impaired.

In looking over the whole group, the psychologist found that there were many problems in addition to hearing loss at an early age: perceptuomotor lags, visual problems, and so on. However, when she tested the older children who had been in the program for a number of years, she found that most of the other problems had been treated and resolved. This was corroborated by the parents' replies to a recent survey questionnaire (see results of the program). Few of them reported the presence of other problems in the older children.

In recent years, funding was not available for psychological testing as a routine part of the program. Rather, the LISTEN Foundation decided to expand funds for the services of the family counselor and the occupational therapist.

Children with severe emotional problems could be referred to local mental health centers or child study centers. For the school age child, the school psychologist was a referral source.

CASE DESCRIPTIONS

The following are examples of cases who have gained varying degrees of benefit from an Acoupedic Program:

KK and JK (Brothers)
KK (born November 5, 1971)

KK was first seen in September 1974 after his brother, JK, was seen in the neonatal screening project as a "high risk" baby. He also had a normal-hearing older brother. K's loss had not been confirmed (although suspected earlier by his parents) until he was 2.5 years old, when he was fitted with aids in another program where his mother felt he was allowed to be very disruptive and was not making any progress. His mother was very nervous, and K was unmanageable: biting people, throwing things, jumping on the table, and so on. Formal evaluation was postponed until behavior modification had taken place. By November 1974, the first Communicative Evaluation Chart was done and his performance development was found to be at a 2–3-year level, and communication at approximately a 1-year level. He was beginning to imitate words but did not understand them. By the new year, he had begun to acquire a vocabulary.

The first reliable audiogram was obtained through play conditioning in January 1975, and subsequent audiograms have shown no significant change.

	250	500	1000	2000	4000	8000	PT/Av.	Aided Speech Detection
Right Ear Unaided	70	95	100	110	NR	NR	102dB	40dB
Left Ear Unaided	65	85	90	NR	NR	NR	95 + dB	40dB
Binaural Aided	20	40	40	55	65			

The K family was then transferred to California for 2 years and the family attended the HEAR Foundation where the boys received an auditory–verbal program.

When KK returned to the acoupedic program in July 1977, he scored only 2.11 years on the PPVT and one point below four years on the Houston Test for Language. Although he had good listening skills, his language development was delayed by his lack of verbs and a failure to form sentences; he spoke in single words or two-word phrases. During the next year this deficiency was corrected and school readiness skills were taught. He now scored one point below a language age of 6 years on the Houston. He understood 16 out of 25 of Boehms' Basic Concepts (form B), and 15 out of 25 on Booklet 2. (He missed such concepts as *almost, between, in order*)

K was admitted to his neighborhood kindergarten in September 1978 and attended therapy 1 hour once a week after school.

At a chronological age of 6.8, K's psychological evaluation report said that he appeared to be a well-adjusted youngster who was easy to work with, with excellent work approach skills, and relating well to time limits in spite of having a broken arm. "He is a self-structuring individual who needs only cursory outside encouragement." He was functioning at age level in visual–motor and gross motor skills. On the WPPSI, a performance score of 129 placed him solidly in the very superior range of nonverbal intellectual functioning. He spontaneously verbalized with the examiner during the entire session.

In July 1980, at the end of second grade and at a chronologic age of 8.8 years, he was tested for progress in language skills using the Brigance Diagnostic Inventory of Basic Skills, and the Myklebust Writing Test, and was found to be performing on a third grade level which was consistent with school achievement tests. For example, classifications, analogies, and homonyms were all passed at the third to fourth grade level. Oral reading rate was 79 words per minute. In writing, in the number of words and sentences he scored at the 85th percentile for his age and sex, but average words per sentence were 9.6 or at the 50th percentile for age and sex. his abstract-imaginative rating was 75–80%. In conversation, he still made morphological errors when nervous.

Audiologically, he began to respond to 2K and 4K at 95 dB and 105 dB in the left ear only. Binaural aided SRT was 45 dB, or the level of a quiet voice, and aided discrimination, using the WIPI test, was 76% at 65 dB HL, that is, a conversational voice. He used an FM unit in the classroom. In 1981 his parents requested ear level aids, but his teachers did not feel he heard as well in the classroom as with his body aids.

K participates in many sports activities in the neighborhood and he has many friends. His report card at the end of firth grade showed Bs in reading and A in independent reading; Bs and Cs in English, As, Bs, and Cs in science and math. K's younger brother presented different problems.

JK (born April 5, 1974)

JK responded to the screening tone as a neonate, but we followed him as a "high risk" baby and were concerned about his hearing levels by 6 months of age. During the next few months, J had many ear infections, but we were able to try loaner aids by his first birthday.

He has a severe to profound loss in the right ear, 95 dB P/T Av., and a steeper, sloping loss in the left ear, 77 dB P/T Av. He was as shy as K was boisterous, and we felt he had some perceptuomotor problems which were confirmed by the occupational therapist. At 6.2 years, his overall gross motor abilities still fell at a 3.10 year level, whereas fine motor skills were within normal limits. J has always preferred reading to physical activities. Of J his mother wrote, "He was very slow in repeating even a single word. Now he is a regular chatterbox. His speech is very clear. At this time I have no concern with J. In Grade 2, his report card showed "Satisfactory" or "S + ." He needs to improve on substraction facts."

In 1983, both boys are still mainstreamed and receiving itinerant services and some private therapy. They have never learned sign language. These two brothers are hearing, talkative boys who take part in all the usual suburban activities with their peers. The father is frequently out of town, and the mother has chosen to stay home although it is difficult financially. The parents have high expectations, but put forth the effort and commitment to help the boys live up to their expectations.

KC (born March 12, 1974)

K's parents had suspected that something was wrong for several months, but it was visiting friends who drew their attention to her unresponsiveness to sound at 9 months. When first seen she also had conductive problems. At 13 months of age, K was a very small, visually alert baby who babbled in a very natural voice quality but showed no startle response to any intensity. She responded to the bone conduction unit only at frequencies and intensities that involved vibration.

KC responded very well to amplification and developed spoken language following the normal sequence.

In December 1978, after three years in the program, K's mother returned to her home state and later remarried. She is now living in a rural area. KC spends part of the year with her mother and part of the year with her father (who moved to a northern state).

KC was brought to Porter's for a reevaluation in October, 1979, with the following results.

	250	500	1000	2000	4000	8000	Unaided P/T Av.	Aided SRT	Aided Disrim.
Right Ear	80	80	100	95	NR	NR	91 dB	45 dB	40% @ 65 dB
Left Ear	85	75	75	80	75	75	76 dB	45 dB	76% @ 65 dB
Binaural Aided	10	30	30	20	40		27 dB	35 dB	95% @ 75 dB (using WIPI)

The etiology of K's loss is unknown. The audiogram looks like rubella. There is some familial hearing loss, and there were reports of other factors during pregnancy which could have affected the fetus.

At a chronologic age of 5 years, 5 months, KC scored as follows on speech and language tests:

PPVT Form A: Raw Score 55. Language age: 5 years, 11 months.

Houston, part 2: Raw Score 54.2. Language age: 6 years. (On this test K made almost two years gain in 7½ months.)

Boehm Test of Basic Concepts, Form b, 1 and 2: 33 correct responses out of 50.

Carrow Test of Auditory Comprehension of Language: Raw Score 87. This is appropriate for a chronologic age of 6 years, 6 months.

Arizona Articulation Proficiency Scale (revised): Total Score 90.5. This is within normal range (some occasional errors in conversation, especially on s, th, and r).

There was some indication of problems in visual perception which might cause problems in learning to read, and later K's mother reported that K did have learning difficulties until third grade. On the other hand, she attended a number of different schools because of her parents' life styles.

The latest report states that K continues to attend normal-hearing schools and fits into the mainstream with little additional help. Her third grade report card shows S + on all academic subjects except handwriting (S −) and art (S). She now loves to read 3 or 4 hours a day. Her favorites: Nancy Drew and Heidi stories. Her conversational skills are such that people do not think she has a hearing loss. K, however, is sometimes frustrated by her hearing loss.

The next two case histories show moderate success, one for a child with a severe to profound loss, and one with a profound loss.

ZR (born April 2, 1969)

ZR was first seen in March 1971, aged 2 years. He had just been tested and given a loaner aid (which was malfunctioning) at another medical center. Subsequently we obtained two body aids through Kiwanis and Public Health. Although the original audiogram showed a severe loss in both ears (approximately 80 dB P/T Av.) the left ear was progressive and eventually Z discarded the aid on that ear. He did not like either a dichotic or a CROS fitting. Etiology was unknown, possibly viral. He had many ear infections and myringotomies.

Z's mother was very young and had just had another son, although her teenage husband had deserted the family. She had little to offer Z in the form of toys. She said he spent hours in the bathtub or in front of the TV, but also enjoyed being outdoors. She complained that he had violent and lengthy temper tantrums.

Because of his erratic, impulsive, and hyperactive behavior, I referred him to the neurology clinic where medication was prescribed. Mrs. R. was resistant to this idea.

In spite of all her personal problems, which continued in different forms for as long as we saw Z, Mrs. R. was persistent in coming to therapy, even coming across town with two little boys on the bus. She received good support from her stepmother.

We were able to arrange financial help and at one point provided volunteers who took Z part of the day to expand his experiences, and a home visitation team from a local mental health center, since both boys were somewhat out of control.

Z responded well to the program. Within 18 months he was speaking words and short sentences clearly, but his memory and recall process seemed poor. He was enrolled in a small preschool and continued to be educated with his normal-hearing peers.

His language scores increased slowly:

January 1974: At Age 4.9, a PPVT score was appropriate for 2.3 years (however his *hearing age* was only 3 years).

At a chronologic age of 6.1 PPVT (form B) 3.6 years, May 1975.

Houston Part 2. Language age 3½ years.

Auditory Memory Test (sentence repetition): below 4 years.

TACL (Carrow Test): 4.11.

Knox Cube Test: 7½ years.

He remained a moody and temperamental child, still medicated for hyperactivity, and we recommended an occupational therapy evaluation. He seemed to be a child who needed time to catch up neurologically as well as experientially.

Occupational Therapy Evaluation: Z evidenced sensorimotor integration dysfunction with delays in postural bilateral integration, form and space perception, and tactile perception. He had problems in motor planning in both fine and gross motor skills and immature inhibition of earlier reflexes. He showed inadequate ability to inhibit extraneous stimuli for his age, causing great problems with attention and arousing much excitory reactions to tactile stimuli.

At Age 8.3 the psychologist noted that Z was a careless worker, wasted time in extraneous movement, and then tried to fudge. He gave up too easily. Performance on the Weschler placed him solidly in the average range with only Coding being below average. She felt that he had good language if he was able to talk spontaneously, but verbal *reasoning* was quite poor in comparison with his performance. On a scale of 1–5, she rated his speech intelligibility as 4.

At his last visit to the clinic at Age 10.3 years, his PPVT score had not improved, showing poor ability to retain new vocabulary. His Peabody Individual Achievement test gave the following scores:

Math	2.2 grade level
Reading Recognition	2.7 grade level
Reading Comprehension	3.0 grade level
Spelling	3.8 grade level
General Information	.3 grade level

Northwestern Syntax Screening Test showed some receptive errors in possessive nouns and passive voice, and expressive errors in possessive *s,* passive voice, singular present verb tense, and indirect objects.

In 1983, his eighth grade report card shows that he is in remedial classes, but receives no help outside school. He still has motor disabilities. Z's mother says he is unsuccessful in sports, and very lazy and irresponsible and she is afraid he is going to have to settle for skilled manual labor, but all in all, he is a very normal teenager despite his handicaps. He has always attended neighborhood schools with normal-hearing children, and is reported to have a large group of friends. "Everyone seems to like him."

Audiologically, his audiogram stabilized at the following levels:

	250	500	1000	2000	4000	8000	P/T Av.	Aided SRT	Aided Discrim.
Right Ear Unaided	65	80	80	80	65	70	80 dB	35	96% at 60 dB HL
Left Ear Unaided	85	95	105	NR	NR		100 dB	65	75% at 75 dB
Binaural Aided	20	30	40	40	40	35		35 dB	90% at 60 dB HL

Z was always able to hold a conversation with someone behind his back. However, last year he caught a severe cold and ear infection at summer camp and lost some hearing in his better ear. His left ear is nonfunctional.

Z has survived many difficulties: hyperactivity and motor problems which have contributed to his learning problems, and a home environment which was constantly changing. The family moved frequently. Z does not know his real father. He has had a stepfather and stepsister who are sometimes part of the family, sometimes not. Since the family prefers to live in the mountains or rural areas, Z would have been sent to the State Residential School if he had not been enrolled in an auditory–verbal program.

LA (born March 19, 1967)

LA may also be said to be a "moderate" success. In contrast to Z, L comes from a very stable family. Her mother is very involved with the social life of her community. There is one younger sister. LA is a rubella baby who was enrolled in Acoupedics at 13 months of age, and her mother continued to drive 70 miles each way to therapy once or twice a week for about 11 years. Despite such commitment, there is a quality of "distancing" or separateness in this family and we often complained that L's assignments were seldom practiced at home. This was especially apparent when she had new vocabulary to learn.

When LA was first seen, she made no overt response to sound, and even when amplified she did not respond very much for almost a year, but she was a bright and charming youngster. An audiogram in 1971 at Age 4 showed minimal hearing in the right ear at 250 and 500 Hz and 110 dB, and a profound loss in the left ear at 90 and 95 dB at the same frequencies. Her aided speech detection threshold was 65 dB. By 1976, we were able to test frequencies 1K–4K at louder levels, and she then showed responses to higher frequencies at 115 dB and 120 dB in both ears, giving a P/T Average of 113 dB. The most recent audiogram in 1981 (conducted at school) shows the following:

	250	500	1000	2000	4000	8000	P/T Av.	Aided SRT	Aided Discrim.
Right Ear Unaided	85	90	100	110	NR	NR	100 dB		
Left Ear Unaided	85	95	105	110	NR	NR	104 dB		
Binaural Aided	15	40	40	55	80	NR	34 dB	50 dB	48% at 65 dB HL (using picture board with WIPI)

This is significantly better than all our previous tests and we question if all the responses were true responses.

LA first attended a Montessori school with normal-hearing children, and her teacher reported that "she fit in very well socially, is very popular and is above average in some areas, for example, she can count to 100." She then transferred to a private school with normal-hearing children.

L's record shows a slow, steady climb to acquire spoken language: at a chronologic age of 4.10, PPVT score was 2.8 years.

Houston Language Test: (administered in a strict, standardized manner) placed her just below the 4-year level.

Laradon Articulation Scales: she articulated all phonemes on a 3-year level. On the 4-year level, she produced *S* but not *J*, and on the 5-year level, *SH* but not *CH*. Her ability to hear and imitate final consonants was the big step forward of that year. I noted that she had a deaf voice quality but had begun to develop some control over her pitch with much more inflection contour.

At 12 years of age, L was tested with the PIAT:

Math	5.7 grade level
Reading Recognition	5.2 grade level
Reading Comprehension	4.4 grade level
Spelling	8.0 grade level

She was making approximately 1 year's gain in 1 year, but was still held back by poor vocabulary gain.

LA is a "moderate success" because until the 9th grade she was able to attend normal-hearing private schools and remained a charming girl who loved to talk. However, in her teens she became interested through summer camp in socializing with other deaf youngsters and her parents made the somewhat surprising decision to send her to the State School for the Deaf where, they said, "she could be accepted as just one of the kids and not someone who was kind of scary because she was different." They now say that she functions very well in the hearing world and is frequently the interpreter for her deaf friends. However, they are "concerned about the academic atmosphere (or lack of it); the expectations are *low*. So next year she will be back in a regular classroom at least part of the time." L's grades were As and Bs with only a C in English. Her teacher stresses her high-quality performance in science, but expresses concern that the "influence of the deaf culture appears to make her less eager to use her speech." The school audiologist commented that "L obtains significant benefit from amplification which places her in the moderate to moderately severe range. She has excellent speech reading skills." Acoupedics at least has given her the ability to live successfully in both worlds: the hearing and the deaf.

The next cases represent children who could not benefit from acoupedics.

CD (born January 25, 1974)

CD was enrolled in the program at Age 3.8 years when the family moved to Colorado. She had meningitis at 11 months of age. She had worn aids for 2 years and had attended a therapy program since 17 months of age. Her coordination had been poor and she fell a great deal. She was described as "willful and stubborn." She was said to use 15 words.

CD's original hearing tests had shown a bilateral severe to profound loss. We had great difficulty eliciting consistent responses until 110–115 dB and any responses at all to soundfield speech with her hearing aids. By July 31, 1978, we did obtain the following:

	250	500	1000	2000	4000	8000	P/T Av.
Right Ear Unaided	100	115	115	125	125	NR	121 dB
Left Ear Unaided	NR	100	120	NR	NR	NR	110 dB

She did identify seven out of eight familiar nouns at 70 dB with her aids on. By February 12, 1979 her left ear had also progressed to a P/T Av. of 123 dB.

Although CD was able to listen and imitate single sounds she did not retain them. Furthermore she was dyspraxic and she was not able to hold on to a pattern and repeat it. The occupational therapy evaluation revealed deficits and poor integration on both sides of the body and problems with visual perception. Weekly therapy was recommended and also a behavioral control program. The psychologist also stressed her extremely poor balance and found her body image to be in the low average range. On the WPPSI she obtained a performance score of 97 but with some disparities: her Picture Completion score (a concept she could not get) was in the mentally retarded range, but other items were in the High Average range.

The psychologist also recommended a complete visual examination by an ophthalmologist. She found her to have too short a visual attention span to comprehend a complete message, with problems in eye contact and very manipulative behavior. "She's very charming but tries to structure the situation herself and tune out other people."

We began to modify the therapy to include visual clues, using the McGinnis method (McGinnis, 1963). On her last evaluation at the clinic in April 1979, the following results were obtained at a chronologic age of 5 years, 3 months:

CED language age: about 2 years, but passing items on the 3rd-, 4th-, and 5th-year levels.

PPVT: 2 years, 5 months

Draw a Man: 7.3 years

Preschool Language Scale:

Auditory Comprehension	3 years, 1½ months
Verbal ability	2 years, 3 months
Language age	2.8 years

We recommended that C be placed in a self-contained classroom for the hearing-impaired. We were doubtful that she would become oral in the local school program, but since she was a bright little girl we did suggest a private residential oral school. The alternative was to learn sign language in a total communication summer program in a neighboring school district in the hopes that she could go to her own school district with a tutor interpreter. This was the parents' choice. Her last report card showed that she has stayed with her age group and is in about the middle of her class. She is below grade level in reading and at grade level in math. The teacher praises her efforts and personality highly but comments that her sentence sense is affected by her disability. Her written work is most accurate when dealing with concrete subjects, but she seems to have more difficulty thoroughly understanding more abstract concepts. Her attention to the interpreters is still inconsistent. Mrs. D writes that she is proud of the way C interacts with hearing people. She feels they gave her every opportunity to talk and would do the same thing again. It was a difficult change from oral to total but learning to sign gave her language. "One thing I have learned is that sign language is fun to learn but difficult to learn and if you do not use it you do not retain it. I would prefer that C be very oral but that was not possible."

In this case Acoupedics had little to offer. We were dealing with a loss which had progressed to the point that, as her mother reported, "We have seen only a few reactions to sound in the last year, once when a low flying jet went over and once when a very loud rock band was playing. She never turns or reacts to her name." C's parents have been investigating cochlear implants. We were also dealing with learning disabilities which sometimes follow meningitis.

If C had started in the program immediately after her illness would the course of treatment have been changed? Based on other postmeningitis cases with similar auditory and speech problems, we would have recommended occupational therapy immediately and our decision to modify the program would have been made earlier. We might have tried Cued Speech (Cornett, 1967) or vibrotactile aids (Proctor and Goldstein, 1983; Sheehy & Hansen, 1983). Not all postmeningitic cases have other problems, but like many of the rubella or CMV children, those with multiple problems continue to challenge us, and of course they take their problems into every method.

DQ (Birthdate Not Available)

This boy had been fitted binaurally at 17 months of age because of a failure to respond consistently to sound. The etiology of the disorder was unknown. He was reenrolled in three different preschool programs within 4 years. Teachers and psychologists observed that he was becoming increasingly hyperactive, and his intelligence test scores deteriorated. When he was brought to the Denver program, he was immediately referred to a neurologist because of his deviant behavior. His electroencephalogram was found to be "paroxysmal" and he was placed on medication. He was also examined by the occupational therapist, who reported that he was able to pass many tests, but in a strange manner. For example, he could only pass the walking board test by running across the board. His motor planning was extremely poor. He seemed to have developed many splinter skills so that he was able to meet the demands of the environment but in a pathologic manner. His true hearing loss remained unknown. He consistently responded to loud sounds after a great deal of conditioning, but those working with him felt that they observed many responses to quiet sounds.

It was not possible to teach him to speak. He used a high pitched, squealing voice. He never retained the sequence of sounds or the motor patterns. He encountered the same problems in finger spelling at Age 9. His main communication skill lay in his ability to retain the visual pattern of words; at an early age he would write words from memory. His drawing was average. At 7.6 years he scored 7.3 years on the Draw-a-Man Test, but only 2.9 on the Peabody Picture Vocabulary Test.

Two other cases will be given next to show the degree of benefit to be gained by acoupedics even when children are of school age.

JR was a rubella baby with a left-corner audiogram bilaterally. She was fitted with aids at 18 months and enrolled in a traditional oral program. She was brought to the acoupedic program at 6 because her mother was concerned about the lack of challenge to this bright child in the "deaf classroom." The family were professional people whose three older children all became college graduates. JR liked to talk, usually much too quickly and quietly, and she had a very deaf voice quality and depended entirely upon visual clues, especially reading. Indeed, she resisted listening and did not believe she could. We fought each other for 2 years. Finally J could listen to a paragraph and answer questions. She loved to work with a tape recorder. The parents, who were going through a divorce, made the difficult decision to transfer J to a normal-hearing parochial school where she has held her own with very good grades (for example, A in American government and biology) although she has had to work hard. She has learned Spanish and financed her own 2-week vacation to Mexico. She works at McDonald's after school. She has friends at work and at school. Her self-concept is such that she commented: "They have accepted some deaf girls from an oral school and these girls keep bugging me to hang around with them. I don't know why. I have nothing in common with them."

Acoupedics has changed her self concept from "deaf" to a "normal teenager with a hearing loss."

On the other hand, TR, who also has a left-corner audiogram and had been fitted at 18 months with aids but enrolled in a total communication program, was brought to acoupedics at Age 6 because "he cannot speak or make sounds nor is he aware of sounds or interested in sound."

We found that TR did not sign well either, and that he had been evaluated in the Kennedy Developmental Center because of his behavior and learning problems. His aids were not appropriate and we changed them and set out to make him aware of sound. We found that he could imitate *auditorily* most phonemes including *t* and *s*. I concluded that he had a language-learning problem and used a modified McGinnis method so that T could relate his listening and speech to reading and writing. At first the school was resistant to his mother bringing him to the clinic once a week, but after they saw his progress they agreed to provide daily speech sessions.

T's mother reported that after entering acoupedics he gained confidence in himself. "He seems to be more mature and more tuned in with his surroundings than his other peers in TC." He was the first of his group to be mainstreamed part of the day. Outside school he is in many other organizations and makes himself understood. He does not let his deafness stand in his way. For example, he was in a dance festival and did well. In sixth grade his grades were Bs and Cs. His SRT with the classroom auditory trainer is 40 dB, but not as good with the ear level aids he is now wearing.

In no way is TR an acoupedic child, but he shows that some of the principles can be applied at a later age. His parents feel strongly about the program and wish TR had been in it at the infant stage.

RESULTS OF ACOUPEDICS

When the program was at the University of Denver, Dr. Joseph Stewart, director of Audiology, received an Office of Education Grant to study a local group of acoupedic children for 5 years and a control group in Cleveland who were receiving a traditional oral approach, that is, with emphasis on lip reading and vision as the main channel of communication (Stewart, 1965). The aspect of acoupedics to be investigated was the extent to which it aided speech and language so that a child might be integrated into the normal classroom. The summary results are indicated in Table 5-3.

TABLE 5-3. Summary of Terminal Data

	Denver	Cleveland
N	12	12
Male	7	6
Female	5	10
Mean age (in months)	60.3	67.6
Range	59–63	58–74
Mean hearing level, better ear	69 dB	71 dB
Range	58–95	43–95
Mean hearing level, poorer ear	77 dB	72 dB
Range	62–95	57–100
Monaural aid	8	2
Binaural aid	4	14
Length of time using aid (months)	19.7	35.1
Range	11–44	16–55
N agreed responses	409	118
Mean	34.0	7.4
Range	0–50	0–35
N agreed words	869	172
Mean	74.4	10.8
Range	0–170	0–75
Mean length of response	1.8	.76
Range	0–3.4	0–2.1
N one word responses	184	92
Mean	15.3	5.8
Range	0–32	0–17
Mean 5 longest responses	3.57	.88
Range	0–7.2	0–4.4
N different words	394	105
Mean	32.8	6.6
Range	0–65	0–45
Mean structural complexity	4.8	.25
Range	0–15	0–1
Parts of speech		
Nouns	367	106
Mean	30.6	6.6
Range	0–61	0–17
Verbs	30	1
Mean	2.5	.06
Range	0–11	0–1
Prepositions	31	5
Mean	2.5	.4
Range	0–14	0–1
Pronouns	158	9
Mean	13.1	.6

	Denver	Cleveland
Range	0–59	0–5
Articles	54	3
Mean	4.5	.18
Range	0–18	0–3
Interjections	48	9
Mean	4.0	.6
Range	0–12	0–5
Templin–Darley Articulation		
Mean	20.3	16.4
Range	0–49	7–30
Socioeconomic classification		
I	0	0
II	6	2
III	3	8
IV	0	0
V	1	4
VI	1	1
VII	0	0
Unclassifiable	1	1

A follow-up study showed that 9 of the 12 children were integrated throughout their school days. In the study, Dr. Stewart made a number of observations.

1. Continuity of treatment throughout the preschool years was of great importance.

2. The control group demonstrated that early amplification and binaural fitting are not the critical factors; any gain made does not persist if future management does not reinforce and build upon these gains. Mere placement of an aid is no guarantee that effective use of the instrument will be learned.

3. Although the most successful children showed measurable hearing across the frequencies and the "failures" did not, the extent to which linguistic and later scholastic achievement can be related solely as a function of hearing loss has not been established. Most publications, as for example Ross, Brackett, and Maxon (1982), quote studies that tend to support this belief. However, one of our most "successful" graduates, SH, has a profound loss and is now a lawyer.

The three notable "failures" in this study do not show any simple cause–effect relationship. Other children with equally severe losses who were not even identified as early as two of the three show strikingly dissimilar results. Stewart (1965) says that a search for common factors relating to success is usually unsatisfactory other than the common factors of intellectual capacity, well-directed parental concern and cooperation, and residual hearing through the high frequencies.

Auditory discrimination, however, is a far more important factor than acuity. In looking at the group at Porter Hospital, some other factors emerged.

1. The presence of additional problems was noted. Many more of this group were of rubella or postmeningitic etiology. By this time we had become aware of sensorimotor problems as a result of the contributions made by occupational therapy to the learning disabled (as in Ayres, 1979). An inspection of the 66 children attending Porter's in 1975–1976 showed that 41 children had additional problems. Nationally, the statistics of the same year showed that 21,424 out of a total number of 49,427 attending classes for the deaf had additional problems.

The degree to which these "other problems" can be remediated seems to be crucial to the outcome of any method. Dinner (1981) found that manual children whom she identified as having learning disabilities made very slow progress.

2. There is often an underlying language-learning difficulty which will cause problems in any method. The children who are most successful seemed to have a natural facility for learning language, regardless of their intellectual capacity or degree of residual hearing.

3. The "successful" cases seem to have certain personality traits which might be described as positive and competitive. Although the personalities can be highly dissimilar, the successful possess a drive to be like everyone else, whereas the less successful are more passive.

There are many factors which can contribute to achievement: age of beginning in the program, configuration of the audiogram, amount of phoneme distortion, maintenance of the hearing aids, quality of the teaching, and so on.

A Survey Questionnaire

Recently a questionnaire was mailed to 122 of the children who were seen until termination was appropriate in the Porter program between 1965 and 1981. Eighty-one replies have been received to date. The names were chosen simply on the basis of being in the telephone book or otherwise available. Many of the children had been lost to follow-up. The following questions were asked which brought the indicated responses:

1. What is your child's primary form of communication?

    Sixty-seven answered "speaks," 13 answered "speaks to hearing people and signs to deaf people," and 1 answered "signs."

2. When did your child learn sign language?

    Of the 14 who use sign language only 4 learned in elementary school. Some did not learn until college when it was a required course. The others learned it in the junior high school years.

3. Does your child attend school? If yes, which school and grade?

    Of the school age population, 35 are mainstreamed and 18 are in special education. Nine are in normal-hearing preschools. (If children were mainstreamed with interpreters, this was counted as special education.) Seven are attending college now, and one is in jail.

4. What kind of help does your child receive during school hours?

    A large percentage receive speech therapy and itinerant help.

    After school hours?

    Those who did receive help quoted "speech therapy, occupational therapy, and tutoring—mainly reading."

5. Would you share the grades on the last report card?

    Grades were usually As, Bc, and Cs. There were few Ds. Other report cards were given as O (outstanding), S (satisfactory), and S + . It is, of course, difficult to evaluate without seeing the average grades of the whole class, but it would seem that they would be similar. It is difficult to evaluate educational achievement since there has been so much public discussion about the decreasing standards and mediocrity in American schools.

6. Does your child have a job?

    Twenty-nine answered *yes*. Of the jobs held after school, or during school vacations, parents listed the following: self-employed housepainter, caddy at the supermarket; a gift wrapper; cleans barber shop, pet sits, paints, mows lawns; busing tables or food preparation; clerical work; crew chief at McDonalds (for 7 years); baby sitting, working on a guest ranch, ground keeper; paper boy, school custodian, auto repair, now drafting trainee; working in truck deliveries for a publishing company; 35–40 lawn jobs; US Youth Conservation Corps at local National Fish Hatchery; salesgirl at a bookstore and maintenance helper for a rental investment company. Of the 11 adults the following occupations were listed: outdoor recreation specialist for the handicapped; precision machinist (tool and die maker); vocational rehabilitation counselor in Virginia; lawyer; teacher at a day care center; computer operator; accounting (bank supervisor); aviation mechanic, secretary, insurance agent, and homemaker.

7. Has your child had any significant change in residual hearing for the worse over the years?

Only 19 answered yes (some only in one ear). Two atresics were reported to have gained significantly more hearing after surgery.

8. Would you please enclose an audiogram?

The author's plan is to compare early audiograms with the most recent ones to verify the parents' statements about significant change. The figure seems too low.

9. What kind of hearing aid is your child wearing?

Answers included: 2 answered on ear level; 60 answered two ear levels; 12 answered two body aids; 3 answered bone conduction (these are atresics); 1 answered none (a retarded autistic child); 1 answered one body aid; and 1 wore a CROS fitting.

10. Does your child have problems other than hearing loss?

Learning disabilities, 14; 9 visual problems (2 are deaf and blind), and 7 emotional problems—(mostly listed as immaturity or upset by divorce, but one boy had been in and out of juvenile detention centers since his early teens. He hears and speaks well and has an older brother who is an excellent achiever in college). Other problems listed included: retardation—(4, two of whom are autistic also); heart defect; motor problems; cerebral palsy; diabetes; Treacher Collins syndrome with paresis of the soft palate; Kallmann's syndrome; allergies, and apraxia.

11. If you had to choose a program for your child again, would you choose acoupedics or another program?

Of 73 who answered: acoupedics; 3 answered yes, or any other oral program; 1 answered maybe, but I think it takes special qualities in family and teacher; 1 answered yes, but I would have placed her in a special oral class earlier instead of mainstreaming; 2 answered yes, but I would have gone to sign language earlier; and 1 answered no, it was not the right program for my child. (This was a multihandicapped, brain-damaged child. At the time, there were no other programs which would accept him. Later he was admitted to the regional deaf and blind program.)

12. What gives you the greatest pride in your child now?

The same words were used over and over again: pride in the child's independence, ability to communicate with everyone, participation in school activities and community activities, personality (works hard, has compassion for others, sense of humor, etc.), school achievement, and athletic prowess. (For example, one girl is an officer in Job's Daughters and has to memorize and say her part in front of a group of people twice a month; another, profoundly deaf, is in the National Honor Society.)

13. What gives you the most concern now?

This showed certain trends: parents of the very young children were concerned with the ability to formulate sentences; of the elementary school children, they were concerned with school performance; of the teen-aged group, concern was high about social life or acceptance by peers, telephone communication, and vocational goals. The parents of the adult group wrote that they had *no* concerns, that all in all everything had turned out well!

There was a tremendous frustration expressed with schools and school personnel, stressing that their children needed quality teaching but did not always get it. They did not like the constant *change* of personnel and methods. Most of all, they felt that schools were comfortable only when they could place all the hearing-impaired children in the deaf classes and teach them sign language. If the Acoupedic children could function quite well in the hearing classroom the help given to them was totally inadequate. One mother even called it "a joke." Many of the parents gave up on the public schools and placed their children, often at great financial sacrifice, into private or parochial schools where, they said, the "basics were emphasized and teachers tried harder with the individual child."

Parents also expressed frustration at the public concepts of "deafness." It was difficult to explain if their child was talking that he did indeed have to work hard to acquire spoken language and that he did have a severe loss. The public always equated "deafness" with the inability to hear or speak.

14. Comment on social life, the program and so on.

The children ranged in age from 5 years to 34 years. The oldest group of 11 adults, many of whom had received their initial training in the first program sponsored by the University of Denver and the Denver Hearing Society but continued to follow the author for their speech therapy or audiological follow-up, had for the most part been fitted with aids at a much later age: from 3 to 5, and monaurally. (As late as their teens for binaural aids.) As a group they tended to have moderately severe to severe losses rather than profound, but there were exceptions. All of them had followed the careers of their choice. Eight were college graduates. Six are married, and four have normal-hearing children.

If it were possible to follow all those early children, there would be a wide range of achievement depending on whether they had gone through special education or had been able to mainstream. The author knows that there are other college graduates in the group.

The next group are of college age with 10 in college either part-time or full-time. One boy is in jail.

The next group are teen-agers. Fourteen are mainstreamed, some with a good deal of help, some with none or very little. Nine are in special education.

The next group are elementary school students. Twenty are mainstreamed. Eight are in special education.

The last group are just ready for school and all nine have been in normal-hearing preschools.

In general, the majority of children in special education are multihandicapped.

DISCUSSION AND SUMMARY

The goals of Acoupedics were stated to be: (1) integration of hearing into the child's total personality development, and (2) mainstreaming to the fullest extent possible.

The first goal can be realized unless there is no residual hearing which is very rare. It takes, however, a commitment during the early years of a child's life which appear to be a sensitive, if not critical, time for the development of the auditory function. As illustrated by Cases JR and TR, it is extremely difficult to achieve similar results after the preschool years when the child's attention has been focused on visual learning. In general it is felt that there are critical periods in a child's life when it is easier to develop certain functions or skills. Some animal research has shown actual morphological changes as a result of lack of stimulation at the appropriate age (Webster & Webster, 1977).

Learning to listen is one of the skills which should occur during the first years of life. Severely impaired adults who have never worn aids before find it almost impossible to tolerate or process amplified sound.

Another aspect of communication which develops in the first year of life is auditory feedback and feedforward; that is, the ability to monitor the sounds we make so that they match the sounds we hear. Thus, by 10 months of age, a German baby sounds German and a Chinese baby sounds Chinese. Deaf babies are born with natural-sounding voices but if they do not hear themselves their vocal tones become more restricted and eventually cease. The "deaf" voice quality which then develops is very difficult to change because the auditory feedback mechanism has never developed—one reason for the unintelligibility of deaf speakers' speech.

It has long been recognized that hearing is the natural and most effective pathway through which to acquire spoken language, but perhaps the most important influence of hearing at an early age is the effect it has on personality development and the ability to "tune in" to other people, to be aware of and responsive to a world that is full of sounds. As Myklebust wrote in 1960, sensory deprivation causes an individual to behave differently. Other psychologists have described the "deaf personality" (Rainer et al., 1969; Myklebust, 1960).

Stewart's report (1965) also described tests by Elkind which dealt with the improved visual perceptual development of Acoupedic children. This confirmed Myklebust's studies (1953) which show that the deaf child has more difficulty interpreting visual experiences than does the hearing child. Auditory perception assists in the interpretation and evaluation of visual experiences. Thus, much of what we see may be interpreted by what we have heard. This is because we hear constantly, whether we pay attention or not. We hear when we are awake or asleep; healthy or in a coma; in the daytime and in the dark; behind our backs and around corners. Hearing is also a temporal sense. In short, there is no substitute for the sense of hearing and it is crucial to develop an auditory function at an early age.

Despite years of evidence to the contrary (Jensema & Trybus, National Demographic Survey, 1974–1978) educators continue to believe that a very young child who knows little or nothing of communication in any mode can learn through several different system simultaneously, because the older children who had started in traditional oral programs were able to add manual communication at a later age.

Psychologists and neurologists, however, point out that we cannot learn different systems simultaneously when one system is defective. The stronger system will become the primary one and the defective one will be inhibited (Krech & Crutchfield, 1959; Negus, 1963). There is a limit to the amount and type of information we can process at one time (Luria, 1973; Schatz, 1977).

It has always required intensive auditory training to integrate hearing into a deaf child's personality. When fitted with aids, the profoundly deaf continue to act as if they do not hear and usually discard their aids after school if audition is not emphasized. Even the hard-of-hearing who wear aids begin to sound and behave as if they are deaf when they are educated in classrooms for deaf children (Berg & Fletcher, 1970).

Another point of controversy is the belief that most children with a severe loss cannot learn to speak intelligibly without sacrificing a large amount of time which could be spent learning "language." In Acoupedics very few children failed to acquire conversational communication and speech development simultaneously with language.

The majority of parents of hearing-impaired children are normal-hearing and it is logical for them to look for a program which promises to prepare their child for participation in a normal-hearing community. They recognize that the ability to use spoken language intelligibly is the key to successful integration.

In questionnaire after questionnaire, the answers to the question: "What gives you the most pride now?" were similar: "I have pride in knowing that K is speaking and learning as a normal child when the textbooks say he shouldn't because of his profound loss." "Capability of communicating with and relating to all people, ages nine days to 99 years." "She has a lot of little friends and plays well. She can have a conversation with anyone, anywhere: it might be at the airport or at McDonald's."

Parents are sometimes accused of being unrealistic or of "denying" the deafness when they express these goals. On the contrary, they are being realistic about the need for communication skills. They are also proud of their children's abilities to deal with a handicap. "When new people meet her they often don't realize she has a hearing problem. On the other hand, she is very accepting of her problem and never tries to hide it." "He readily explains to people who ask 'What is that thing on your head?'"

The second goal, that of participating in the community to the fullest extent possible, depends upon many factors not the least being the expectations of the community or the school system where the child spent so many formative years. At the present time, school personnel place a great deal of pressure upon hearing-impaired children to learn sign language. As LA's mother reported, parents feel that expectations in the special schools are far too low.

The field of deaf education has long been immersed in methodological controversy, with certain groups believing that the handicap of deafness is irreversible and that educationally it is only important for the child to learn language, that is, *manual* language, with the tradition of schools for the deaf playing an important role in the maintenance and transmission of the deaf subculture (Meadow K. & Schlesinger, 1972). Mindel and Vernon (1971) were even more emphatic against auditory-verbal education, stating that continuous efforts to expose a child to sound are an exercise in futility, and that the children who were thought to have significant losses but who eventually develop greater vocabulary and language ability are usually children who were originally misdiagnosed.

There are other groups who feel just as strongly that education should try to prepare children to become fully participating citizens within the normal community to the degree permitted by their abilities and capacities, and with a consistent and continuous interaction within the home, community, school, and church, that is, in the mainstream of life (Bitter & Mears, 1973).

Which Option for Which Child?

Although it is generally agreed that there should be different options for the hearing-impaired, the question arises as to *which* option for *which* child? Attempts to predict the outcome at an early age have led some audiologists to use rating scales, while the schools offer Total Communication which they equate with oralism since it is supposed to offer all forms of communication simultaneously (Dicker, 1970).

The problems in decision making stem from several unknowns: the potential for learning in very young children with severe to profound loss; their response to amplification; the presence of other deficits; and the response of parents after they recover from the initial trauma.

In discussing the factors which make for success among the children in the University of California Total Communication program, Meadow (1980) described them as "parent–child interaction that was marked by enjoyment; by varying degrees of residual hearing (from moderate to profound hearing loss) but no handicapping conditions in addition to deafness; parents who were very much involved in their development and committed to working closely with their children and the professionals." This description applies exactly to the families of the Acoupedic Program whose children have been able to mainstream without sign language or without having to identify with a subculture, and indeed, some of the children with additional handicapping conditions have also achieved this kind of success. (See the case of CM who is legally deaf and blind [Pollack, in Mencher, 1981], and the case studies by Ernst, 1974.) Meadow also suggests that where there are additional handicaps or problems with busy or noninvolved parents, the Total Communication approach may not be optimum.

There are also other problems to be considered: the non-English-speaking parent, the physically handicapped child, the isolated rural child whose entry into a program may be late, and the abused child. Foster homes have been suggested as a solution for these children. Because the total number of severely impaired children is only a small percentage of the total school age population, the problem of appropriate or least restrictive educational placement continues to frustrate parents.

It is the philosophy of Acoupedics that *every* young child with residual hearing should be given the opportunity to use that hearing optimally. There is no substitute for the information we process through hearing, and the influence of hearing upon personality development, voice quality, communication skills, independence, and general responsiveness to the environment in which we live is inestimable.

However, evaluations of the child's development must take place at regular intervals. It is always possible to modify a program or change methodology to fit the child's needs. Advocates of manual communication do not, of course, want "failures" from other programs, but acoupedic children are not failures. In the survey questionnaire, parents noted that their children who were now in Total Communication programs were the interpreters for the Total Communication children because *they spoke so well*. I do not believe we should look at children as "successes" or "failures." Children with hearing losses are not a homogeneous group. Some are very intact apart from the hearing loss, and others have additional problems, some of which are more serious than the hearing impairment. Many can overcome the original handicap to the point that it is "an inconvenience, not a handicap" as MB wrote. Other children will have many limitations. For example, in the case of JM who spent the years from 5 to 20 in a residential state school, he is reported to have learned only 91 signs in that time; or RH, an attractive teen-ager in a Total Communication program of whom her mother wrote, "She is very slow to learn reading, which impairs all other areas. Learning is her biggest problem. She simply doesn't learn, and no one has been able to explain why. Bad memory?"

There is no panacea for all deaf children. In view of the present "state of the art," choice of programs should be, first and foremost, the responsibility of the parents. But since many parents have had no prior experience with deafness it is the responsibility of the professional community to inform them of all the programs available and to encourage parents to visit them and meet the *graduates* of these programs and their parents.

The Acoupedic Program is one of the options open to parents. By commitment to its principles and by quality teaching, its goals can be achieved for the majority of infants with severe to profound hearing loss. Every child deserves this opportunity to participate fully and independently in his community, and to be the kind of person he was meant to be.

REFERENCES

Arenberg, I. K. (1979). Endolymphatic sac implant surgery. *Laryngoscope* (Suppl. 17), *1*(2), 48–53.

Ayres, J. (1979). *Sensory integration and the child,* Los Angeles: Western Psychological Services.

Berg, F., & Fletcher, S. (1970). *The hard of hearing child.* New York: Grune & Stratton.

Bitter, G., & Mears, E. (1973). Facilitative integration of hearing impaired students into regular public school classes in Washington, DC. *Volta Review, 75*(1), 13–22.

Bloom, L. (1973). *One word at a time.* The Hague: Mouton.

Bloom, L. (1975). *Structure and variation in child language.* Chicago: Society for Research in Child Development, (Monograph).

Brackmann, D. (1977). Electric response audiometry in a clinical practice. *Laryngoscope,* (Suppl. 5), *87*(5, part 2), 1–33.

Brown, R., & Bellugi, U. (1964). *New directions in the study of language.* Cambridge, MA: MIT Press.

Cornett, R. O. (1967). Cued speech. *American Annals of the Deaf, 112,* 3–13.

Dale, D. M. C. (1979). *Applied audiology for children.* Springfield, IL: Thomas.

Dicker, L. (1970). *The rationale for total communication.* Paper delivered at the third annual dinner meeting for principals and teachers of the deaf, Milwaukee, WI, November.

Dinner, B. (1981). *A proposed sign language battery for use in differential diagnosis of language/learning disabilities in deaf children.* PhD thesis, Boulder, CO: University of Colorado.

DuBard, E. (1974). *Teaching aphasics and other language deficient children.* Jackson: University of Mississippi.

Eilers, R., & Minifie, F. (1975). Fricative discrimination in early infancy. *Journal of Speech and Hearing Research, 18,* 158–167.

Eisenberg, R. (1976). *Auditory competence in early life.* Baltimore: University Park Press.

Ernst, M. (1974). Report of the Porter Hospital study of hearing-impaired children born during 1964–1965. In C. Griffiths (Ed.), *Proceedings of the international conference on auditory techniques,* Springfield, IL: Thomas.

Finitzo-Hieber, T. (1982). Auditory brainstem response: Its place in infant audiologic evaluations. In J. Marlowe (Ed.), *The evaluation and management of communication disorders in infants* (Vol. 3, No. 1, 76–87), New York: Thieme-Stratton.

Fria, T. (1983). The assessment and middle ear function in children. In C. Bluestone & S. Stool (Eds.), *Pediatric audiology,* (Vol. 1, pp. 152–185). Philadelphia: Saunders.

Gantenbein, A. (1979). Sorting it out through a language learning program. In *Proceedings of the Second International Conference on Auditory Techniques.* Alexander Graham Bell Association/HEAR Foundation.

Hanners, B. (1976). The audiologist as educator: The ultimate aide. In G. Nix (Ed.), *Mainstream education for hearing impaired children.* New York: Grune & Stratton.

Hardy, W. (1965). In H. Davis (Ed.), The Young Deaf Child, Identification and Management. *Acta Otolaryngologica* (Suppl. 206), *36,* 95–97.

Harris, E. & Pollack, D. (1979). Parents in the auditory approach. In *Proceedings of the Second International Conference on Auditory Techniques,* Pasadena, CA: HEAR Foundation/Alexander Graham Bell Association for the Deaf.

Horton, K. (1976). Mainstreaming the primary-aged child. In B. Watrous (Ed.), *Developing home training programs for hearing-impaired children.* Albuquerque: Indian Health Service and the University of New Mexico.

Howie, V. M., Ploussard, J. H., & Sloyer, J. (1975). The 'otitis-prone' condition. *American Journal of the Disabled Child, 129,* 676–678.

Huizing, H. (1959). Deaf-mutism—Modern trends in treatment and prevention. *Advances in Oto-Rhino-Laryngology, 5,* 74–106.

Jensema, C. J., & Trybus, R. (1978). Communication patterns and educational achievement of hearing impaired students. Washington, DC: Office of Demographic Studies, Gallaudet College, Series T, No. 2.

Krech, E., & Crutchfield, R. (1959). *Elements of psychology.* New York: Knopf.

Kretschmer, R. (Ed.) (1982). *Reading and the hearing-impaired individual.* Washington, DC: Alexander Graham Bell Association.

Leckie, D. (1973). Creating a receptive climate in the mainstream program. In W. Northcott (Ed.), *The hearing-impaired child in a regular classroom.* Washington, DC: Alexander Graham Bell Association.

Ling, D. (1976). *Speech and the hearing-impaired child.* Washington, DC: Alexander Graham Bell Association.

LISTEN Foundation. *Does Your Baby Hear?* and *They Do Belong,* available from 2525 S. Downing St., Denver, CO 80210.

Luria, A. (1973). *The working brain.* New York: Basic Books.

Luterman, D. (1979). *Counseling parents of hearing-impaired children.* Boston: Little, Brown.

McGinnis, M. (1963). *Aphasic children.* Washington, DC: Alexander Graham Bell Association.

Meadow, K., & Schlesinger, H. (1972). *Sound and sign.* Berkeley: University of California Press.

Meadow, K. (1980). *Deafness and child development.* Berkeley: University of California Press.

Mencher, G., & Gerber, S. (Eds.). (1981). *Early management of hearing loss.* New York: Grune & Stratton.

Mindel, E., & Vernon, M. (1971). *They grow in silence.* Silver Spring, MD: National Association of the Deaf.

Moses, K., & Van Hecke Wulatin, M. (1981). The socio-emotional impact of infant deafness. In G. Mencher, & S. Gerber (Eds.), *Early management of hearing loss.* New York: Grune & Stratton.

Moskowitz, B. (1978, November). The acquisition of language. *Scientific American,* 92-108.

Myklebust, H., & Brutten, M. (1953). A study of the visual perception of deaf children. *Acta Otolaryngologica,* Suppl. 105, 9-122.

Myklebust, H. (1960). The psychological effects of deafness, *American Annals of the Deaf, 105*(4), 372.

Negus, V. (1963). Purposive inattention to olfactory stimulation. *Acta Otolaryngologica, 162* (Suppl. 99), 183, 99-102.

Nix, G. (Ed.). (1977). The rights of hearing-impaired children. *Volta Review, 79*(5), 263-349.

Northcott, W. (1978). UNISTAPS: Reports on the early education program for hearing-impaired children 0-6. Minnesota State Dept. of Education.

Northern, J., & Downs, M. (1974). *Hearing in children.* Baltimore: Williams & Wilkins.

Pollack, D. (1970). *Educational audiology for the limited-hearing infant* (1st Ed.). Springfield, IL: Thomas. (New edition in press.)

Pollack, D. (1974, April). Denver's acoupedic program. *The Peabody Journal of Education, 51,* 180-185.

Pollack, D. (1981). Acoupedics: An approach to early management. In G. Menscher, & S. Gerber (Eds.), *Early management of hearing loss.* New York: Grune & Stratton.

Pollack, D. (1981). Teaching Strategies for the development of auditory verbal communication (videotapes). Washington, DC: Alexander Graham Bell Association.

Pollack, D., & Ernst, M. (1973). Don't set limits: Learning to listen in an integrated pre-school. *Volta Review, 75,* 359-367.

Proctor, A., & Goldstein, M. (1983). Development of lexical comprehension in a profoundly deaf child using a vibro-tactile communication aid. *ASHA, Language, Speech and Hearing Services in the Schools, 14,* 138-149.

Quigley, S., & Kretschmer, R. (1982). *The education of deaf children,* Baltimore: University Park Press.

Rainer, J., Altshuler, K., & Kallman, F. (1969). *Family and mental health problems in a deaf population.* Springfield, IL: Thomas.

Reichenstein, J. (1978). Integrated kindergartens for severely hearing impaired children. In E. Cohen (Ed.), *Proceedings of the International Conference on*

Pre-School Education of the Hearing Impaired Child, 1978, and after. Tel Aviv: Micha.

Ross, M., with Brackett, D., & Maxon, A. (1982). *Hard of hearing children in regular schools.* Englewood Cliffs, NJ: Prentice–Hall.

Ross, M., & Lerman, J. (1970). *Word intelligibility by picture identification.* Pittsburgh, PA: Stanwix House.

Shatz, M. (1977). *The relationship between cognitive processes and the development of communication skills.* Nebraska Symposium on Motivation, University of Nebraska Press.

Sheehy, P., & Hansen, S. (1983). Programs in action: The use of vibrotactile aids with pre-school hearing impaired children. *Volta Review, 85*(1), 14–26.

Stewart, J. (1965). *Effectiveness of educational audiology on the language development of hearing handicapped children.* Washington, DC: Office of Education, Project 969.

Suzuki, T., & Ogiba, Y. (1961). Conditioned orientation audiometry. Archives of Otolaryngology, 74, 192–198.

Van Uden, A. (1980). *A world of language for deaf children* (P. I). Amsterdam: Swets & Zeitlinger, 1977.

Webster, D., & Webster, M. (1977). Neonatal sound deprivation affects brainstem auditory nuclei. *Archives of Otology, 13,* 392–396.

APPENDIX 5-A
A DEVELOPMENTAL APPROACH:
Curriculum Guideline for the Development of Auditory, Speech and Language Milestones

AUDITORY	SPEECH	LANGUAGE
Understanding	Spontaneous Speech Articulation Development	Receptive and Expressive Language
Processing Patterns	Jargon	Development of Syntax
Sequencing	First Words	Symbolic Language: Concrete and Abstract
Auditory Memory Span	Blowing and Whispering	Functional Words, Often Associated with Gestures
Auditory Feedback	Echolalia	
Discrimination	Babbling and Lalling	
Localization	Vocal Play	Sounds have Meaning
Distance Hearing	Cooing and Smiling	
Attention or Listening		
First Level: Awareness	Crying	Sound is used for Communication

TEST MATERIAL
Early Developmental Tests

Communication Evaluation Chart from Infancy to Five Years, Ruth M. Anderson, Madeline Miles, Patricia Matheny, Educators Publishing Services, Inc., Cambridge, MA, 1963.

Denver Developmental Screening Test, William J. Frankenburg and Josiah B. Dodds, University of Colorado Medical Center, Denver, CO, 1966.

Koontz Child Developmental Program, Chas. W. Koontz, Western Psychological Services, Los Angeles, CA, 1974.

Receptive–Expressive Emergent Language Scale, Anhinga Press Asso. Publications, Inc., Gainsville, FL.

Vineland Social Maturity Scale, E. A. Doll, American Guidance Service, Inc., Publishers Building, Circle Pines, MN 55014.

Early Language Tests

Houston Test for Language Development, Margaret Crabtree, 10133 Bassoon, Houston, TX, 1963.

Pre-School Language Scale, I. Zimmerman, V. Steiner, and R. Pond, Columbus, OH, Chas. E. Merrill Pub. Co., 1979.

Utah Test of Language Development, M. J. Meacham, J. L. Lex, and J. D. Jones, Communication Research Association, Salt Lake City, UT, 1967.

Verbal Language Development Scale (Ages 1–16), M. Mecham, American Guidance Service, Inc., Circle Pines, MN, 1958, 1971.

Speech Tests

Arizona Articulation Proficiency Scale (Revised), Western Psychological Services, 12031 Wilshire Boulevard, Los Angeles, CA 90025.

Goldman-Fristoe Test of Articulation (Ages 2 and over), American Guidance Service, Inc., Circle Pines, MN.

Phonetic Speech Evaluation Sheets, Planbook and Guide to the Development of Speech Skills, D. Ling, Alexander Graham Bell Assn., Washington, DC, 1978.

Auditory Tests

Test of Auditory Comprehension of Language, Elizabeth Carrow, Educational Concepts, Austin, TX.

Goldman-Fristoe and Woodcock Test of Auditory Discrimination, American Guidance Services, Inc., MN.

Detroit Test of Learning Aptitude, (3 years to Adult), Baker and Leland, Bobbs-Merrill Company, Inc., 4300 West 62nd Street, Indianapolis, IN 46268, 1935.

Lindamood Auditory Conceptualization Test (Preschool to Adult), P. Lindamood, Teaching Resources Corporation, 100 Boylston Street, Boston, MA 02116.

Roswal-Chall Test of Auditory Blending (1st to 5th grade), Essay Press, P.O. Box 5, Planetarium Station, New York, NY 10024.

Wepman Test of Auditory Discrimination, Auditory Memory Span Test, and Auditory Sequential Memory Test (5 through 13 years), J. Wepman, Language Research Associates, 175 East Delaware Place, Chicago, IL 60611.

More Advanced Tests for Conceptual, Language and Perceptual Development

The Basic Concept Inventory, Siegfried Engelman, Follet Educational Corp., Chicago, IL, 1967.

Boehm Test of Basic Concepts, A. E. Boehm, The Psychological Corporation, New York.

Bracken Basic Concept Scale, Bruce Bracken, Chas. E. Merrill Pub. Co., Columbus, OH, 1983.

Illinois Test of Psycholinguistic Abilities, Samuel A. Kirk, James J. McCarthy, and Winifred D. Kirk, University of Illinois Press, Urbana, IL, 1968.

Northwestern Syntax Screening Test, Laura Lee, Northwestern University Press, Evanston, IL, 1969.

Goodenough–Harris Drawing Test, Dale Harris, Harcourt Brace Jovanovich, Inc., New York, 1963.

School Readiness Tests

First Grade Screening Test, John E. Pate, Ph.D. and Warren W. Webb, Ph.D., American Guidance Service, Circle Pines, MN, 1966.

Metropolitan Readiness Tests, Gertrude H. Hildreth, Nellie L. Griffiths, Mary McGaurian, Harcourt, Brace, and World, Inc., New York, 1964.

Frostig Developmental Test of Visual Perception (Pre-Kindergarten—Grade 3), Consulting Psychologist Press, Inc., Palo Alto, CA, 1963.

Academic Achievement Tests

Brigance Diagnostic Inventory of Basic Skills, Brigance, Curriculum Associates, Woburn, MA, 1977.

Peabody Individual Achievement Test, Dunn, American Guidance Service, Inc., Circle Pines, MN, 1970.

Wide Range Achievement Test, J. J. Jastak and S. R. Jastak, Guidance Associates, Wilmington, DE, 1965.

Picture Story Language Test, Helmer R. Myklebust, Grune & Stratton, New York, 1965.

Screening Test for Identifying Children with Specific Language Disability, Beth Slingerland, Educators Publishing Service, Cambridge, MA, 1967.

PROBLEM-ORIENTED RECORD

Form 1:   Listing of Problems and dates when first observed and when resolved.

Form 2:   Treatment Plan with dates of initiation of each step and dates of completion.

Form 3:   Progress Notes: brief description of each treatment session and results.

Form 4:   Parameter Summary Record: Dates, Tests used, Scores obtained. Initials of Tester.

Form 5:   Chronologic account of significant events during treatment, as for example, dates of audiologic rechecks; staffings; parent counseling sessions; speech and language evaluations; preschool visits, telephone calls, etcetera.

OBSERVATION SHEET OF TRAINEE

1. Trainee's level of language

    Very simple   Very complex
        1 ☐   2 ☐   3 ☐   4 ☐   5 ☐

2. Trainee's coordination of language with action

    Never used   Overused
        1 ☐   2 ☐   3 ☐   4 ☐   5 ☐

3. Trainee's coordination of language with child's action

    Never used   Overused
        1 ☐   2 ☐   3 ☐   4 ☐   5 ☐

4. Appropriateness of trainee's play for child's developmental level

    Below child's level   Above child's level
        1 ☐   2 ☐   3 ☐   4 ☐   5 ☐

5. Relative status (trainee's)

    Submissive   Domineering
        1 ☐   2 ☐   3 ☐   4 ☐   5 ☐

6. Child's activity level

    Very passive   Very active
        1 ☐   2 ☐   3 ☐   4 ☐   5 ☐

7. Tone of trainee's interaction

    Rejective   Overly affectionate
        1 ☐   2 ☐   3 ☐   4 ☐   5 ☐

8. Tone of child's interaction

    Rejective   Overly affectionate
        1 ☐   2 ☐   3 ☐   4 ☐   5 ☐

		YES	NO
1.	Call attention to sounds heard during the session.	☐	☐
2.	Use varied and interesting intonational patterns when talking to child.	☐	☐
3.	Demonstrate two acceptable methods of getting child's auditory attention.	☐	☐
4.	Use repetition to teach new language.	☐	☐
5.	Use phrases and short sentences when talking to child.	☐	☐
6.	Use synonym or new phrase for language child already knows.	☐	☐
7.	Respond to (reinforce) child's vocalizations.	☐	☐
8.	Wait to intervene until child asks for help.	☐	☐

9. Wait for child's response and listen to child. ☐ ☐

10. Talk when using gestures. ☐ ☐

11. Give praise and social reinforcement when child gives a desired behavior. ☐ ☐

12. Watch to see what child is interested in and talk to him/her about that. ☐ ☐

OTHER COMMENTS:

_____
_____
_____
_____

SUGGESTIONS FOR IMPROVEMENT TO BE DISCUSSED WITH PARENTS:

1. _____

2. _____

3. _____

4. _____

5. _____

TEAM MEMBERS (psychologist, speech therapist, physical therapist, audiologist, or social worker) that may need additional information:

_____
_____

RECOMMENDATIONS GIVEN TO PARENTS:

DATE:

BY WHOM:

OBSERVATION EVALUATION FORM

CHILD'S NAME _____   EXAMINER _____
DATE_____   LESSON _____
TRAINEE_____   MATERIAL USED _____

CIRCLE ONE: Infants   Prekindergarten   1st Grade
               Language   Kindergarten   Multiple Handicapped

1. Needs significant improvement.   3. Effective but minimal changes needed.
2. Several changes needed.   4. Highly Satisfactory

	1	2	3	4	COMMENTS

1. TOTAL SESSION

2. RAPPORT WITH CHILD

   (a) Give and take interchange.

   (b) Discipline.

   (c) Ability to maintain a confident manner in the face of behavioral disruptions.

   (d) Application of limits dealing with inappropriate behaviors.

   (e) Reinforcement.

   (f) Is perceptive of child's social and emotional needs.

3. RAPPORT WITH PARENT

   (a) During therapy.

   (b) After therapy.

   (c) Listening to them.

4. DEVELOPMENT OF AUDITORY SKILLS

5. DEVELOPMENT OF SPEECH

   (a) Elicit from child.

   (b) Therapist: 1) natural inflection; 2) voice quality; 3) rate.

6. DEVELOPMENT OF LANGUAGE

   (a) Appropriate for child's level.

   (b) Elicit from child.

   (c) Appropriate amount of talking by therapist.

7. PLANNING OF THERAPY

   (a) Develops appropriate rationale.

   (b) Develops appropriate written objectives.

(c) Develops organized sequence of procedures.

(d) Selects appropriate materials.

(e) Is responsive to parent's and child's input in planning expectations.

---

8. IMPLEMENTATION OF THERAPY

(a) Ability to motivate child.

(b) Clueing (auditory and visual).

(c) Use of materials, equipment and clinic setting.

(d) Application of procedures (creativity).

(e) Flexibility.

(f) Effective use of time.

---

9. SELF ANALYSIS OF SESSION

(a) Initiates communication with supervision in developing therapy plans and evaluating self-performance.

(b) Accepts supervision positively.

(c) Initiates to devising of new methods for the basic problem.

(d) Follow through for next session.

---

10. DIAGNOSTIC SKILLS

(a) Administers and scores diagnostic tests according to standardization criteria.

(b) Administers appropriate tests in an organized manner.

(c) Exhibits skill in client observation.

(d) Scores and interprets results of testing accurately.

(e) Exhibits skill in integration of test results.

(f) Makes appropriate recommendations and/or referrals.

(g) Exhibits skill in giving/eliciting information through family member/client interviews.

---

11. REPORTING SKILLS

(a) Includes information in written form that is pertinent and accurate.

(b) Demonstrates adequate organization of report.

(c) Uses acceptable professional writing style.

(d) makes appropriate recommendations and/or referrals.

Adapted from the University of Denver's Professional Training Evaluation forms.

6
COMMENTS AND CONCLUSIONS

Daniel Ling

The well-documented material presented with the program descriptions in the preceding chapters makes it unnecessary to enter into extensive discussion. This chapter, therefore, is brief. Its purposes are to comment on some of the similarities and differences among the four programs, to provide notes of explanation on matters that appear to require clarification, and to suggest certain conclusions that are indicated by this text and related literature.

The programs described in the preceding chapters were all initiated by professionals with exceptionally high levels of personal drive who found themselves in circumstances that were conducive to the further development of their skills. Their programs grew from small beginnings and have now come to serve as models for others. The philosophy of treatment in all four programs emphasizes interactive intervention that is centered on the parents and on the family as the major agents of the child's spoken language development. Consistent use of residual hearing is basic to all that they do. Each contributor provides a detailed description of the competencies required of the professionals involved in early oral intervention and stresses the need for both attention to detailed programming and high levels of expectation. Their contributions offer excellent guidelines for those who wish to set up similar programs in areas where none exist.

Ideally, programs for early oral intervention should be funded by local government (health and education) authorities, since the cost of providing such programs is higher than most parents can afford. However, the variety of settings in which these programs are based and the diversity in their sources of funding indicate that where the need for such provision can be demonstrated, funding can be arranged through one or more private agencies within the community. Staff in the four programs described are all involved in providing information about their work to other professionals and to the public. Many of their referrals as well as much of their funding results from such publicity.

The involvement of students is part of all four programs. This is important in any field if it is to grow and to persist beyond the span of a professional's career. A great deal of theoretical knowledge is required of students for efficient functioning in this type of work, but such knowledge without a variety of practical skills is grossly inadequate. The practical skills of students who wish to become teacher/clinicians can only be developed through experience, preferably under the supervision of master teachers working in exemplary programs.

DIAGNOSTIC TEACHING

All four oral options described in this book are open to hearing-impaired children from infancy regardless of their hearing levels or the presence of additional handicaps. Parental decision to participate is the only criterion for the child's enrollment. This is typical of programs that focus on evaluation and assessment in the course of ongoing treatment. Diagnostic intervention in early oral options is considered by the preceding authors to maximize the opportunity for hearing-impaired children to begin learning spoken language at an early age. Mindel and Vernon (1971) caution that failure to learn to speak and understand speech in infancy may adversely affect the mother–child bond and subsequent psychological development. They further suggest that such adverse effects are inevitable with early oral intervention. Some professionals support this view, but others do not (see MacLean, 1983).

The contributors focus on diagnostic appraisal in the course of early oral training. This focus is reasonable, since there are no tests that can be considered as reliable guides to a child's potential abilities. Absence of an auditory response, even to the best "objective" physiological tests, does not necessarily indicate total deafness (Berlin, 1978; Finitzo-Hieber, 1982) and the extent to which a handicap additional to deafness will impair learning by speech can not be known in advance (Ling, 1976).

It has been suggested that giving primary emphasis to speech communication implies that sign language is less desirable than spoken language, and that parents who seek speech and hearing development for their children may not be accepting the fact of their deafness (Mindel & Vernon, 1971). Such suggestions may be true for some people in the early stages of treatment. However, counseling is provided in all four programs to help parents understand and accept the facts and implications of their children's hearing problems. The greatest difficulty in early diagnostic intervention in oral options appears to be in deciding when it would be better for a child to follow another type of treatment. There are no absolute guidelines on this question, since much depends on the quality of available alternatives as well as what parents and staff consider satisfactory rates of progress.

TREATMENT PROCEDURES

The initial steps following enrollment in all four programs are evaluation and hearing aid selection for the children, and counseling education and guidance for the parents. All four of the contributors describe the programs in detail. The purpose here is to summarize them briefly and then point up noteworthy differences and similarities. The contributors differ in the evaluation procedures they employ, in the type of hearing aids they prefer, and in several aspects of the counseling, education and guidance they provide. All, however, accept children who are profoundly hearing-impaired in their programs. Indeed, many such children are reported as being among their most successful.

Description of Procedures

Authors of all four chapters described *what* they did in detail, but, like those who contributed to the companion volume, they did not place as much emphasis on *how* material was presented to either parents or children. The dynamics of counseling, education, and guidance are, nevertheless, equally as important to the success of a program as the materials and information presented. The process of teaching and therapy is, however harder to describe than to demonstrate. Videotaped materials, such as those prepared by Pollack (chap. 5) and by Ling (1982) can do much to overcome such difficulty. The dynamics of teaching and learning in early intervention work have not received as much research attention as the outcome of such work. Considerable improvement in methodology could be expected to result if more research effort were directed toward the outcome of early intervention in relation to how rather than what materials are presented. The Lincoln profile described by Clezy (chap. 3) is a step in this direction.

Hearing Aid Selection

The types of hearing aid recommended vary from one program to another. Whereas Clezy (chap. 3) employs mainly radio frequency hearing aids, which present the same signal to both ears, the other authors prefer binaural hearing aids which the children wear either on their bodies or behind their ears. Sound falls in intensity by about 6 dB with every doubling of distance. Since the speaker (usually the mother) wears the microphone of the radio aid, its distance from her mouth, and hence the input to the child, are relatively constant. The resulting speech signal can, under these conditions, be generally maintained above ambient noise levels (most noise being further away from the microphone than the speech). This can be an advantage, as Clezy points out, when it is difficult for mothers to be consistently close to their children. An additional advantage is that feedback is rarely encountered with radio aids because the microphone is at a distance from the child's ear.

Fewer feedback problems occur with body-worn as compared with head-worn hearing aids. Children's ears grow quickly at times during infancy and cause earmolds to become loose. Leakage of sound from the earmold, if detected and reamplified by the hearing aid, is the main cause of feedback, which results in a squealing noise. Of course, ear level hearing aids can be worn without feedback by young children if they have very well-fitting earmolds or if the hearing aid is not exceptionally powerful. Under these conditions, ear level, head-worn hearing aids can be advantageous, because they can be used with special earmold adjustments to provide better high-frequency amplification of sounds like /s/. More details on the relative merits of different types of hearing aids are provided in Ling and Ling (1978).

Development of Residual Audition

There were clear differences in the way that the four contributors approached the development of residual audition. Three concentrated on using audition alone in some activities from the beginning. However, this was not so in the exemplary case described by Cole and Paterson. The child they described responded to low-frequency sounds during the first evaluation at levels which suggest that, when provided with hearing aids having an average 60 dB gain, he would have been able to hear voice over a distance of a few yards. Nevertheless, considerable emphasis was initially placed on attracting his attention in nonauditory ways. Only later did they use techniques involving audition alone. This procedure was apparently adopted for two reasons, both of which would be questioned by those who place a strong primary emphasis on audition: first, to ensure that interactive communication between mother and child would begin immediately even if the aided residual hearing was inadequate; and second, to encourage the child to develop eye-to-eye contact when communicating. In more traditional oral programs, persistent use of vision-plus-audition would be the norm, and, for very profoundly hearing-impaired and totally deaf children, the use of vision would of necessity be emphasized. Such emphasis might include the use of cued speech as an oral option, although it does not belong in the particular programs described. For certain children it can, however, be a viable system when residual hearing is too limited to permit development of spoken language through auditory techniques.

Frequency of Training Sessions

The frequency of individual sessions varied greatly from one early intervention program to another. The reasons for this included the characteristics of the population served, the geographical distribution of the families enrolled, their distance from the intervention center, the center's facilities, staff availability, and the staffs' philosophy of treatment. All programs scheduled more frequent sessions in the early stages of treatment. In the two centers offering a residence for out-of-town families, intensive work over several days at less frequent intervals was provided. Home visits were substituted for sessions in the intervention center by some on the grounds that it was helpful if the teacher/clinician was able to relate the intervention program to the real life situations afforded children in their homes. More frequent sessions were usually scheduled by those professionals who personally worked a great deal with the child than by those who saw the parents as the main agents in the child's treatment. Professionals in all early intervention programs are apt to enjoy interacting with the child more than working with and through the parents. If professionals succumb to such temptations, their work, in the long run, can become counterproductive (Luterman, 1967).

Speech Teaching

The manner in which speech skills were developed also differed among the programs reported. In some programs, considerable care was taken to ensure systematic growth of component skills (Ling, 1976), whereas in others emphasis appeared to be on growth of competence almost exclusively through meaningful language units (words, phrases, sentences). The differences in speed of acquisition and levels of competence achieved under the two conditions could be evaluated through research. Speech acquisition is important in its own right, but it has also been found to be a positive influence on auditory perception in hearing-impaired children (Novelli-Olmstead & Ling, in press). Of course, children who can hear well (and those who hear badly but are taught to listen well) can approximate normal feedforward and feedback control of their speech. The more profoundly hearing-impaired the children, however, and the later they are enrolled in oral options, the more likely it is that carefully structured speech development will be required (Ling, 1976).

Personnel

The complexity of the problems related to hearing impairment in early infancy makes it virtually impossible for a teacher/clinician to undertake or to supervise all aspects of early intervention. All authors acknowledge that audiologists, psychologists, psychiatrists, physicians, and regular teachers are essential support personnel. Adequate support services add not only to the quality of a program, they increase its efficiency in that a greater caseload can be carried by the teacher/clinician. There is a danger that parents can misunderstand the results of their consultations with support staff, a situation that can cause problems unless the teacher/clinician has an excellent liaison with others on the team and can interpret their findings as necessary. Only in the program described by Beebe, Pearson, and Koch (chap. 3) is more than one teacher/clinician responsible for the management of a child. Particularly good communication among staff members and between them and the parents is required for such an arrangement to work smoothly.

Parent Participation

Parents participated in the four programs by choice. Because early oral options were not available in certain localities some families either occasionally used the residential facilities provided by two of the programs or moved to be permanently closer to these early intervention centers. All four of the programs were described as parent centered rather than child centered. Parents were therefore expected to participate in guidance sessions on a regular basis, take part in educational planning, accept primary responsibility for maintenance of the children's hearing aids, and carry out specific activities with the children at home. These activities, in addition to the pursuit of their own interests and those of other family members, placed many demands on parents, particularly on mothers. These demands were not simply the outcome of their choosing oral options. Such tasks were, indeed, similar to those accepted by parents who participated in the total communication options described in the companion volume, except that they also had to become fluent in the use of signs.

GOALS AND PHILOSOPHIES

One of the goals in many early oral options is to enable children to enter regular schools and participate in lessons alongside their hearing peers with minimal, if any, support services. In the programs reported in this book educational mainstreaming is seen not so much as a goal but as one part of the process, which prepares the child, step by step, to be integrated as far as possible into regular school life, not only from early childhood but at any stage of schooling. There are many reports of excellent results in mainstreaming programs, but it is not enough to simply place hearing-impaired children in regular classes. Most require extensive support services to maintain optimum progress once adequate skills for mainstream placement have been achieved (Leckie, 1973).

All four authors integrate the many aspects of their programs in such a way that each aspect complements the other. The main aspects are good quality professional work, involvement of parents, intervention beginning in the early years (although the average age on admission to these programs is still unacceptably high), and reaching and utilizing remnants of audition through the selection of appropriate hearing aids and effective auditory training techniques. It may be said that these are also features included in visual oral options and the total communication options described in the companion volume. There are differences, however. All oral options exclude sign language and finger spelling, and auditory oral options focus on the use of residual hearing alone to the greatest extent possible so that it becomes a major avenue (if not *the* major avenue) of learning during training and in real life situations. Total communication cannot, by definition, incorporate these aspects of oral intervention. Some of the outstanding results of the oral options described here may be largely due to the exclusion of sign language, but this can never be proven. It can, at best, only be inferred through comparisons with children who are similar in every respect but who have been enrolled in exemplary total communication programs from the same age. Such comparisons are very difficult to make.

Finally, the contributors to this volume were all able to demonstrate the efficiency of their programs in relation to results achieved. Such noteworthy results are more widespread than generally recognized, and equally compelling descriptions of procedures and results could also have been obtained from other and similar early oral options. It is regrettable that, in the space available, a wider focus was impossible, and thus some types of early oral intervention were mentioned but briefly. Readers who wish to know how to locate options that offer early spoken language development for hearing-impaired children are recommended to contact the Alexander Graham Bell Association for the Deaf, 3417 Volta Place, NW, Washington, DC 20007. The International Committee on Auditory–Verbal Communication of this association has an extensive listing of early oral options and those engaged in this type of work. A substantial number of periodicals, journals, and books are also available through this association, membership in which is open to anyone.

SUMMARY

The descriptions of oral options and the results obtained by authors in this volume suggest that the goals of early oral intervention can be achieved by the majority of (but not by all) hearing-impaired children, given a number of conditions. These include enrollment in a well-staffed program which stresses the importance of parents being involved as partners in the habilitation process, the optimal use of residual hearing, and high expectation levels among professionals and parents. Less than optimal achievements may be expected if these conditions are not met. Children unlikely to succeed in acquiring fluent spoken language through auditory verbal strategies in exemplary programs are those with dual or multiple problems that lead to language learning difficulties and those who are totally or near totally deaf. Alternative auditory–visual or visual–oral options (such as cued speech) can be effective with some totally deaf children, but some of those with multiple problems may find it difficult to master any system of communication. The provision of diagnostic teaching/therapy within early oral intervention can help to determine which children have good potential for spoken language development and to define the nature of additional problems. The contributors recognize that sign language may be the most efficient means of communication for some children, but recommend auditory oral programs as the first option for most. All stress that the choice of option (oral or total communication) should rest with the parents and should be made following sufficient exposure to the facts and implications of each type of intervention. It is hoped that this book and its companion volume *Early Intervention for Hearing-Impaired Children: Total Communication Options* will assist both professionals and parents in making appropriate choices to meet particular children's individual needs.

REFERENCES

Berlin, C. (1978). Electrophysiological indices of auditory function. In F. N. Martin (Ed.), *Pediatric audiology*. Englewood Cliffs, NJ: Prentice-Hall.

Finitzo-Hieber, T. (1982). Auditory brainstem response: Its place in infant audiologic evaluations. In J. Marlow (Ed.), *The evaluation and management of communication disorders in infants* (Vol. 3, pp. 76–87). New York: Thieme-Stratton.

Leckie, D. J. (1973). Creating a receptive climate in the mainstream program. In W. Northcott (Ed.), *The hearing-impaired child in a regular classroom*. Washington, DC: Alexander Graham Bell Association.

Ling, D. (1976). *Speech and the hearing-impaired child: Theory and practice*. Washington, DC: Alexander Graham Bell Association.

Ling, D. (1982). Five videotapes relating to speech development in hearing-impaired children. Montreal: Instructional Communications Center, McGill University.

Ling, D., & Ling, A. H. (1978). *Aural habilitation: The foundations of verbal learning*. Washington, DC: Alexander Graham Bell Association.

Luterman, D. (1967). A parent centered program for preschool deaf children. *Volta Review, 69*, 515–520.

MacLean, G. (1983). Teacher ratings of behavior in hearing-impaired orally taught mainstreamed children. *Journal of the American Academy of Child Psychiatry, 22*, 217–220.

Mindell, E. D., & Vernon, M. (1971). *They grow in silence*. Silver Spring, MD: National Association of the Deaf.

Novelli-Olmstead, T., & Ling, D. (1984). Speech production and speech discrimination by hearing-impaired children. *Volta Review 86*, 72–80.

AUTHOR INDEX

SUBJECT INDEX